Public Utility Accounting

Public Utility Accounting: Theory and Application

by

James E. Suelflow

1973

MSU Public Utilities Studies

Institute of Public Utilities
Division of Research
Graduate School of Business Administration
Michigan State University

The Institute of Public Utilities, Graduate School of Business Administration, Michigan State University, publishes books monographs, and occasional papers as part of its program of promoting academic interest in the study of public utilities and regulation. The views and opinions expressed in these works are solely those of the authors, and acceptance for publication does not constitute endorsement by the Institute, its member companies, or Michigan State University.

ISBN: 0-87744-118-9
Library of Congress Catalog Card Number: 72-619568

Second Printing, 1974

Printed in the United States of America

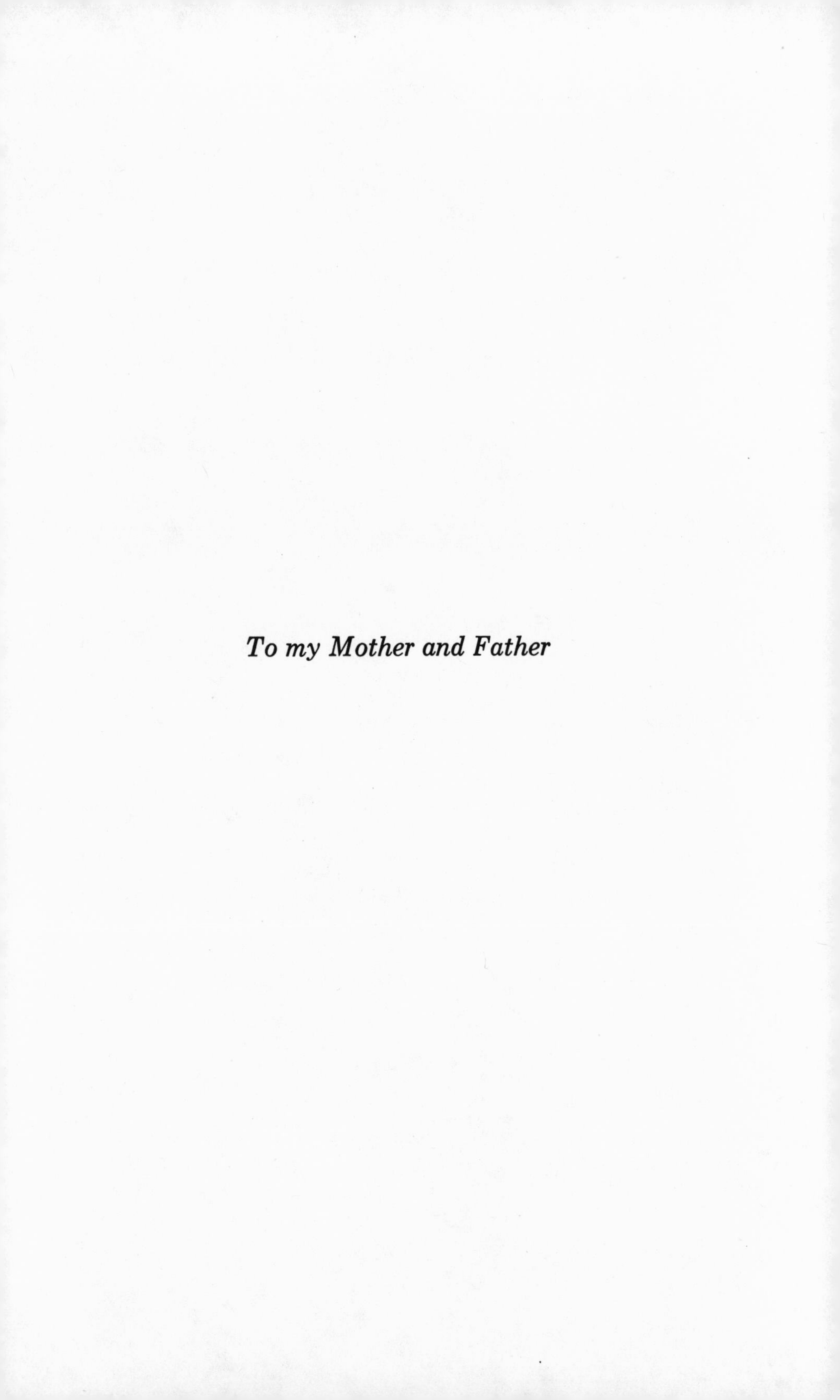

To my Mother and Father

Contents

List of Tables

List of Figures

Preface

Concern regarding public utility services looms large in our lives today. Consumer protection, ecological imbalances, and governmental influence as well as rising costs bear heavily upon public utility consumers and utility owners, managers, and regulators.

The use of accounting information in regulated industries is vital not only to management planning and control but also to owners and regulators. The peculiar accounting techniques of regulated industries always are not understood by individuals particularly interested in a public utility's operations; this book is designed as a reference guide and is directed toward those people. It is intended to acquaint interested parties with the public utility concept and the attendant uniform accounting systems, whose rules and regulations are so important to a utility's financial success. This volume has not been written as an introductory accounting text, and it presupposes a basic knowledge of accounting theory and application. Accounting books are available for this latter purpose at all levels of sophistication and degrees of difficulty; some emphasize simple bookkeeping techniques, whereas others are oriented toward detailed accounting theory.

No book is a single-handed endeavor, and I wish to acknowledge the assistance and encouragement of a number of individuals. The Institute of Public Utilities at Michigan State University and Professor Harry M. Trebing, Director, provided the necessary financial support and continued encouragement. Professor L. L. Waters, my colleague at Indiana University, and several unknown referees offered valuable criticism, assistance, and encouragement. Their comments were reviewed with interest, and many of their suggestions and improvements have been incorporated into the text; others were stubbornly challenged or resisted. Thus, any shortcomings or errors which remain must be mine. Further criticism is always welcomed.

1

The Economics of Public Utilities

Required accounting principles and techniques bear heavily upon a public utility's economic success. The consequences of using a uniform system of accounts as specified by regulatory commissions should be explored in relation to the economic and legal characteristics of the public utility enterprise. Furthermore, there is a strong correlation between the tenets of accounting and their influence on the future behavior of the various institutions with which the public utility comes in contact. Laymen and new initiates to the field of public utilities must be aware of the powerful tools of accounting and their economic effects not only on the utility itself but also on financial institutions, taxing powers, creditors, consumers of utility services, and even upon regulatory commissions. Understanding is dependent upon awareness of the economic and legal peculiarities of regulated industry.

Introduction

The impact of utility services as one part of our total economic activity is more easily grasped if one relates investment in public utilities with other forms of industrial investment. Table 1 displays the net total assets of all active nonfinancial corporations in the United States for fiscal 1969. These data were taken from corporate income statements filed with the Internal Revenue Service. While the figures given for public utility services—particularly electricity, gas, and sanitation—are somewhat incomplete when one considers the many public- (government-)owned utilities which are not required to file tax returns, the facts still are startling. If the net assets of electricity, gas, and sanitation are combined with communications, public utilities as a group rank second in size and constitute about 17 percent of the total net assets tabulated. Furthermore, investment in utility net assets is almost one-third as great as that of all manufacturing facilities. If regulated transportation were added to these data, the results would be even more profound.

TABLE 1. *Net Total Assets of Active Nonfinancial Corporations, by Major Industry Classification, 1969*

Major industry group	*Net total assets (billions of dollars)*
Manufacturing	509.5
Electric, gas, and sanitation	110.9
Retail	86.9
Transportation	51.6
Wholesale	71.6
Communications	66.2
Services	36.3
Construction	31.1
Mining	16.5
Agriculture, forestry, and fisheries	6.8
Other	000.1
Total	988.0

SOURCE: Internal Revenue Service, Department of the Treasury, *Preliminary Statistics of Income—1969, Corporation Income Tax Returns,* Publication no. 159 (12–71) (Washington, D.C.: U.S. Government Printing Office, 15 October 1970), Table 3, pp. 27–31.

NOTE: The sum of individual industries does not equal the total due to rounding.

For some years utilities have been responsible for approximately 40 percent of new corporate security flotations.[1] While most of these firms are not labor intensive, they do employ about 3.1 percent of all full-time workers in private industry,[2] and they con-

[1] *Statistical Bulletin* 31 (February 1972): 22.

[2] *Employment and Earnings* 18 (March 1972): 50, 55.

tribute an average of 20–25 cents out of every revenue dollar to meet local, state, and federal tax requirements.[3]

Economic Characteristics

The public utility concept is not new. Indeed, it can be traced to the early church fathers of the Holy Roman Empire, who recognized the need for certain elements of control in the name of social justice. In transactions between buyer and seller where common advantages and benefits existed, the church decreed that the exchange was to be consummated at a "just price." Somewhat later, English common law added the legal concept of common calling.[4] From these far-flung beginnings the concept has matured to its present state, changing slightly but remaining wedded to surprisingly similar benchmarks. Although criteria are essentially the same today, certain more recent contributions are evident in rigorous mathematical and logical evaluations of the public utility institution.

The public utility concept, a creature of the legal mind, identifies a certain class or type of economic activity which shares many common and basic economic characteristics. For almost a century economists have been detailing such supply characteristics as natural monopoly, declining average unit costs with increased outputs, utilization economies, substantial scale economies, technological limitations, large amounts of capital investment, and vertical integration. Demand characteristics include service to various customers who have varying price and income elasticities through direct physical connection in market areas with few, if any, direct substitutes. One might enumerate any number of nonregulated economic activities which display one or more of these characteristics, but only when these appear in concert does one usually find a full-fledged utility.

---

[3]Data derived from *Moody's Public Utility Manual, 1971* (New York: Moody's Investors Service, 1971).

[4]*Common calling* or public employment is to be distinguished from private employment. This medieval term was used to identify that individual who offered his services to anyone desiring them. It is in contrast to *private employment*, in which an individual was employed by another solely for the latter's private account.

Supply Characteristics

Reference has been made to the concept of *natural monopoly*. Although the term may be somewhat misleading, it implies that a single firm of substantial size serving a given market is able to provide service at a lower average unit cost than could several competing firms supplying the same market area by employing duplicate physical facilities. To explain further, as output increases to meet demand, average unit costs decline. This can be illustrated in both the economic short- and long-run situations. The former refers to utilization economies available to most firms, regulated and unregulated, with excess capacity; in the latter case (economies of scale) larger and larger facilities are capable of supplying a service at lower unit costs. As the size of plant or capacity increases and output increases correspondingly, costs and, subsequently, prices decline.

The analysis must be carried at least one additional step. Logic argues that any industry or firm is capable of showing short-run utilization economies, and undoubtedly one can find several examples of unregulated firms which display scale economies. To qualify as a public utility the assumption must be made that even if unit costs of supplying utility service increase with output, the characteristics of supplying the service are such that technological limitations still make it most economical to use a single utility plant. At the same time, the fact cannot be ignored that utilities, like all business enterprises, compete for labor, capital, and other raw material inputs. Of the three, capital appears most critical. The large quantities of capital investment in property and plant necessary to produce a given volume of revenue were illustrated earlier. The magnitude necessary before the utility can supply even a single unit of output is closely related to the concept of declining costs and economies of scale. For example, an electric firm must have substantial generating facilities, the means for transporting or transmitting electric energy, and a rather complete distribution system capable of serving all anticipated consumers before it begins operations. Other utilities face similar situations.

Closely allied with the element of natural monopoly is the situation in which the producer and ultimate distributor are the same entity. This type of supplier generally has been identified as a vertically integrated business. Vertical integration is much more difficult to identify in a public utility. The concept appears to have taken on at least two different meanings. According to the first interpretation, raw materials are converted into equipment to produce the product or service which, in turn, is sold by the producer to the final consumer. One of the best examples in the utility field is the American Telephone and Telegraph Company, which produces much of the equipment used in telephone operations through its subsidiary, Western Electric. The second interpretation, and the one generally used in the public utilities context, implies that raw materials (coal, oil, and so forth) are converted into a finished product (electric energy) and are sold to the final consumer, thereby eliminating the initial step of equipment manufacturing. The former is a better explanation of vertical integration in the usual economic sense, but to cite this phenomenon as a standard utility characteristic is open to considerable question.

Demand Characteristics

In addition to the supply considerations of regulated firms, a number of demand considerations must be explored. It is essential for a utility to have available capacity in property and plant to meet customer requirements whenever they occur, but it is important to realize that all customer requirements do not occur simultaneously. Some can be short-term, peak type demands which occur at specific hours of the day, week, month, or year; others may be average demands over longer periods of time. Inasmuch as demand is not continuous and these firms are supplying a nonstorable service (the only exception might be the limited storage facilities of natural gas and water utilities), public utilities cannot take advantage of off-peak periods of time for producing an inventory to satisfy some later requirement. As a result, firms often may have investments lying idle.

The concept of price elasticity of demand adds a further refinement to our definition. In order to take advantage of this phenomenon, utilities generally classify customers by type and occurrence of demand, such as industrial, commercial, and residential consumers. One might discuss income elasticities of consumers as well as price elasticities of the service and, depending upon the particular customer or customer group under discussion, demand elasticities may be inelastic or elastic.[5] Residential customers usually are classified as having an inelastic demand. Regardless of increase in prices or rates, it is doubtful that these customers would substantially change the amount of utility service consumed; at the same time, it is questionable whether or not they would increase consumption in a marked way if the price or rate for the service was reduced. Furthermore, the rise and fall of the particular consumer's income (income elasticity of demand) probably has little bearing on the amount of utility service consumed in a given period. Industrial consumers present a different picture since electric energy is one among other costs in the production process. Therefore, when considering rates to be charged to large industrial users, utilities are aware that the pricing structure is critical. Most industrial consumers have very elastic demands.

One might then logically ask: If prices change and demands are elastic, would the consumer substitute some other service? In the past the general consensus was that substitute services in regulated industries were rather indirect, but this attitude is not held as unanimously today. It seems reasonable to assume that some classes of customers might find ready substitutes more easily than others. If a residential customer is contemplating purchasing a new water heater, he might consider whether or not gas fired or electrically heated water may be to his advantage. However, once the purchase is consummated and until such time as the heater again requires replacement, the possibilities of calling upon a substitute service are minimal. Energy substitution is more likely with large industrial customers, particularly since problems of air pollution and ecological considerations may make substitution a necessity, regardless of costs.

Ratio Analysis

The interaction of the supply-demand or cost-revenue conditions just outlined gives rise to some rather common characteristics of utilities, but also produces some unique characteristics as compared to many firms and industries not included in the public

---

[5]*Economic elasticity* is defined as the percentage change in quantity demanded divided by the percentage change in price. If the result is greater than one, demand is elastic; if less than one, demand is inelastic.

utility category. This uniqueness best might be illustrated by analyzing certain accounting or financial ratios. These include the capital turnover, operating, and debt ratios, as well as dividend yields and payouts.

CAPITAL TURNOVER RATIO. The capital turnover ratio, which measures the relationship between a firm's investment in operating assets and total gross revenues derived from these assets, exemplifies the common element peculiar to most utilities but different from most nonregulated economic activity. It generally is maintained that, on the average, public utilities require from three to four dollars of investment in operating assets to derive one dollar of revenue. To illustrate another way, a utility would have to operate between three and four years to produce revenues equal to the original investment in operating assets. Thus, during a single year's operation, between 25–30 percent of the investment is recovered by gross operating revenues. Although the above is a generally accepted utility industry average, obviously the capital turnover of a particular type of utility may vary dramatically. Table 2 illustrates the capital turnover ratios for utilities as well as for nonutility economic endeavors.

TABLE 2. *Capital Turnover Ratios of Active Nonfinancial Corporations, by Major Industry Classification, 1969*

Major industry group	*Capital turnover ratio*
Manufacturing	1.21
Electric, gas, and sanitation	0.32
Retail	2.66
Transportation	0.72
Wholesale	2.88
Communications	0.45
Services	1.19
Construction	2.16
Mining	0.74
Agriculture, forestry, and fisheries	1.39
Other	2.55
All nonfinancial corporations	1.31

SOURCE: Internal Revenue Service, Department of the Treasury, *Preliminary Statistics of Income—1969, Corporation Income Tax Returns,* Publication no. 159 (12–71) (Washington, D.C.: U.S. Government Printing Office, 15 October 1970), Table 3, pp. 27–31.

NOTE: *Capital turnover* is defined as the ratio of gross revenue to net capital investment in assets.

Operating Ratio. Operating ratios for public utilities also are rather unique. The operating ratio, which relates operating expenses to operating revenues to show that percentage or cents of every dollar of revenue used to pay operating expenses, is rather low in the utility industries as opposed to other economic activity. Depending on the precise definition of the operating ratio, which will be discussed in more detail in chapter 11, and the particular utility being analyzed, approximately 50–70 percent of each dollar of revenue will be used to pay operating expenses. The remaining 30–50 percent properly can be identified as the gross profit margin, which in utility parlance is designated for payment of bond interest, dividends on both preferred and common stock equities, and amounts to be retained by the utility. Table 3 illustrates operating ratios of various utilities and selected industries outside this regulated sector.

TABLE 3. *Operating Ratios of Active Nonfinancial Corporations, by Major Industry Classification, 1969*

Major industry group	*Operating ratio (percent)*
Manufacturing	92.6
Electric, gas, and sanitation	88.2
Retail	96.9
Transportation	94.8
Wholesale	97.3
Communications	82.0
Construction	96.2
Mining	83.2
Agriculture, forestry, and fisheries	94.4
Other	98.0
All nonfinancial corporations (weighted)	93.9

Source: Internal Revenue Service, Department of the Treasury, *Preliminary Statistics of Income—1969, Corporation Income Tax Returns,* Publication no. 159 (12–71) (Washington, D.C.: U.S. Government Printing Office, 15 October 1970), Table 3, pp. 27–31.

Note: *Operating ratio* is defined as the ratio of all operating expenses and taxes, except interest and income tax, to gross operating revenues.

An analysis of Tables 2 and 3 shows essentially the following relationship. If an industry or firm has a slow capital turnover, in order for that industry or firm to be an economically viable institution, it also must possess a relatively low operating ratio or high profit margin. Only in this way will the investors in such an enterprise receive an adequate or reasonable return on their securities. Likewise, those firms or industries which require relatively small amounts of capital for each dollar of revenue generated also require relatively lower profit margins and are able to sustain high operating ratios. In this latter case, during any particular accounting period, generally identified as the calendar year, a firm might earn a low profit margin on each revenue dollar but might turn over its capital investment in gross revenues several times, thus earning a reasonable and satisfactory return for its investors.

Debt Ratio. Among the several additional financial indicators peculiar to the public utility sector is the debt ratio. It indicates the percentage of debt type capital to all capital invested in operating assets, and when utility debt ratios are compared to those of nonregulated industry, the former are substantially higher. In the nonregulated sector from 15–25 percent of investment may be in the form of debt capital, but utilities have debt ratios which range from 30–60 percent or more of total investment. The ability of the public utility firm to attract such large amounts of debt capital at reasonable interest rates often is accounted for by the utility's stable earning power. As a result of this stability, investors are not as wary of the utility's defaulting on payment of bond interest. Since demands for utility services are less volatile when compared to nonregulated enterprises, ample revenue generation is more assured.

Dividend Payout. A public utility's dividend payout, or that relationship between dividends declared and subsequently paid, and earnings on equity investment are relatively high when compared with the nonregulated enterprise. Undoubtedly, the stability of earnings and the ability for the utility firm to attract new outside capital are partially responsible for the higher portions of earnings being paid out as dividends.

Recently it has been suggested that the phenomena we have discussed up to this point are indeed interesting, but such characteristics might be apparent in many industries whether or not identified as regulated public utilities. Professor James Bonbright of Columbia University, in his book on public utility rates, says that he does seem to find one particular distinction which is not evident in unregulated firms: the close physical connection between the producer and consumer of the utility's output. The consumer is directly connected to the electric company, the telephone company, the water utility, and the gas utility, and this, in many ways, provides a limited and well-defined market.[6] Professor Bonbright's view substantiates our previous arguments related to the technological limitations of public utility services.

Legal Characteristics

Our legal system effectively created the public utility phenomenon as we know it today. Briefly stated, legal identification, interpretation, and control of regulated utilities evolve from the U.S. *Constitution.* The commerce clause allows for the regulation of activity between states, including regulation of public utilities. A residual authority known generally as police power, which is designed to protect the health, safety, sanitation, morale, and general welfare of the citizens of individual states, allows for intrastate control. Utilities operating in interstate commerce are subject to regulation by federal agencies, and those firms operating in intrastate commerce are controlled by state agencies.

The Congress and state legislatures, functioning within the constitutional framework, have passed legislation creating regulatory agencies and have provided these agencies or commissions with guidelines for operation. The principle function of the commission is to interpret and apply the legal mandate of regulations. These regulations include: (1) the granting of permission through franchise and/or certificate to the utility for performing its specified public service; (2) the setting of standards, both safety and economic, under which the utility must function; and (3) the approving of rates or prices which utilities are allowed to charge for their service. The legal aspects of the public utility concept have been hewn from these general regulatory provisos. Thus, at both the intra- and interstate level, if laws have been properly written and interpreted, businesses supplying a necessary service under legally sanctioned monopolistic conditions within the scope of general activity affected with the public interest are identified as regulated public utilities.

These regulatory devices are not without safeguards or curbs. A review of legal interpretations of intra- and interstate commerce generally reveals decisions based on the denial of the harmed

---

[6]James C. Bonbright, *Principles of Public Utility Rates* (New York: Columbia University Press, 1961), pp. 12–13.

party's right to due process of law. Of particular interest in the due process clause is the substantive interpretation. This may be identified with the substance of the case, as opposed to generally accepted legal procedures of administering regulation, and usually is referred to as property confiscation. Since regulation controls not only entry and exit but also rates or prices charged, regulation might involve the taking or denial of utility property without due process. Such taking away or denial results when the rate regulation imposed upon the utility produces total revenues which provide an inadequate return on investment, thus reducing the value of that investment (where value is derived through capitalization of earnings). It must be admitted that whenever regulation of price is imposed a firm is likely to suffer property confiscation in some degree. The courts have ruled that when economic activity of the type described above is performed under regulatory constraints, the regulated firm does so knowing full well that it has relinquished certain private property rights (profits and property value) in exchange for the authority to operate.

Rights and Duties

When a utility is sanctioned for operation and is issued a franchise or permit to provide a utility service, the agreement normally sets forth a number of obligations or duties expected from that utility as well as certain rights accorded to it. Among the former, the utility is expected to supply service to all who are ready and willing to pay. Furthermore, this service must be adequate and must be distributed under interpreted safe conditions. The utility also is obligated to supply this service at reasonable rates and without undue or unjust discrimination. Note that this does not preclude the charging of differentiated or legally sanctioned discriminatory prices.

Finally, the utility is obligated to obey and follow all reasonable regulatory commission orders and rulings. Such regulation has been authorized by statute through proper governmental channels and these orders and rules have the effect of law. One particular rule important to this study is that which requires and obligates utilities to maintain proper accounting and financial records in accordance with prescribed uniform accounting systems and procedures. These records, in turn, provide critical data needed by the regulatory authorities in performing their economic control functions.

In return for these obligations, the utility is given the right to charge reasonable prices and to render service subject to reasonable regulations and rules. The utility is virtually assured freedom from direct competition of service distribution, although a number of indirect substitutes are available, such as coal or gas for electricity or oil. Finally, the utility is entitled to exercise the right of eminent domain, which allows for orderly and adequate development.

Utilities in Our Capitalistic Economy

Having identified the public utility concept, it is important to determine how this particular segment fits into our overall economy. We have suggested that the market structure in the public utility sector is something less than competitive. In fact, a utility appears to be a natural monopoly, or a monopoly which, economically speaking, operates in the declining portion of the firm's average total unit cost curve; that is, it operates under conditions whereby increased output is produced at lower unit costs. At the same time, resource allocation and the supplying of these necessary services dictate that regulation be substituted for the marketplace, and that prices charged by the utility should be similar to those which would be charged under competitive conditions. The latter situation is illustrated in Figure 1.

In that figure,

MC = marginal cost or added cost for each added unit of output;
$ATUC$ = average total unit cost for the entire output;
MR = marginal revenue or added revenue for each added unit of output;
AR = average revenue or revenue per unit of output based on total output;
D = demand;
P = price; and
Q = quantity of output.

Under these conditions, average revenue equals average cost and marginal revenue equals marginal cost, all of which are equal to the

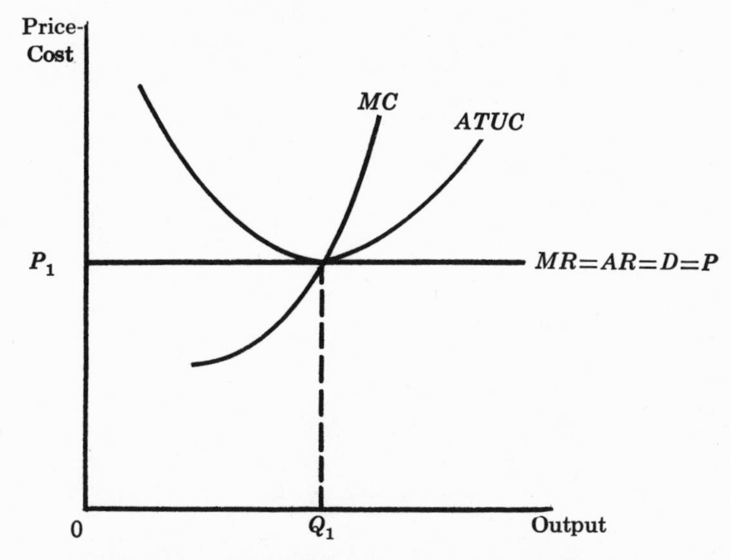

FIGURE 1. *Equilibrium in a Competitive Market*

price being charged. One goal of regulating a public utility appears to be that of achieving similar results in a less than competitive market situation.

Figure 2 illustrates the market structure of a less than perfect, or pure, competitive enterprise and is the type of cost configuration usually presented to depict the public utility enterprise. The figure displays several important phenomena. Plants AC_1, AC_2, and AC_3 range from smallest to largest output; each succeeding larger plant is capable of producing a larger output at lower average unit costs under declining cost conditions. Given a utility's demand function and derived marginal revenue function, a firm desiring to maximize profits would provide output at Q_1 and set price at P_1, that point where marginal cost is equal to marginal revenue.

Such a single pricing scheme, however, provides for excessive or monopolistic profits (area $P_1\ RST$). Since regulation is designed to eliminate excessive profits while producing as much service as is economically feasible, this obviously is neither the best (socially optimal) price nor output position for a public utility. Regulation substituting, if it does, for competition would suggest producing at output Q_2 and pricing this production at P_2, or at the point on the diagram (Figure 2) where average total unit cost is equal to

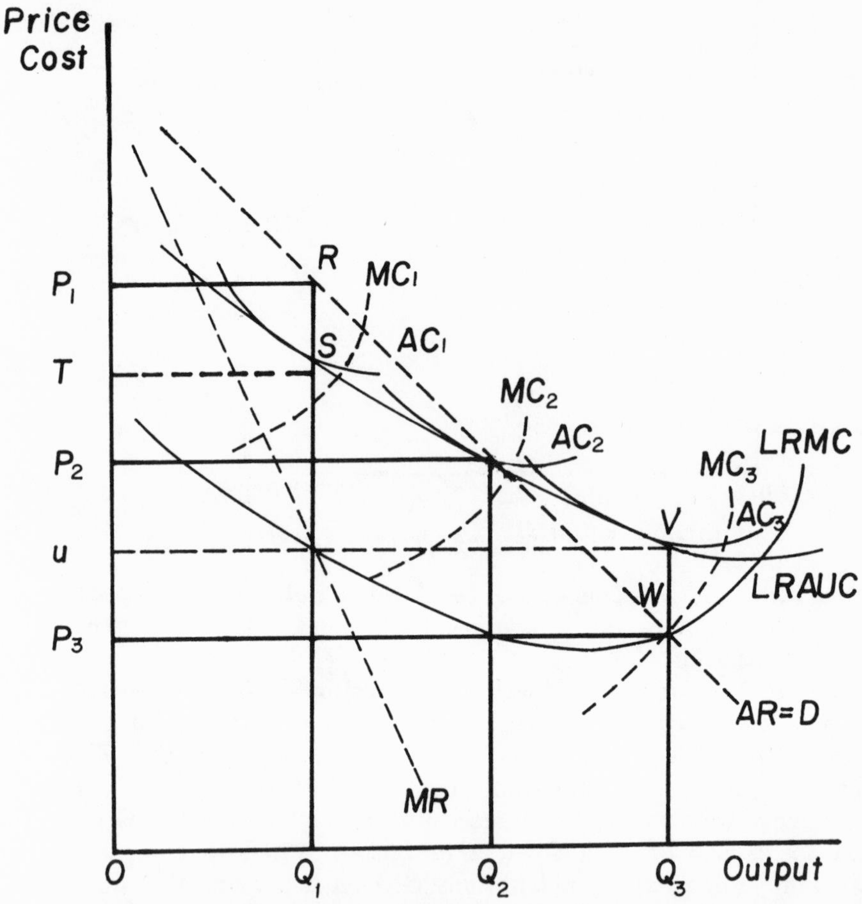

FIGURE 2. *Monopolistic Firm with Declining Unit Costs*

average revenue. Here it is assumed that average total unit cost includes a reasonable or normal profit element. This solution generally is referred to as the theory of the second best. While setting a price P_2 and output Q_2 eliminates the so-called monopolist profit, the utility still is not meeting the critical requirement of competition whereby price equals marginal cost, or the social optimum where demand equals marginal cost.

The modern economist would suggest that output should be further extended to Q_3 and price reduced to P_3, with average revenue or demand equaling marginal cost. This average price, however, introduces an additional consideration, namely, that under a single pricing system, price P_3, at output Q_3, produces total revenues which are less than total costs (indicated by the area P_3 UVW). Those economists who recently have argued that public utilities are a special class of public goods would say that the loss or difference between total revenue and total cost should be obtained by subsidization. An alternative is to allow the utility to practice price discrimination, and utilities are granted this privilege, enabling it to increase output to Q_3 where long-run marginal cost equals demand price. If the differentiated price structure is well conceived the utility will be able to cover all costs.

To summarize, the entire public utility concept—social, economic, and legal—obviously is one of degree. The various economic tests or characteristics enumerated certainly can be found in industries other than those identified as regulated utilities. Likewise, the legal interpretation of the utility concept is subject to debate. Furthermore, those industries identified as utilities at one period of a nation's development certainly may not be utilities at other points in time. The accountant must be aware of these economic and social conditions as well as those legal constraints which are imposed upon public utility firms.

Selected References

Bonbright, James C. *Principles of Public Utility Rates.* New York: Columbia University Press, 1961.

Clemens, Eli W. *Economics and Public Utilities.* New York: Appleton-Century-Crofts, Inc., 1950.

Garfield, Paul, and Lovejoy, Wallace. *Public Utility Economics.* Englewood Cliffs, N.J.: Prentice-Hall, Inc., 1964.

Glaeser, Martin G. *Public Utilities in American Capitalism.* New York: Macmillan, 1957.

Phillips, Charles. *The Economics of Regulation.* Rev. ed. Homewood, Ill.: Richard D. Irwin, Inc., 1969.

2

The Role of Accounting in Public Utilities

Public utilities within the United States are operated under various forms of ownership. In absolute figures there are a substantial number of publicly owned facilities; that is, municipalities, townships, counties, states, public utility districts (PUDs), and the federal government own and operate facilities supplying utility services. By contrast, although the number may be smaller, private, investor-owned utilities provide the bulk of utility services, and in terms of output as well as revenues generated these firms are the chief contributors. Within the investor-owned sector, one finds single proprietorship, partnership, and corporate forms of organization. The latter is undoubtedly the most popular, and it is this form around which most accounting systems have been developed.

Uses of Accounting Data

Regardless of the type of ownership, accounting data become extremely useful tools for those individuals interested in a particular utility organization. Among these are managers, creditors and potential creditors, stockholders and potential stockholders, consumers, employees, regulatory personnel of the Internal Revenue Service, the Securities and Exchange Commission, local taxing authorities, governing bodies which supervise certain health and safety standards, and state and federal public service regulatory commissions.

Accounting Data and Management

The need for accounting data by management of any business enterprise is paramount. Efficient operation demands that financial data be collected, assembled, and disseminated in such a fashion that managers will have information available for both day-to-day operations and long-range planning. While the former may require elaborate breakdowns for use in cost comparison and analysis, reports and financial statements prepared for longer range planning purposes may be presented in aggregate form. Similarly, differing levels of management within the organization will require reports of varying detail. Operations and middle management are oriented toward day-to-day data and detailed cost analysis. Responsibility accounting by departments of daily operations enable managers to measure actual performance with budgeted figures. Planning for future expansions, financial commitments, and so forth, as well as reviewing past performance belongs to higher management, and for these purposes data aggregation with highlighted features is often satisfactory.

Accounting Data and Creditors

Present and potential creditors are vitally interested in accounting reports. Firms which sell products and services to the utility want to assure themselves that services rendered or products delivered will be paid for on time. Short-term creditors, such as commercial banks, are interested in reviewing accounting data to ascertain that outstanding or prospective loans will be paid promptly. To the extent that public utilities engage in short-term financing, creditors obviously are interested in the cash position of the business as well as working capital requirements.

Suppliers of long-term debt, including bonds or debentures, place substantial demands upon a utility's earnings. The creditors' concern not only involves the probability of prompt payment of interest, but also the repayment of principal at maturity. Thus, a long-term creditor is particularly interested in the earning ability of the firm—the profit margin on one hand (the difference between gross operating revenues and operating expenses), and the annual revenue requirements to meet the costs of senior creditor obligations on the other.

While some long-term securities are of the debenture variety, whose security is based solely on the earning capacity of the firm, many other long-term bonds are secured through open-end mortgage provisions whereby the investment in property and plant obtained from the borrowed funds provides security to the debt holder.

Accounting Data and Stockholders

As in most corporate organizations, the majority of individual utility stockholders have minor interests in the organization and rarely exercise the prerogative of reviewing or inspecting the utility's books of account; their curiosity is satisfied by perusing the annual report supplied to them by the corporation. Although the stockholder assumes much of the risk for the corporation's success, his participation in managing the firm is minimal. His part in electing the board of directors, which subsequently appoints management answerable to that board, is the extent of his management function. One might postulate that the abundance of absentee ownership magnifies the needs for increased accounting responsibility and reliable accounting standards.

The stockholder might better be viewed in yet another role, that of an investor, which is similar to a long-term creditor. From a practical standpoint, the stockholder will investigate a particular company when considering purchasing securities or disposing of those already owned. The intelligent investor requires complete accounting information not only for his appraisal of the company as an investment, but also for his comparison of one potential investment with another.

Accounting Data and Rate Payers

A proper system of financial accounting must be extended into cost accounting systems, which detail much information used by utilities in cost of service studies. These studies consider the total cost of service or revenue requirements of a utility, including all expenses of operation, and a just and reasonable return on the rate base and apportion these economic costs to the consumers of the utility's service. This analysis becomes the basis for establishing individual rates (prices) or rate structures for specific classes of utility customers. The established prices paid by the consumer for utility services are heavily dependent upon accounting procedures and methods used by the utility and authorized by regulatory bodies. (This particular topic is discussed in detail in chapter 12.) Furthermore, financial accounting data are useful for determining both the amount of revenue received from various customer classes or groups and the expenses incurred in providing these services.

Accounting Data and Employees

Any worthy employee should be interested in the success of the company for which he works since his ultimate welfare depends upon adequate performance by the utility. Furthermore, accounting data usually are necessary for collective bargaining and wage negotiations; in fact, such information often is required by law.

Accounting Data and Regulatory Bodies

Regulatory agencies requiring accounting information are numerous and varied; the types of data demanded are dependent upon the purposes for which they are used.

SECURITY ISSUES. Some agencies are interested in the issuance of securities by a public utility. They have as their goal the obtaining and publicizing of information to assure the investing public that the firm is engaged in an honest and legal business and that the company meets certain minimum financial standards. This is not to say that the regulatory agency approves of the issuance of such securities; it merely provides the assurance that accounting data have fully disclosed all pertinent information relevant to their issue. At the state level this information is required under blue-sky laws. The Securities and Exchange Commission is the approving agency for all security sales in interstate commerce regardless of the fact that the firm might be regulated. However, in the case of interstate sale of securities for electric utilities, the Federal Power Commission must give its approval prior to the issue.

TAXATION. Taxing authorities at local, state, and federal levels require information provided through proper accounting to assess various forms of taxes. Among these are unemployment, social security, ad valorem, excise, gross revenue, and sales taxes, and the familiar income tax.

Rate Making. The federal regulatory commissions, including the Federal Power Commission, Federal Communications Commission, and, in the case of transportation, the Interstate Commerce Commission and the Civil Aeronautics Board, as well as the commissions at state levels rely heavily upon detailed accounting information.[1] The demands are so great that the general design of accounting systems used by public utilities is based upon regulatory requirements and is modified so that other interested parties may receive their needed information. This situation is obvious when one peruses the financial statements of a utility, particularly as compared to most nonregulated firms. The differences are dependent upon and dictated by the use of accounting information in the context of a utility's general rate level. Indeed, accounting data are imperative for good economic regulation. The information required by various commissions most often is taken from the utility's income statement and balance sheet.

The Income Statement

We have noted that public utility accounting data generally are provided in a format required by the regulatory commission; that agency possesses the authority and assumes the responsibility for exercising economic control of the firm offering public utility services. All expenses and revenues must be classified to enable the regulator to separate utility operating revenues from any income received from activity outside the control of the commission. The same is true with regard to expenses. The regulatory commission must be apprised of and can control only those expenses pertinent to the firm's operations in providing a regulated public utility service; all expenses for nonregulated activities must be segregated.

Table 4 shows a composite income statement for Class A and B electric utilities in the United States for fiscal 1968. Because it is a composite, specific utilities may not utilize each of the items detailed, but most items that a utility would encounter are illustrated.

---

[1]State regulatory agencies are identified by a variety of names, including public service commission, railway commission, and corporation commission.

TABLE 4. *Composite Income Statement for Fiscal Year 1968, Class A and B Electric Utilities, in Millions of Dollars*

Utility operating income		
Operating revenues[a]		19,405
Operating expenses:		
Operation expense	8,208	
Maintenance expense	1,191	
Depreciation and amortization expense	2,034	
Taxes other than income taxes	1,969	
Income taxes:		
Federal—current	1,655	
Other—current	86	
Provision for deferred income taxes	134	
Income taxes deferred in prior years—cr.	(59)	
Investment tax credit adjustment (net)	81	
Total operating expenses		15,299
Net operating revenue		4,106
Income from utility plant leased to others		3
Total utility operating income		4,109
Other income		
Income from merchandising, jobbing, and contract work	.5	
Income from nonutility operations	1.0	
Nonoperating rental income	(1.0)	
Interest and dividend income	96.5	
Miscellaneous nonoperating income	27	
Total other income		124
Total income		4,233
Miscellaneous income deductions		
Miscellaneous amortization	4	
Other income deductions	28	
Total income deductions		32
Income before interest charges		4,201
Interest charges		
Interest on long-term debt	1,365	
Amortization of debt discount and expense	5	
Amortization of premium on debt—cr.	(7)	
Interest on debt to associated companies	6	
Other interest expense	111	
Interest charged to construction—cr.	(275)	
Total interest charges		1,205
Net income		2,996
Dividends declared, preferred stock		279
Dividends declared, common stock		1,919

SOURCE: Federal Power Commission, *Statistics of Privately Owned Electric Utilities in the United States, 1968, Class A and B* (Washington, D.C.: U.S. Government Printing Office, 1969), Table 11, pp. XXIII and XXIV.

[a] Utilities often display gross operating revenue and expenses by utility function. Thus, any individual utility may have electric revenue and expenses, gas revenue and expenses, and so forth.

Operating Revenues

The first item of the income statement, "Utility operating income," is subtitled "Operating revenues." It represents the dollars that were earned from utility functions, and it includes only revenue from regulated operations.[2] At the time a regulatory commission sets a utility's revenue requirements or general rate level, it is the gross operating revenue figure which is determined. Operating revenues may be further subdivided if the utility engages in several regulated activities. The most common such subdivisions would include operating revenue from sales of electricity, gas, and steam.

Operating Expenses

The second major division of the income statement is entitled "Operating expenses." This is a category of many items as opposed to being identified with a particular account title. Expenses included in the income statement under this category consist of those made in producing the utility's primary regulated service(s), for example, electricity, gas, steam, telephone communication, and so forth.

OPERATIONS EXPENSE. The first subdesignation of operating expenses is entitled "Operation expense."[3] Again, this is a summary account taken from many subaccounts including labor costs, fuel costs, rent, meter reading expenses, other customer record keeping expenses, and sales expenses, all of which are classified as legitimate to the operation of the utility.

MAINTENANCE EXPENSE. "Maintenance expense" also is a summary and encompasses maintenance of generating, transmission, distribution, and general administrative facilities. It involves labor and any materials and supplies utilized in maintaining utility property and plant.

---

[2]This figure, in an accounting sense, is the total shown in the Federal Power Commission's accounting system for Class A and B electric utilities under control account 400, or the summation of suboperating revenue accounts 440 through 456 (see chap. 3, p. 50 ff., for further discussion of operating revenues). Federal Power Commission, *Uniform System of Accounts Prescribed for Public Utilities and Licensees* (Washington, D.C.: U.S. Government Printing Office, 1 January 1970 [hereafter cited as *Uniform System*]).

[3]Ibid. This is account 401 in the *Uniform System.*

DEPRECIATION AND AMORTIZATION EXPENSES. "Depreciation and amortization expenses" summarizes all depreciation and amortization calculated on property and plant used and useful in providing the public utility service. It does not include depreciation or amortization on plant which is used for purposes other than providing a utility function.[4]

TAXES. The remaining classifications of expenses completing total operating expenses are tax items. The first, "Taxes other than income taxes," is self-explanatory, but one of the first major differences encountered in viewing a public utility income statement, the item "Income taxes," is perhaps the most confusing. The nonregulated firm's income statement usually places income taxes much later in the statement, after all taxable items have been accounted for, and the income tax actually is deducted from a preceding net taxable income figure. Only the item's position on the utility's income statement is different; by Supreme Court dicta, income taxes have been identified as a proper operating expense and are so reflected on the income statement.[5] Rearranging the balance of the income statement to accommodate the Supreme Court's decision, however, does not indicate that a public utility calculates income taxes in any different manner than does a nonregulated firm. Neither the Supreme Court nor the regulatory commission have dictated to the Internal Revenue Service how a firm's taxable income is to be calculated. Consequently, the position of this item is merely shifted in the published financial record.

ABOVE AND BELOW THE LINE. Total operating expenses now can be indicated which, when deducted from operating revenues, yield net operating revenues. This point is extremely critical in regulation and deserves particular emphasis since it is the demarcation in the

---

[4]The *Uniform System* provides a number of accounts to aid in identifying specific depreciation and amortization expenses. All accounts may or may not be utilized by a specific utility. Detailed discussion of these accounts is found in chapter 5.

[5]In 1922, in the *Galveston* case, Justice Brandeis said: "In calculating . . . proper return, it is necessary to deduct from gross revenue the expenses and charges; and all taxes which would be payable if a fair return were earned are appropriate deductions. There is no difference in this respect between state and federal taxes, or between income taxes and others." *Galveston Electric Company* v. *Galveston* (1922) 258 U.S. 388, 399 (U.S. Supreme Court).

income statement which separates costs and expenses into above- and below-the-line categories.

The above- and below-the-line concept probably is explained best by identifying the *line* as that drawn beneath operating expenses in the mechanical process of deducting these expenses from operating revenues. Operating expenses occurring and tabulated above this line are chargeable to the rate payer since, recalling the previous discussion, all legitimate operating expenses must pertain solely to the supplying of a utility's primary regulated service or services. Any item that is accounted for and displayed above the line with commission approval will be utilized in determining the rate structures or prices paid by the consumer. Although accounting does not control rate making, nor rate making accounting, their mutual influence is apparent.

If expenditures are not chargeable to rate payers, the alternative is to charge them to the utility owners. An example may be helpful. Although a regulatory commission cannot pronounce whether or not an expenditure can be made, it can tell the utility whether or not the expense is chargeable to the rate payer. The question of a utility advertising the sale of its services is a case in point. Some commissions have ruled advertising is a legitimate above-the-line expense, whereas others have ruled that it is unnecessary and, consequently, is a below-the-line item. Commissions are not indicating that the utility does not have the right to advertise; what is at issue is the accounting method used.[6]

Other Items. The utility may lease certain of its property to other utilities. Although this is income for the accounting utility, it is not income derived from the accounting utility's rate payer. In fact, it is an operating expense for the lessee when the lessee accounts for its expenses of utility operation.[7] "Total utility operating in-

[6]For further discussion of legitimate above-the-line expenses, see chapter 4.

[7]Under certain circumstances income from leased property may be considered above the line. The treatment of this income is dependent upon the regulatory commission's decision either to include or exclude leased assets in or from the rate base. Differences of opinion exist among regulatory agencies. For example, those in favor of including leased property in the rate base and subsequent incurred expenses above the line include: *Re City Gas Company of Florida* (1966) 64 PUR 3d 518 (Florida), a ruling on appliance leases;

come" is followed by "Other income," which is income derived from activities of a nonutility nature such as merchandising, the selling of appliances, job order work, and contract work. These are functions over which the regulatory commission has no direct control as far as revenues or expenditures are concerned. Nonutility income is followed by nonutility expenses to arrive at "Income before interest charges." Nonutility expenses are followed by interest on outstanding debt and amortization of attendant expenses. "Net income," the residual available for stockholders (preferred and common), generally is transferred to the retained earnings (earned surplus) statement.

The Balance Sheet

Table 5 illustrates a typical balance sheet for a public utility; for illustrative purposes it is a composite balance sheet of Class A and B electric utilities for 1968, hence all items may not be found on a particular utility's balance sheet. Regulatory influence in the construction of this financial statement, like the income statement, is very much in evidence.

Assets and Other Debits

The left-hand portion of the balance sheet, "Assets and other debits," includes all items owned by the firm whether utility property or not.

UTILITY PLANT. A closer analysis reveals that the item occupying

---

and *Re Southern Union Gas Company* (1961) 40 PUR 3d 481 (New Mexico), a ruling on gas plant leased to others.

Other commissions specifically have excluded leased utility property from the rate base. The resulting expenses and revenues are then below-the-line items. These decisions include: *Re City Gas Company of Florida* (1966) 64 PUR 3d 518 (Florida). This case involved a utility leasing gas turbines to an apartment house while the other utility customers received no benefits; *Re Blair Academy Water Department* (1967) 70 PUR 3d 467 (New Jersey). Utility property was leased to others and the rental income was excluded from operating income; therefore, the rental property was excluded from the rate base; *Re Central Indiana Gas Company* (1960) 37 PUR 3d 138 (Indiana). Gas plant leased to others was excluded from the rate base; and *Re Wood County Telephone Company of Wisconsin* (1950) 85 PUR NS 142 (Wisconsin), a decision where telephone building that was leased to others was excluded from the rate base, and rental income therefrom was excluded from the income accounts above the line.

TABLE 5. ***Composite Balance Sheet, 31 December 1968, Class A and B Electric Utilities, in Millions of Dollars***

Assets and other debits		
Utility plant (at original cost)		
Electric utility plant	76,026	
Other utility plant	7,914	
		83,940
Less: Accumulated provisions for depreciation and amortization		19,040
Net total utility plant		64,900
Utility plant adjustments		1
Investments		
Nonutility property less accumulated provisions for depreciation and amortization	155	
Investment in associated companies	1,092	
Other investments	198	
Special funds	19	
Total other property and investments		1,464
Current and accrued assets		
Cash	603	
Special deposits	143	
Working funds	30	
Temporary cash investments	223	
Notes and accounts receivable less accumulated provisions for uncollectible accounts	1,673	
Receivables from associated companies	95	
Materials and supplies	1,297	
Prepayments	207	
Other current and accrued assets	168	
Total current and accrued assets		4,439
Deferred debits		
Unamortized debt discount and expense	87	
Extraordinary property losses	15	
Preliminary survey and investigation charges	24	
Clearing accounts	12	
Other deferred debits	156	
Total deferred debits		295
Total assets and other debits		71,099

SOURCE: Federal Power Commission, *Statistics of Privately Owned Electric Utilities in the United States, 1968, Class A and B* (Washington, D.C.: U.S. Government Printing Office, 1969), Table 8, pp. XVIII, XIX.

TABLE 5.—*Continued*

Liabilities and other credits		
Capitalization		
Common stock issued	11,764	
Preferred stock issued	5,982	
Premium on capital stock	2,734	
Other capital stock items	2	
Other paid-in capital	615	
Capital stock discount and expense	(88)	
Retained earnings	7,742	
Reacquired capital stock	(3)	
Total proprietary capital		28,748
Bonds (less bonds reacquired)	32,845	
Advances from associated companies	82	
Other long-term debt	592	
Total long-term debt		33,519
Total capitalization		62,267
Current and accrued liabilities		
Accounts payable	988	
Notes payable	1,961	
Payables to associated companies	144	
Customer deposits	252	
Taxes accrued	1,330	
Interest accrued	384	
Dividends declared	249	
Tax collections payable	68	
Other current and accrued liabilities	270	
Total current and accrued liabilities		5,646
Deferred credits		
Unamortized premium on debt	70	
Customer advances for construction	69	
Accumulated deferred investment tax credits	430	
Other deferred credits	95	
Total deferred credits		664
Reserves, and so forth		
Property insurance reserve	34	
Injuries and damages reserve	39	
Pensions and benefits reserve	33	
Other operating reserves	42	
Total operating reserves		145
Contributions in aid of construction		386
Accelerated amortization	875	
Liberalized depreciation	1,115	
Other	1	
Total liabilities and other credits		71,099

the primary position in the asset column is utility property, both plant and equipment, sometimes called utility plant in service. Just as the income statement was segregated to identify revenues and expenses concerned with utility operations, so, too, the balance sheet meticulously distributes assets to indicate those that are used in the production of utility service. A further distinguishing characteristic is that the property and plant are listed at original cost.

Original cost in public utility regulation has a very special meaning. At some time in the utility's history all property and plant included in this account originally were placed in public service, that is, in some form of service providing a public utility function. The cost expended at that particular time is the original cost of property and plant to that first owner, who placed the property into public use. If at any time the property is purchased by another utility, the purchaser must record the acquisition in the account entitled "Property and plant" at the seller utility's original cost. Any difference between this original cost and the actual price paid by a subsequent purchaser is segregated as an "Acquisition adjustment." The full import of this concept will be discussed later, but it is important to mention at this time that this interpretation was made part of the uniform system of accounts developed in the 1930s, when many utilities were involved in rather unhappy financial problems. In an effort to alleviate potential financial wrongdoing, such as increasing property values through resales among subsidiaries of a parent holding company's organization, the original cost concept was instituted.

The "Accumulated provisions for depreciation and amortization" item also must reflect the separation between utility and nonutility property. "Net investment in utility property and plant" is self-explanatory.

INVESTMENTS. Following utility plant and plant acquisition adjustments is a listing of any other property and investments which a utility may possess. Included are any nonutility property, together with its attendant provisions for depreciation and amortization, investments in associated companies, and investments in any other securities or business ventures with which the utility may be involved. Also in this category are any funded accounts which are more financial than operational; thus, while these possess fixed asset characteristics, they are separated from operating assets because of their financial implications.

Current and Accrued Assets and Deferred Debits. Fixed assets are followed by "Current and accrued assets" and, finally, by "Deferred debits," sometimes referred to as deferred charges. The latter items usually occupy a relatively small percentage of a utility's total asset value and reemphasize several of the peculiar economic characteristics of a public utility. First, a utility is designated as one in which most investment is in the form of fixed assets. Since utilities usually are classed as supplying a service rather than a product, inventory, which in most nonregulated industrial firms is a substantial item of total investment as well as current assets, is relatively minor in utility organizations. Since a utility's revenue requirements are based upon the revenues generated from the fixed assets, their importance again is stressed. Commission rule through the uniform system of accounts has stressed the peculiar configuration of the balance sheet to emphasize the important items. Contrary to conventional accounting, a utility's balance sheet begins with fixed items and moves to those which are more liquid.

Liabilities and Other Credits

The right-hand side of the balance sheet, including "Liabilities and other credits," has a similarly inverted arrangement.

Capitalization. Among the accounts occupying a primary position are the capitalization items, with common stock equity holding the number one position. This category, together with its attendant stated or par value and retained earnings accounts, is followed by any preferred stock accounts, which precede a summary of long-term debt. This latter illustrates another peculiarity of the utility's financial statement. Conventional accounting tends to separate long-term debt into a category of long-term liabilities. However, utilities incorporate long-term debt as one of the items under "Capitalization," including debt capital with preferred stock and common equity.

There appears to be a rather logical explanation for this grouping; it not only conforms to the uniform accounting system and regulatory requirements, but also stresses the importance of bond indebtedness, which comprises a substantial portion of total securities issued. In fact, depending upon the utility being analyzed, long-term debt comprises from one-third to more than one-half of all securities outstanding. When long-term debt matures, rather than retiring and removing it from the capital structure, it oftentimes is refinanced by the issuance of new debt capital. Like stock, the dollar amount of long-term debt becomes a permanent form of outside utility financing.

Current and Accrued Liabilities, Deferred Debits, and Reserves. To complete the symmetry of the balance sheet, capitalization is followed by current liabilities and other deferred credits. While the principles of uniform accounting are evident, the requirements of the regulator dominate.

Statement of Retained Earnings

Table 6 illustrates a typical retained earnings (earned surplus[8]) statement of a public utility, again based upon 1968 composite data

TABLE 6. *Composite Statement of Retained Earnings (Earned Surplus), in Millions of Dollars*

Balance, 31 December 1967		6,997
Add:		
Net income for the year	2,996	
Miscellaneous credits to retained earnings	13	
		3,009
		10,006
Deduct:		
Dividends on preferred stock	279	
Dividends on common stock	1,919	
Appropriations of retained earnings	3	
Miscellaneous debits to retained earnings	63	
		2 264
Balance, 31 December 1968		7,742

Source: Federal Power Commission, *Statistics of Privately Owned Electric Utilities in the United States, 1968, Class A and B* (Washington, D.C.: U.S. Government Printing Office, 1969). Author's calculations based on Section II, pp. 101-53.

[8]The accounting profession in recent years has frowned upon the term *surplus*, which implies excess. Today, accepted accounting practice has replaced the term with *retained earnings*. This more nearly explains the fact that the company has earnings rightfully belonging to equity capital holders, but these earnings have not been distributed. Thus, any actual dollars as represented by this account may have been used for a multiplicity of purposes. Retained earnings may be used to reinvest in new plant and equip-

for Class A and B electric utilities. This statement plays the same role for the regulated utility that it does in any nonregulated business. That is, it provides the link between the income statement and balance sheet by showing the balance in retained earnings at the beginning of the year, the addition of net income after interest and tax deductions and any miscellaneous credits to surplus, the deductions for stock dividends and other surplus appropriations, and ending with the retained earnings balance reflected in the utility's balance sheet.

---

ment, to pay the president's salary, or may exist in the form of cash. Throughout the discussion in this book the newer term, *retained earnings,* will be taken to mean the now considered obsolete *earned surplus.* The Federal Power Commission formally has authorized this change in all FPC uniform accounting systems effective 1 January 1970 (FPC, Docket R-344, Order No. 389, January 1970).

3

Uniform Systems of Accounts

If accounting information is to aid in the regulatory process, and this is one of the purposes for developing utility accounting systems, uniformity is paramount. In fact, uniformity is a prerequisite for comparability, that is, comparisons within the utility as well as among various utility enterprises, which is one of the techniques used in the regulatory process.

Comparability

Various uniform systems have been developed so that gas, electric, telephone, telegraph, and water utilities all have their specific systems. Several forms of regulated transportation also must be included. One uniform accounting system for all utilities of a specific type would be too broad and cumbersome to cope with problems for the wide range of firm sizes. To overcome this difficulty, utilities have been categorized by various regulatory agencies on the basis of gross operating revenues. The larger the firm, the greater the detail demanded by the accounting system. For example, electric utilities are divided by the Federal Power Commission into four classes based upon the magnitude of their annual gross operating revenues. Class A electric utilities include all those with gross annual revenues of $2,500,000 or more; Class B those with between $1,000,000 and $2,500,000; Class C those with between $150,000 and $1,000,000; and Class D those with between

$25,000 and $150,000.[1] Given a particular utility, it is possible to classify it not only by type but also by size, thus helping to identify it with other comparable firms.

The analyst also must be able to compare accounting data of a particular utility from one period to another. Among other reasons, uniformity over a substantial time span is important because it indicates a utility's growth, change in magnitude and type of operating expenses, plant investment, and securities issued.

Further refinement is available if selected comparable operating utilities are confined to a given geographical area. This may be some arbitrary regional designation or political subdivision, such as a state or group of states, or it may encompass the entire nation. Uniformity is important when the responsibility for regulation is designated to various political units. If utilities are of similar size, home rule or local regulation should provide accounting uniformity with state regulation requirements, and state requirements of accounting regulation should be uniform with interstate regulation by federal authorities.

A word of caution is demanded: Geographic, market composition, and cost variations, among others, make it virtually impossible to find identical firms supplying the same type of utility service under the same operating conditions. Furthermore, since varying interpretations are given to the uniform system of accounts by different regulatory agencies, intracompany uniformity is probably most important to the regulator. Only when this atmosphere of uniformity is maintained from year to year is it possible for the commission to intelligently analyze data from a company's balance sheet and income statement to apply proper regulating procedures.

History

The state of Massachusetts was probably the first political subdivision to take steps toward uniformity in public utility account-

[1]Gas utilities have a similar classification, while water and telephone utilities have the following classifications: Class A companies have annual operating revenues exceeding $250,000; Class B companies have annual operating revenues exceeding $100,000, but not more than $250,000; Class C have annual operating revenues exceeding $50,000, but not more than $100,000; and Class D includes those companies having annual operating revenues not exceeding $50,000.

ing. In 1876 the state directed its Board of Railroad Commissioners to prescribe "a system in which the books and accounts of corporations, operating railroads or street railroads should be kept in a uniform manner."[2] This same admonition was extended to gas utilities in 1885 and electric companies in 1887.

The modern era of administrative commission regulation began early in the twentieth century, and with it came jurisdiction over the accounting of public utilities in such states as New York in 1905 and Wisconsin in 1907. As an example, the state of Indiana provided for similar regulatory requirements by legislative act in 1913, when it incorporated into its statutes the following: "Paragraph 54-207 (12684). *Accounts of business—System—*Every public utility shall keep and render to the Commission, in the manner and form prescribed by the Commission, uniform accounts of all business transacted. In formulating a system of accounting for any class of public utilities, the Commission shall consider any system of accounting established by any federal law, commission, or department, and any system authorized by a national association of such utilities" (*Acts 1913*, ch. 76, Para. 13, p. 167).[3]

Part III, Section 301A, of the Federal Power Act says:

> Every licensee and public utility shall make, keep, and preserve for such periods, such accounts, records of cost accounting procedures, correspondence, memoranda, papers, books, and other records as the Commission may by rules and regulation prescribe as necessary or appropriate for purposes of the administration of this Act, including accounts, records, and memoranda of the generation, transmission, distribution, delivery, or sale of electric energy, the furnishing of services or facilities in connection therewith, and receipts and expenditures with respect to any of the foregoing: *provided, however,* that nothing in this Act shall relieve any public utility from keeping any accounts, memoranda, or records which such public utility may be required to keep by or under authority of the laws of any state. The Commission may prescribe a system of accounts to be kept by licensees and public utilities and may classify such licensees and public utilities and prescribe a system of accounts for each class. The Commission, after notice and opportunity for a hearing, may determine by

[2]*Re Montana Power Company* (1962) 42 PUR 3d 252 (Montana). See also Martin G. Glaeser, *Public Utilities in American Capitalism* (New York: Macmillan, 1957), p. 255.

[3]*Burns' Indiana Statutes Annotated,* vol. 10, Part II, 1951 replacement (Indianapolis: Bobbs-Merrill, 1951), p. 720.

> order the accounts in which particular outlays and receipts shall be entered, charged, or credited. The burden of proof to justify every account entry questioned by the Commission shall be on the person making, authorizing, or requiring such entry, and the Commission may suspend a charge or credit pending submission of satisfactory proof in support thereof.[4]

Table 7 indicates the extent of commission accounting authority as it applies to electric, gas, and telephone utilities at both federal and state levels and with respect to private or investor-owned utilities, and public- (government-)owned as well as cooperative forms of operation. All commissions which have the authority to regulate rates of electric, gas, or telephone services of the investor-owned utilities also have the authority to prescribe a uniform system of accounts.

The basic systems of accounts utilized today can be traced to the 1930s. During this period there was a general revision in most statutes covering the utility regulatory process. At that time jurisdiction at the federal and state level was more clearly delineated, and accounting reforms were made a part of the revised regulatory process.[5] With minor exceptions, such as those occurring in the late 1950s and the more recent changes initiated by the Federal Power Commission which were due to the introduction of new technology or accounting interpretations by professional accounting organizations or regulatory bodies, these same systems of accounts are enforced today.

Interpretations of Accounting Systems

Accounting uniformity, however detailed, cannot become a reality with the mere publication of orders and requirements; it can be achieved only with proper regulatory enforcement. Uniformity of requirements and uniformity in fact are never the same. There is

[4]Federal Power Act, Part III (Washington, D.C.: U.S. Government Printing Office, 1963), p. 40.

[5]In November 1936, the National Association of Regulatory Utility Commissioners (NARUC) recommended a uniform accounting system for electric and gas utilities. In that same year it approved a new classification for telephone utilities which was prescribed by the FCC. Also in 1936, the SEC prescribed an accounting classification for holding companies, and in the following year the FPC prescribed systems for electric and gas utilities under their jurisdiction and control.

TABLE 7. *Accounting Jurisdiction of Federal and State Regulatory Commissions*

State	The commission has: *Authority to prescribe a uniform system of accounts*						*Prescribed a uniform system of accounts*			*Authority to make interpretations of uniform systems of accounts*						*Made interpretations of the prescribed system of accounts*
	Electric			*Gas*			*Electric*	*Gas*	*Telephone*	*Electric*			*Gas*			
	Private	Public	Cooperative	Private	Public	*Telephone*				Private	Public	Cooperative	Private	Public	*Telephone*	
FPC	×[1]	—[5]		×[1]			FPC	FPC		×[1]	—[5]		×[1]			×
FCC						×			FCC						×	×
Alabama	×			×		×	NARUC	NARUC	FCC	×			×		×	×
Alaska	×		×	×		×	—[15]	—[15]	—[15]	×		×	×		×	
Arizona	×		×	×		×	NARUC	NARUC	No	×		×	×		×	
Arkansas	×			×		×	FPC	FPC	FCC[17]	×			×		×	×
California	×		×	×		×	FPC	FPC	FCC	×		×	×		×	×
Colorado	×	—[6]	×	×	—[6]	×	NARUC	NARUC	FCC	×	—[6]	×	×	—[6]	×	
Connecticut	×	×	—[3]	×	×	×	NARUC	NARUC	FCC	×	×	—[3]	×	×	×	×
Delaware	×		×	×		×	FPC	FPC	FCC	×		×	×		×	×
District of Columbia	×	—[3]	—[3]	×	—[3]	×	FPC	FPC	FCC	×	—[3]	—[3]	×	—[3]	×	×
Florida	×			×		×	NARUC	NARUC	FCC	×			×		×	×
Georgia	×			×		×	NARUC	NARUC	FCC	×			×		×	×
Hawaii	×	—[3]	—[3]	×	—[3]	×	NARUC	NARUC	FCC	×	—[3]	—[3]	×	—[3]	×	×
Idaho	×			×		×	NARUC	NARUC	FCC	×			×		×	×

Illinois	×			×		×	OWN[16]	OWN[16]	OWN	×			×		×	×
Indiana	×	×	×	×	×	×	NARUC	NARUC	FCC	×	×	×	×	×	×	×
Iowa	×	×[7]	×[7]	×	×[7]	×[12]	NARUC[17]	NARUC[17]	FCC[17]	×	×	×	×	×	×	
Kansas	×		×	×		×	FPC	FPC	FCC	×		×	×		×	×
Kentucky	×		×	×		×	FPC[18]	FPC[18]	FCC[18]	×		×	×		×	×
Louisiana	×			×		×	FPC[17]	FPC[17]	FCC	×			×		×	
Maine	×	×		×	×	×	OWN	NARUC	OWN	×	×		×	×	×	×
Maryland	×	×	×	×	×	×	FPC	FPC	FCC	×	×	×	×	×	×	×
Massachusetts	×	×	—[3]	×	×	×	FPC[17]	FPC[17]	FCC	×	×	—[3]	×	×	×	×
Michigan	×	×	×	×	×	×	NARUC	NARUC	FCC	×	×	×	×	×	×	×
Minnesota	—[2]	—[2]	—[2]	—[2]	—[2]	×	—[2]	—[2]	FCC	—[2]	—[2]	—[2]	—[2]	—[2]	×	×
Mississippi	×			×		×	No	No	No	×			×		×	
Missouri	×			×		—[13]	FPC	FPC	FCC	×			×		—[13]	×
Montana	×	×		×	×	×	NARUC	NARUC	FCC	×	×		×	×	×	×
Nebraska	—[3]	—[2]	—[3]	—[2]	—[3]	×	—[2]	—[2]	OWN	—[3]	—[2]	—[3]	—[2]	—[3]	×	×
Nevada	×		×	×		×	FPC	FPC	FCC							
New Hampshire	×	×	×	×	—[3]	×	OWN	OWN	OWN	×	×	×	×	—[3]	×	×
New Jersey	×	×	×	×	—[3]	×	NARUC[17]	NARUC[17]	FCC	×	×	×	×	—[3]	×	×
New Mexico	×	—[8]	×	×	×	×	—[19]	—[19]	FCC	×	—[8]	×	×	×	×	×[26]
New York	×	×	—[9]	×	×	×	OWN	OWN	OWN	×	×	—[9]	×	×	×	×
North Carolina	×			×		×	NARUC	NARUC	FCC	×			×		×	
North Dakota	×			×		×	NARUC	NARUC	FCC	×			×		×	×
Ohio	×			×		×	FPC[20]	FPC[20, 23]	FCC[20]	×			×		×	×
Oklahoma	×			×		×	NARUC[21]	NARUC[21]	FCC[21]	×			×		×	×
Oregon	×			×		×	NARUC	NARUC	FCC[22]	×			×		×	×
Pennsylvania	×			×		×	FPC	FPC	FCC[22]	×			×		×	×
Puerto Rico	—[3]		—[3]	×	—[3]	×	No	NARUC	FCC	—[3]		—[3]	×	—[3]	×	×
Rhode Island	×	×	—[3]	×	—[3]	×	NARUC[17]	NARUC[17]	No[24]	×	×	—[3]	×	—[3]	×	×
South Carolina	×			×		×	NARUC	FPC	FCC	×			×		×	

TABLE 7.—*Continued*

State	*Authority to prescribe a uniform system of accounts*						*The commission has Prescribed a uniform system of accounts*			*Authority to make interpretations of uniform systems of accounts*						*Made interpretations of the prescribed system of accounts*
	Electric			*Gas*			*Electric*	*Gas*		*Electric*			*Gas*			
	Private	Public	Cooperative	Private	Public	*Telephone*				Private	Public	Cooperative	Private	Public	*Telephone*	
South Dakota	—[2]	—[2]	—[2]	—[2]	—[2]	×	—[2]	—[2]	FCC	—[2]	—[2]	—[2]	—[2]	—[2]	×	
Tennessee	×			×		×	NARUC	NARUC	FCC							
Texas	—[2]	—[2]	—[2]	×		—[2]	—[2]	No	—[2]	—[2]	—[2]	—[2]	×		—[2]	—[27]
Utah	×		×	×		×	NARUC	NARUC	FCC[22]	×		×	×		×	×
Vermont	×	×		×	×	×	FPC	NARUC	FCC	×	×		×	×	×	×
Virginia	×		×	×		×	NARUC	NARUC	OWN	×		×	×		×	
Virgin Islands	—[4]	—[4]	—[4]	—[11]	—[11]	×	—[4]	—[11]	FCC	—[4]	—[4]	—[4]	—[11]	—[11]	×	
Washington	×			×		×	NARUC	NARUC	FCC	×			×		×	×
West Virginia	×	×	×	×	×	×	NARUC	FPC	FCC	×	×	×	×	×	×	×
Wisconsin	×	×	—[10]	×	×	×	NARUC[17]	NARUC[17]	—[25]	×	×	—[10]	×	×	×	×
Wyoming	×	—[6]	×	×	—[6]	—[14]	FPC[22]	FPC[22]	FCC[22]	×	—[6]	×	×	—[6]	—[14]	×[28]

SOURCE: Federal Power Commission, *Federal and State Jurisdiction and Regulation of Electric, Gas, and Telephone Utilities* (Washington, D.C.: U.S. Government Printing Office, 1967), pp. 16, 17, 18.
NOTE: X = "Yes."

[1]For utilities engaged in interstate commerce and licensees other than state or municipal licensees.
[2]Not regulated by a state commission.

[3]No systems in this ownership classification.
[4]Electric facilities are government owned and operated and are not regulated by the commission.
[5]U.S. agencies must follow FPC accounting.
[6]"No," except outside corporate limits of municipalities.
[7]Only accounts for revenues are prescribed.
[8]"No," unless authorized by municipal election.
[9]"No": Cooperatives are required to file annual statistical report only.
[10]"No," unless a cooperative extends its activities to include functions that make it a utility (or unless a portion of cooperative service are within an incorporated municipality as a result of annexation).
[11]No natural gas service in the Virgin Islands other than bottled gas, which is not regulated by the commission.
[12]Entire system of accounts prescribed for privately owned utilities with more than 2,000 stations. Only revenue accounts are prescribed for the others.
[13]"Yes," for all utilities except mutuals.
[14]"Yes," except for cooperative telephone operations serving only members with out tolls, which are exempt by law.
[15]Commission is presently considering a uniform system of accounts.
[16]Adaptation of NARUC.
[17]With modifications.
[18]Classification different.
[19]NARUC or FPC.
[20]Commission may require additional accounts.
[21]State system of accounts also prescribed.
[22]State system of accounts required for smaller utilities.
[23]Not for interstate companies.
[24]FCC, but not prescribed.
[25]Class A and B, modified FCC, and Class C and D, state system.
[26]"No" for telephone.
[27]Not reported.
[28]Basically FPC and FCC interpretations are relied upon; if requested, clarifications are made informally.

always room for many sincere differences of interpretation of the various provisions of a uniform system of accounts. Uniformity, in fact, only can be achieved with mutual understanding between the regulatory body and the utilities being controlled, and this may be a slow and painful road.

While the prerequisites of a good accounting system are founded on sound economic principles, it seems reasonable, at least at this point of development, to view accounting classification merely as a means of providing the regulatory body with information in a standard form. Interpretation of this information comes from the regulatory commission. Thus, a regulatory body cannot be bound in its interpretation of results by the prescribed system of accounts, and "a regulatory body must not be restrained in regulation by the art of accounting."[6]

At the same time, well-established accounting techniques must not be violated. This was expressed in the *Southwest Gas Corporation* case when the Nevada Public Service Commission stated that "good accounting procedures must have as their foundation sound economic principles . . . and . . . such . . . principles must be accorded due consideration when interpreting *loosely stated* accounting procedures . . . . [But] mere economic consequences alone, regardless of their gravity or magnitude, can [not] justify a blatant violation of the well established and *clearly expressed* rules of either accounting behavior or any other kind of behavior."[7]

The postulates and generally accepted principles of the accounting profession apply to nonregulated and regulated industries alike. Any differences that arise usually are due to the rate-making processes of the regulator. One of the main differences that occurs is in the timing of when certain items enter into net income—matching of expenses and revenues. For example, extraordinary losses are recognized by nonregulated firms in the accounting period in which they occur; regulated utilities often defer these items, amortizing them over a future time period. While at variance with generally accepted principles, the practice is acceptable, but only if cost recovery is sure. The other possible difference which exists between regulated and nonregulated firms concerns certain charges that may be written off to retained earnings when generally accepted

[6]*Re Montana Power Company* (1962) 42 PUR 3d 253 (Montana).

[7]*Re Southwest Gas Corporation* (1967) 69 PUR 3d 360 (Nevada).

accounting principles would consider the item as a charge against current income of the nonregulated firm.[8]

One cannot ignore the fact that state and federal commission accounting requirements may differ. In this regard, the Federal Power Commission's decision in the *Appalachian Power* case clearly stated that when such conflicts occur the FPC requirements take precedence. Likewise, the Securities and Exchange Commission also will accept FPC interpretations.[9]

The Uniform Systems

The accounting systems used by regulated public utilities are more than mere listings of account numbers and titles. The following is the Table of Contents for the Class A and B electric utility accounting system issued by the Federal Power Commission:[10]

CONTENTS

Included are legal authority for prescribing the system as found in the Federal Power Act, definitions of peculiar accounting terms used within the system, and general, operating, and particular accounting instructions concerning the recording of various transactions.

---

[8]American Institute of Certified Public Accountants, *APB Accounting Principles* (New York: Commerce Clearing House, 1971), Section 6011, "Accounting Principles for Regulated Industries," pp. 5001–5012.

[9]*Re Appalachian Power Company* (1962) 28 FPC 1199, 46 PUR 3d 440 (Federal Power Commission).

[10]FPC, *Uniform System,* p. v.

The preceding detailed evaluations are followed by a listing of the accounts. The uniform system, based on functional accounting, is comprised of specific accounts in which all transactions are recorded at cost. Each account is numbered and titled and contains a description of the general class of items to be included therein as well as a specific listing of these items. Many accounts specify items *not* to be included or other specific accounts into which items must be placed. Account number 370, "Meters," is presented in Exhibit 1 and illustrates the extent of information found in most uniform systems.

Balance Sheet Accounts

The first accounts to be listed are the balance sheet items. Exhibit 2 shows a general breakdown of the balance sheet accounts, including account numbers and titles. In fact, the arrangement of the balance sheet described in chapter 2 is taken from this classification. All balance sheet accounts assigned numbers from 100 to 199 are asset and other debit accounts; all accounts numbered 200 to 299 are liabilities and other credits, including capital accounts, current and accrued liabilities, and reserves. The accounts begin with the utility plant in service, the most fixed assets, and end with those items which are considered more liquid—current and accrued assets and deferred debits. The same arrangement is true for liabilities, beginning with equity capital and ending with the more current type of liabilities followed by specific reserves and customer contributions.

ELECTRIC PLANT. Account number 101, "Electric plant in service," is critical for rate making and rate base delineation. Exhibit 3, "Electric Plant Accounts," is a subdivision of the summary account number 101 shown in the balance sheet. Account numbers 300 to 399 have been assigned to the electric plant accounts. Separate accounting records are maintained for intangible, production, transmission, distribution, and general plant. Since electric energy is produced by a variety of sources, the production plant accounts are further subdivided into steam, nuclear, hydraulic, and other production. Except for the numbers, many of the accounts repeat themselves in each subcategory. To summarize, plant accounts in the 300 series are a more detailed breakdown of account number 101, utility plant in service.

EXHIBIT 1. *Account 370, Meters*

A. This account shall include the cost installed of meters or devices and appurtenances thereto, for use in measuring the electricity delivered to its users, whether actually in service or held in reserve.

B. When a meter is permanently retired from service, the installed cost thereof shall be credited to this account.

C. The records covering meters shall be so kept that the utility can furnish information as to the number of meters of various capacities in service and in reserve as well as the location of each meter owned.

ITEMS

1. Alternating current watt-hour meters.
2. Current limiting devices.
3. Demand indicators.
4. Demand meters.
5. Direct current watt-hour meters.
6. Graphic demand meters.
7. Installation, labor of (first installation only).
8. Instrument transformers.
9. Maximum demand meters.
10. Meter badges and their attachments.
11. Meter boards and boxes.
12. Meter fittings, connections, and shelves (first set).
13. Meter switches and cut-outs.
14. Prepayment meters.
15. Protective devices.
16. Testing new meters.

Note A.—This account shall not include meters for recording output of a generating station, substation meters, etc. It includes only those meters used to record energy delivered to customers.
Note B.—The cost of removing and resetting meters shall be charged to account 586, Meter Expenses.

SOURCE: Federal Power Commission, *Uniform System of Accounts Prescribed for Public Utilities and Licensees* (Washington, D.C.: U.S. Government Printing Office, January 1970), pp. 101-55 and 101-56.

EXHIBIT 2. ***Balance Sheet Accounts***

ASSETS AND OTHER DEBITS

1. UTILITY PLANT

ELECTRIC PLANT

101 Electric plant in service.
102 Electric plant purchased or sold.
103 Electric plant in process of reclassification.
104 Electric plant leased to others.
105 Electric plant held for future use.
106 Completed construction not classified—Electric.
107 Construction work in progress—Electric.
108 Accumulated provision for depreciation of electric plant in service.
109 Accumulated provision for depreciation of electric plant leased to others.
110 Accumulated provision for depreciation of electric plant held for future use.
111 Accumulated provision for amortization of electric plant in service.
112 Accumulated provision for amortization of electric plant leased to others.
113 Accumulated provision for amortization of electric plant held for future use.
114 Electric plant acquisition adjustments.
115 Accumulated provision for amortization of electric plant acquisition adjustments.
116 Other electric plant adjustments.
118 Other utility plant.
119 Accumulated provision for depreciation and amortization of other utility plant.
120.1 Nuclear fuel in process of refinement, conversion, enrichment and fabrication.
120.2 Nuclear fuel materials and assemblies—Stock account.
120.3 Nuclear fuel assemblies in reactor.
120.4 Spent nuclear fuel.
120.5 Accumulated provision for amortization of nuclear fuel assemblies.

2. OTHER PROPERTY AND INVESTMENTS

121 Nonutility property.
122 Accumulated provision for depreciation and amortization of nonutility property.
123 Investment in associated companies.
124 Other investments.

SPECIAL FUNDS

125 Sinking funds.
126 Depreciation fund.
127 Amortization fund—Federal.
128 Other special funds.

3. CURRENT AND ACCRUED ASSETS

131 Cash.

EXHIBIT 2—*Continued*

SPECIAL DEPOSITS

132 Interest special deposits.
133 Dividend special deposits.
134 Other special deposits.
135 Working funds.
136 Temporary cash investments.

NOTES AND ACCOUNTS RECEIVABLE

141 Notes receivable.
142 Customer accounts receivable.
143 Other accounts receivable.
144 Accumulated provision for uncollectible accounts—credit.

RECEIVABLES FROM ASSOCIATED COMPANIES

145 Notes receivable from associated companies.
146 Accounts receivable from associated companies.

MATERIAL AND SUPPLIES

151 Fuel stock.
152 Fuel stock expenses undistributed.
153 Residuals.
154 Plant materials and operating supplies.
155 Merchandise.
156 Other materials and supplies.
157 Nuclear materials held for sale.
158 Nuclear fuel assemblies and components—Stock account.
159 Nuclear byproduct materials.
163 Stores expense undistributed.
165 Prepayments.

OTHER CURRENT AND ACCRUED ASSETS

171 Interest and dividends receivable.
172 Rents receivable.
173 Accrued utility revenues.
174 Miscellaneous current and accrued assets.

4. DEFERRED DEBITS

181 Unamortized debt discount and expense.
182 Extraordinary property losses.

OTHER DEFERRED DEBITS

183 Preliminary survey and investigation charges.
184 Clearing accounts.
185 Temporary facilities.
186 Miscellaneous deferred debits.

LIABILITIES AND OTHER CREDITS

5. PROPRIETARY CAPITAL

COMMON CAPITAL STOCK

201 Common stock issued.
202 Common stock subscribed.
203 Common stock liability for conversion.

PREFERRED CAPITAL STOCK

204 Preferred stock issued.
205 Preferred stock subscribed.
206 Preferred stock liability for conversion.

OTHER PAID-IN CAPITAL

207 Premium on capital stock.
208 Donations received from stockholders.

EXHIBIT 2—*Continued*

209 Reduction in par or stated value of capital stock.
210 Gain on resale or cancellation of reacquired capital stock.
211 Miscellaneous paid-in capital.
212 Installments received on capital stock.
213 Discount on capital stock.
214 Capital stock expense.
215 Appropriated retained earnings.
216 Unappropriated retained earnings.
217 Reacquired capital stock.

6. LONG-TERM DEBT

BONDS

221 Bonds.
222 Reacquired bonds.
223 Advances from associated companies.
224 Other long-term debt.

7. CURRENT AND ACCRUED LIABILITIES

231 Notes payable.
232 Accounts payable.

PAYABLES TO ASSOCIATED COMPANIES

233 Notes payable to associated companies.
234 Accounts payable to associated companies.
235 Customer deposits.
236 Taxes accrued.
237 Interest accrued.

OTHER CURRENT AND ACCRUED LIABILITIES

238 Dividends declared.
239 Matured long-term debt.
240 Matured interest.
241 Tax collections payable.
242 Miscellaneous current and accrued liabilities.

8. DEFERRED CREDITS

251 Unamortized premium on debt.
252 Customer advances for construction.
253 Other deferred credits.
255 Accumulated deferred investment tax credits.

9. OPERATING RESERVES

261 Property insurance reserve.
262 Injuries and damages reserve.
263 Pensions and benefits reserve.
264 Amortization reserve—Federal.
265 Miscellaneous operating reserves.

10. CONTRIBUTIONS IN AID OF CONSTRUCTION

271 Contributions in aid of construction.

11. ACCUMULATED DEFERRED INCOME TAXES

281 Accumulated deferred income taxes—Accelerated amortization.
282 Accumulated deferred income taxes—Liberalized depreciation.
283 Accumulated deferred income taxes—Other.

SOURCE: Federal Power Commission, *Uniform System of Accounts Prescribed for Public Utilities and Licensees* (Washington, D.C.: U.S. Government Printing Office, January 1970), pp. 101-18–101-19.

EXHIBIT 3. *Electric Plant Accounts*

1. INTANGIBLE PLANT

Sec.
301 Organization.
302 Franchises and consents.
303 Miscellaneous intangible plant.

2. PRODUCTION PLANT

A. STEAM PRODUCTION

310 Land and land rights.
311 Structures and improvements.
312 Boiler plant equipment.
313 Engines and engine driven generators.
314 Turbogenerator units.
315 Accessory electric equipment.
316 Miscellaneous power plant equipment.

B. NUCLEAR PRODUCTION

320 Land and land rights.
321 Structures and improvements.
322 Reactor plant equipment.
323 Turbogenerator units.
324 Accessory electric equipment.
325 Miscellaneous power plant equipment.

C. HYDRAULIC PRODUCTION

330 Land and land rights.
331 Structures and improvements.
332 Reservoirs, dams and waterways.
333 Water wheels, turbines and generators.
334 Accessory electric equipment.
335 Miscellaneous power plant equipment.
336 Roads, railroads and bridges.

D. OTHER PRODUCTION

340 Land and land rights.
341 Structures and improvements.
342 Fuel holders, producers and accessories.
343 Prime movers.
344 Generators.
345 Accessory electric equipment.
346 Miscellaneous power plant equipment.

3. TRANSMISSION PLANT

350 Land and land rights.
351 [Revoked and reserved.]
352 Structures and improvements.
353 Station equipment.
354 Towers and fixtures.
355 Poles and fixtures.
356 Overhead conductors and devices.
357 Underground conduit.
358 Underground conductors and devices.
359 Roads and trails.

4. DISTRIBUTION PLANT

360 Land and land rights.
361 Structures and improvements.
362 Station equipment.
363 Storage battery equipment.
364 Poles, towers and fixtures.
365 Overhead conductors and devices.
366 Underground conduit.
367 Underground conductors and devices.
368 Line transformers.
369 Services.
370 Meters.

EXHIBIT 3—*Continued*

371 Installations on customers' premises.
372 Leased property on customers' premises.
373 Street lighting and signal systems.

5. GENERAL PLANT

389 Land and land rights.
390 Structures and improvements.
391 Office furniture and equipment.
392 Transportation equipment.
393 Stores equipment.
394 Tools, shop and garage equipment.
395 Laboratory equipment.
396 Power operated equipment.
397 Communication equipment.
398 Miscellaneous equipment.
399 Other tangible property.

SOURCE: Federal Power Commission, *Uniform System of Accounts Prescribed for Public Utilities and Licensees* (Washington, D.C.: U.S. Government Printing Office, January 1970), p. 101-41.

RETAINED EARNINGS. The current uniform system issued by the FPC places retained earnings accounts in a subclassification. This segregation includes accounts 216, "Unappropriated retained earnings (at beginning of period)," and those attendant accounts which may alter the beginning balance of prior period's earnings retained before reaching the retention at period's end. Exhibit 4 illustrates.

EXHIBIT 4. ***Retained Earnings Accounts***

216 Unappropriated retained earnings (at beginning of period).
433 Balance transferred from income.
436 Appropriations of retained earnings.
437 Dividends declared—Preferred stock.
438 Dividends declared—Common stock.
439 Adjustments to retained earnings.
216 Unappropriated retained earnings (at end of period).

SOURCE: Federal Power Commission, *Uniform System of Accounts Prescribed for Public Utilities and Licensees* (Washington, D.C.: U.S. Government Printing Office, January 1970), p. 101-67.

Income Accounts

The income-expense accounts within the uniform system are categorized and subdivided similar to balance sheet items. The broadest classification includes utility operating income, other income, miscellaneous income deductions, interest charges, and retained earnings (earned surplus). Exhibit 5 illustrates the income accounts.

EXHIBIT 5. *Income Accounts*

INCOME ACCOUNTS

1. UTILITY OPERATING INCOME

400 Operating revenues.

OPERATING EXPENSES

401 Operating expense.
402 Maintenance expense.
403 Depreciation expense.
404 Amortization of limited-term electric plant.
405 Amortization of other electric plant.
406 Amortization of electric plant acquisition adjustments.
407 Amortization of property losses.
408 Taxes other than income taxes.
408.1 Taxes other than income taxes, utility operating income.
409 Income taxes.
409.1 Income taxes, utility operating income.
410 Provision for deferred income taxes.
410.1 Provision for deferred income taxes, utility operating income.
411 Income taxes deferred in prior years-Cr.
411.1 Income taxes deferred in prior years-Cr., utility operating income.
411.3 Investment tax credit adjustments.
411.4 Investment tax credit adjustments, utility operations.
Total utility operating expenses.

OTHER OPERATING INCOME

412 Revenues from electric plant leased to others.
413 Expenses of electric plant leased to others.
414 Other utility operating income.
Net utility operating income.

2. OTHER INCOME AND DEDUCTIONS

A. OTHER INCOME

415 Revenues from merchandising, jobbing, and contract work.
416 Cost and expenses of merchandising, jobbing and contract work.
417 Revenues from nonutility operations.
417.1 Expenses of nonutility operations.

EXHIBIT 5—*Continued*

418 Nonoperating rental income.
419 Interest and dividend income.
421 Miscellaneous nonoperating income.
421.1 Gain on disposition of property.
Total Other Income.

B. OTHER INCOME DEDUCTIONS

421.2 Loss on disposition of property.
425 Miscellaneous amortization.
426 Miscellaneous income deductions.
426.1 Donations.
426.2 Life insurance.
426.3 Penalties.
426.4 Expenditures for certain civic, political and related activities.
426.5 Other deductions.
Total other income deductions.
Total Other Income and Deductions.

C. TAXES APPLICABLE TO OTHER INCOME AND DEDUCTIONS

408.2 Taxes other than income taxes, other income and deductions.
409.2 Income taxes, other income and deductions.
410.2 Provision for deferred income taxes, other income and deductions.
411.2 Income taxes deferred in prior years-Cr., other income and deductions.
411.5 Investment tax credit adjustments, nonutility operations.
Total taxes on other income and deductions.
Net other income and deductions.

3. INTEREST CHARGES

427 Interest on long-term debt.
428 Amortization of debt discount and expense.
429 Amortization of premium on debt-Cr.
430 Interest on debt to associated companies.
431 Other interest expense.
Total interest charges.
432 Interest charged to construction-Cr.
Income before extraordinary items.

4. EXTRAORDINARY ITEMS

434 Extraordinary income.
435 Extraordinary deductions.
409.3 Income taxes, extraordinary items.
Net income.

SOURCE: Federal Power Commission, *Uniform System of Accounts Prescribed for Public Utilities and Licensees* (Washington, D.C.: U.S. Government Printing Office, January 1970), p. 101-59.

OPERATING REVENUES. Account 400, "Operating revenue accounts," is divided into sales of electricity by customer type. Accounts 440 through 448 represent different sales classifications including residential, commercial, industrial, and public street and highway lighting categories. Accounts 450 through 456 represent other operating revenues which are not primary revenue sources, but which arise through financial transactions or through the utility's mere existence as an operating entity. Forfeited discounts on utility bills (account 450) which were not paid by a designated deadline (a financial item), rent from utility property (account 454), and interdepartmental rents (incidental revenues, account 455) are illustrative examples. A total listing is given in Exhibit 6.

EXHIBIT 6. *Operating Revenue Accounts*

1. SALES OF ELECTRICITY

440	Residential sales.
442	Commercial and industrial sales.
444	Public street and highway lighting.
445	Other sales to public authorities.
446	Sales to railroads and railways.
447	Sales for resale.
448	Interdepartmental sales.

2. OTHER OPERATING REVENUES

450	Forfeited discounts.
451	Miscellaneous service revenues.
453	Sales of water and water power.
454	Rent from electric property.
455	Interdepartmental rents.
456	Other electric revenues.

SOURCE: Federal Power Commission, *Uniform System of Accounts Prescribed for Public Utilities and Licensees* (Washington, D.C.: U.S. Government Printing Office, January 1970), p. 101-69.

The arrangement of income accounts provides the basis for the income statement configuration placing all revenues and expenses from utility operations first, thus denoting their above-the-line position. These are followed by other income from nonutility operations as well as expenses involved in any nonutility work. Next are charges for fixed income securities (interest) and accounts needed to record extraordinary items. Income accounts are numbered consecutively and begin with account 400.

OPERATING EXPENSES. Operating expenses, a classification rather than an accounting title, precedes a list of the various operating expense items (see Exhibit 5). Accounts 401, "Operating expense," and 402, "Maintenance expense," are subdivided into functional categories. In conformity with the breakdown of balance sheet accounts, operation and maintenance expense items are categorized into power production expenses, including generation by steam, nuclear, hydraulic, and miscellaneous other forms. Each of these subcategories is further divided into operation and maintenance expenses. These encompass accounts 500 through 557 and are illustrated in Exhibit 7.

EXHIBIT 7. ***Operation and Maintenance Expense Accounts***

1. POWER PRODUCTION EXPENSES

A. STEAM POWER GENERATION

Operation

500 Operation supervision and engineering.
501 Fuel.
502 Steam expenses.
503 Steam from other sources.
504 Steam transferred—Cr.
505 Electric expenses.
506 Miscellaneous steam power expenses.
507 Rents.

Maintenance

510 Maintenance supervision and engineering.
511 Maintenance of structures.
512 Maintenance of boiler plant.
513 Maintenance of electric plant.
514 Maintenance of miscellaneous steam plant.

B. NUCLEAR POWER GENERATION

Operation

517 Operation supervision and engineering.
518 Nuclear fuel expense.
519 Coolants and water.
520 Steam expenses.
521 Steam from other sources.
522 Steam transferred—Cr.
523 Electric expenses.
524 Miscellaneous nuclear power expenses.
525 Rents.

Maintenance

528 Maintenance supervision and engineering.
529 Maintenance of structures.
530 Maintenance of reactor plant equipment.
531 Maintenance of electric plant.
532 Maintenance of miscellaneous nuclear plant.

C. HYDRAULIC POWER GENERATION

Operation

535 Operation supervision and engineering.
536 Water for power.
537 Hydraulic expenses.
538 Electric expenses.
539 Miscellaneous hydraulic power generation expenses.
540 Rents.

EXHIBIT 7—*Continued*

Maintenance

541 Maintenance supervision and engineering.
542 Maintenance of structures.
543 Maintenance of reservoirs, dams and waterways.
544 Maintenance of electric plant.
545 Maintenance of miscellaneous hydraulic plant.

D. OTHER POWER GENERATION

Operation

546 Operation supervision and engineering.
547 Fuel.
548 Generation expenses.
549 Miscellaneous other power generation expenses.
550 Rents.

Maintenance

551 Maintenance supervision and engineering.
552 Maintenance of structures.
553 Maintenance of generating and electric plant.
554 Maintenance of miscellaneous other power generation plant.

E. OTHER POWER SUPPLY EXPENSES

555 Purchased power.
556 System control and load dispatching.
557 Other expenses.

2. TRANSMISSION EXPENSES

Operation

560 Operation supervision and engineering.
561 Load dispatching.
562 Station expenses.
563 Overhead line expenses.
564 Underground line expenses
565 Transmission of electricity by others.
566 Miscellaneous transmission expenses.
567 Rents.

Maintenance

568 Maintenance supervision and engineering.
569 Maintenance of structures.
570 Maintenance of station equipment.
571 Maintenance of overhead lines.
572 Maintenance of underground lines.
573 Maintenance of miscellaneous transmission plant.

3. DISTRIBUTION EXPENSES

Operation

580 Operation supervision and engineering.
581 Load dispatching.
582 Station expenses.
583 Overhead line expenses.
584 Underground line expenses.
585 Street lighting and signal system expenses.
586 Meter expenses.
587 Customer installations expenses.
588 Miscellaneous distribution expenses.
589 Rents.

Maintenance

590 Maintenance supervision and engineering.
591 Maintenance of structures.

EXHIBIT 7—*Continued*

592 Maintenance of station equipment.
593 Maintenance of overhead lines.
594 Maintenance of underground lines.
595 Maintenance of transformers.
596 Maintenance of street lighting and signal systems.
597 Maintenance of meters.
598 Maintenance of miscellaneous distribution plant.

4. CUSTOMER ACCOUNTS EXPENSES

901 Supervision.
902 Meter reading expenses.
903 Customer records and collection expenses.
904 Uncollectible accounts.
905 Miscellaneous customer accounts expenses.

5. SALES EXPENSES

Operation

911 Supervision.
912 Demonstrating and selling expenses.
913 Advertising expenses.
914 Revenues from merchandising, jobbing and contract work.
915 Cost and expenses of merchandising, jobbing and contract work.
916 Miscellaneous sales expenses.

6. ADMINISTRATIVE AND GENERAL EXPENSES

Operation

920 Administrative and general salaries.
921 Office supplies and expenses.
922 Administrative expenses transferred—Cr.
923 Outside services employed.
924 Property insurance.
925 Injuries and damages.
926 Employee pensions and benefits.
927 Franchise requirements.
928 Regulatory commission expenses.
929 Duplicate charges—Cr.
930 Miscellaneous general expenses.
931 Rents.

Maintenance

932 Maintenance of general plant.

SOURCE: Federal Power Commission, *Uniform System of Accounts Prescribed for Public Utilities and Licensees* (Washington, D.C.: U.S. Government Printing Office, January 1970), pp. 101-72–101-73.

The other major divisions of operation and maintenance expense, as was true in the electric plant accounts, include transmission, distribution, customer accounts, sales, and administrative and general expenses. Transmission and distribution expenses are subdivided into operation and maintenance and include accounts 560 through 598. Customer accounts and sales expenses are concerned only with operations and are covered by accounts 901 through 916. Administrative and general expenses, the final operation and maintenance subcategories, include accounts 920 through 931, which cover operations, and account 932, which covers maintenance of the general plant.

Obviously, different types of utilities will require different account titles, but this discussion will familiarize the reader with uniform accounting systems. Furthermore, the accounts listed might be considered as minimum requirements for the particular utility's class size; the utility is free to pursue a more detailed classification if it so desires. Thus a Class D electric company is free to use a Class A and B uniform system; or a Class A utility is free to add more subaccounts to provide further detail to uniform accounting requirements.

Selected References

Foster, J. Rhoads, and Rodey, B. S. *Public Utility Accounting*. New York: Prentice Hall, Inc., 1951.

Hay, Leon E., and Grinnell, D. J. *Water Utility Accounting*. New York: Municipal Finance Officers Association and American Water Works Association, 1970.

The reader is urged to consult the uniform systems of accounts which are available. Accounting systems for electric, gas, and water utilities are available from the National Association of Regulatory Utility Commissioners, P.O. Box 684, Washington, D.C., 20044. Similar accounting systems for electric and gas utilities as prescribed by the Federal Power Commission, and accounting systems for telephone, radiotelegraph, wire-telegraph and ocean-cable carriers as prescribed by the Federal Communications Commission are available through the Superintendent of Documents, U.S. Government Printing Office, Washington, D.C., 20402.

4

Accounting for Operating Expenses

Economic regulation essentially monitors two major functional areas of accounting. The first is all expenses of operation, the topic of the present chapter, and the second is a reasonable and just return on invested capital, or the rate base. Accounting for the rate base—utility property and plant in service—will be detailed in later chapters.

Regulation of operating expenses appears to be a simple task, and indeed it is for the many repetitive and reasonable disbursements determined by normal competitive forces. The regulator's task under such circumstances is to assure that these expenses are just and reasonable.[1] Hence, general instructions in the uniform system state that "all amounts included in the accounts prescribed herein for electric plant and operating expenses shall be just and reasonable and any payments or accruals by the utility in excess of just and reasonable charges shall be included in account 426, Miscellaneous Income Deductions."[2] While it may be forcefully

---

[1]See, for example, *City of Norfolk et al.* v. *Chesapeake & Potomac Telephone Company of Virginia* (1951) 89 PUR NS 33, 192 Va 292, 64 SE 2d 772 (Virginia Supreme Court of Appeals); and *Wisconsin Telephone Company* v. *Public Service Commission* (1939) 30 P.U.R.(N.S.) 65, _______ Wis _______, 287 N.W. 122 (Wisconsin Supreme Court).

[2]FPC, *Uniform System,* p. 101-1.

argued that items should not be charged to above-the-line accounts because they later will be disallowed by commission proceedings, one might present an equally strong case for misinterpretation if amounts are not allocated initially. There are a number of items which bear close scrutiny. These not only must be reviewed for reasonableness, but also, and more importantly, they must be identified as legitimate, above-the-line expenses by the commission.

In 1936 the Supreme Court identified the role of the regulatory commission in reviewing a utility's operating expenses: "A contention that the amount to be expended is purely a question of managerial judgment overlooks the consideration that when a charge is for a public service regulation cannot be frustrated by a requirement that the rate be made to compensate extravagant or unnecessary cost."[3]

One must remember that commissions cannot usurp management's function of how to spend its money. Rather, it is the commission's duty to pass judgment on legitimacy and reasonableness. The Alabama Supreme Court stated: "The Commission has a reasonable discretion to disallow expenses actually incurred by a public utility company only where affirmative evidence is offered challenging the reasonableness of the expenses, on the ground that they are exorbitant, unnecessary, wasteful, extravagant, or incurred in the abuse of discretion or in bad faith, or of a nonrecurring nature."[4] This judgment in the public interest generally is evident in formal rate proceedings or under specific circumstances which may be brought to the commission's attention. While most of the legal evidence cited in the following discussion will involve rate proceedings, the citations certainly should be weighed carefully by the utility in making accounting decisions with reference to potentially questionable items.

Among those items which raise questions of classification as above-the-line expenses of operation or below-the-line income deductions are: (1) advertising, promotion, and publicity; (2) contributions to charitable organizations; (3) dues to professional and nonprofessional organizations; (4) maintenance; (5) merchandis-

---

[3]*Acker* v. *United States* (1936) 298 U.S. 426, 80 L. ed. 1257, 56 S. Ct. 824 (U.S. Supreme Court).

[4]*Alabama Public Service Commission* v. *Southern Bell Telephone & Telegraph Company* (1949) 84 PUR NS 221, ______ Ala ______, 42 So2d 655 (Alabama Supreme Court).

ing products; (6) commodity costs such as natural gas; (7) certain nonrecurring items including (a) property acquisition adjustments, (b) legal fees, (c) extraordinary property losses, and (d) expenses of rate case proceedings; (8) payments to affiliates; (9) pensions for employees; (10) wages and salaries; (11) depreciation; and (12) taxes. Discussion of the latter two is reserved for chapters 5 and 6.

Classifying Operating Expenses

Operating expenses basically are classified among functional groups of accounts. For electric utilities these include power production, transmission, distribution, customer accounts, sales, and administrative and general expenses. Extensive subclassification occurs under each major functional class. These not only aid in reporting but also are critical for management understanding and control of the utility's operations, for rate-making cost analysis, and for general regulatory purposes.

Control of operating expenses by the regulatory commission is achieved by (1) disallowance of improper charges already incurred through formal rate proceedings and (2) by prohibiting expenditures before they occur; the latter is best done through budget approvals.

The items mentioned above, if found acceptable for rate making, may be classified as legitimate above-the-line expenses; however, if the expenditure is found to be exorbitant or for some other reason unnecessary, the item is a below-the-line income deduction. The uniform system of accounts provides for the classification of these expenditures in either way. Table 8 details the expenditure as well as the accounts to which the item must be charged. This may be altered upon commission interpretation, or the utility may provide further detail through additional subaccounts.

Analysis and Interpretation of Expenditures

The utility accountant, as well as the regulatory commission, has the obligation to analyze thoroughly each expenditure as to its appropriateness and reasonableness and to record it in the best interest of the public.

TABLE 8. *Accounting for Specific Expenditures*

Expenditures	*Above-the-line account*	*Below-the-line account*
Advertising	913, 930	416
Charitable contributions	930	426
Dues	930	426
Maintenance	—[a]	426
Merchandising	914, 915	415, 416
Commodity costs	—[a]	426
Nonrecurring items:		
Acquisition adjustment	406	425[b]
Legal fees	—[a]	426
Extraordinary losses	407	425[b]
Rate case proceedings	928	426
Payments to affiliates	—[a]	—[c]
Pensions	926	426
Labor costs	—[a]	426
Depreciation	—[a]	—[c]
Taxes	—[a]	416, 417

[a] There are a number of operating accounts to which this item is allocated.
[b] May at times be charged to account 439, "Adjustment to retained earnings," rather than expense account.
[c] Generally direct commission control and/or approval before expenditures.

Advertising, Promotion, and Publicity

The merits of expenditures by public utilities for advertising of various types long has been an issue for economists and regulators. If one assumes that such expenditures are made in order to increase demands for service, the question is raised as to whether or not a public utility which enjoys a monopolistic market position, free of the competition of identical services or products, can, indeed, increase demand. If the answer is negative, one might readily conclude that such expenditures are unnecessary and not in the public interest.

On the other hand, even though a particular utility has a designated market area which is assigned solely to that firm, two counterarguments might be made. First, within any given market it is quite possible to encourage the sale of additional utility services. For example, a person who realizes that it is less expensive to make additional use of the telephone during given periods of the day might be encouraged through proper advertising to use this service. Second, most economists would concede that although directly substitutable services may be rare, indirect substitutes are available. Examples include substituting electric energy for coal, fuel oil, or natural gas heating, using natural gas in place of electricity for cooking and water heating, and microwave communication or telegraph service rather than telephone service. Under such circumstances, one could argue that increased demand also would aid a utility in taking advantage of greater long-run scale economies. Addressing itself to this topic, the North Carolina Public Service Commission said: "Sound competition among utilities should be founded upon efficiency of management techniques, productive skills, technological improvements, superiority of service, and economy of costs to the consumer rather than by high promotional expenditures."[5]

Uniform accounting systems make specific reference to advertising, promotion, and publicity expenses in several accounts, depending upon the circumstances surrounding the expenditure. Subaccounts of "Operation and maintenance expense," including accounts 911, "Supervision"; 912, "Demonstration and selling expenses"; 913, "Advertising expenses"; and 930, "Miscellaneous general expenses," all refer to costs of performing a sales function. Accounts 911, 912, and 913 are specifically identified with expenditures designed to increase demands for electric service.

Account 930, "Miscellaneous general expenses," includes the cost of labor and expenses incurred in connection with the general management of a utility not provided for in other accounts. Among the several examples listed are institutional and goodwill advertising. The latter forms might be described as methods used by a utility to bring its name before the consumer or general public. This usually is done to establish rapport between the utility and public to demonstrate that the utility is performing its assigned functions well and in the public interest.

Regulatory commissions and the courts generally have allowed as above-the-line operating expenses those advertising, promotion, and publicity items which will increase service demands. The Supreme Court has said that a state commission's action in reducing an allowance claimed by a gas utility for new business expense, without evidence of inefficiency or improvidence in making

[5]*Re Piedmont Natural Gas Company, Inc.* (1960) 34 PUR 3d 1 (North Carolina).

such expenditures for such purposes, was arbitrary.[6] In another decision, the Arkansas Supreme Court stated: "Advertising expenses of a gas company directed at promoting sales of gas were properly included in utility expenses for ratemaking purposes; on the same basis expenses incurred in connection with the operation of a wholly-owned finance company handling only the accounts of the gas company's customers were properly allowed."[7]

Advertising may appear promotional in nature—that is, encouraging the use of additional service—but benefits derived from such advertising are questionable. In a decision before the North Carolina Public Service Commission, the Duke Power Company was not allowed to reimburse the advertising expense of home builders after homes equipped with electric heating were completed and open to prospective buyers. Since these payments would be made to the home builder, the commission interpreted the builder, not the rate payer, as the benefactor and decided that rate payers should not be required to underwrite expenses of others, advertising or otherwise.[8] The New York Public Service Commission has ably summarized current thinking on allowable advertising expenses: "So long as advertising expenditures, including institutional advertising to promote good will, do not exceed what is reasonably necessary and proper in the particular case, they are allowable as a necessary and proper expense for rate-making purposes."[9]

Another form of publicity, political lobbying, is prevalent in many areas of the country. The California Public Service Commission ruled that "political expenditures are not properly includable in operating expenses."[10] The Wisconsin commission, addressing itself specifically to public versus private power, said: "Expenditures devoted to influencing public opinion either for or against

[6]*West Ohio Gas Company* v. *Public Utilities Commission of Ohio* (1935) 6 P.U.R.(N.S.) 449, 294 U.S. 63, 79 L. ed. 761, 55 S.Ct. 316 (U.S. Supreme Court).

[7]*City of El Dorado et al.* v. *Arkansas Public Service Commisson et al.* (1962) 235 Ark 812, 47 PUR 3d 354, 362 SW2d 680 (Arkansas Supreme Court).

[8]*Re Duke Power Company* (1964) 54 PUR 3d 574 (North Carolina).

[9]*Re Consolidated Edison Company of New York, Inc.* (1961) 41 PUR 3d 305 (New York).

[10]*Re Pacific Lighting Gas Supply Company* (1962) 44 PUR 3d 177 (California)

public ownership of power facilities are not allowable operating expenses of utilities."[11] In a more sweeping statement, the Federal Power Commission in a decision concerning the Alabama Power Company said: "Expenditures for advertising of an institutional and political nature by private electric companies in an effort to combat alleged competition by the advocates of public power are not, for accounting purposes, ordinary and necessary expenditures in the operation of the company's businesses so as to be chargeable to operating expenses."[12]

While these interpretations of advertising are rate-making decisions, the question arises as to the proper accounting procedures to be employed in recording such expenditures. The National Association of Regulatory Utility Commissioners (NARUC) poses the following question and answer.

> *Question:*
> What is the proper account to be charged with non-promotional advertising of the type sometimes referred to as institutional advertising or goodwill advertising, the purpose of which is to foster and maintain public goodwill rather than for any immediate and direct promotion of sales of electricity or appliances?
>
> *Answer:*
> Such advertising should be charged to Account 930, Miscellaneous General Expenses; however, Account No. 426, Other Income Deductions, should be charged with the cost of any advertising for the purpose of influencing public opinion as to the election of public officers, referenda, proposed legislation, proposed ordinances, repeal of existing laws or ordinances, approval or revocation of franchises; for the purpose of influencing decisions of public officers; or having any direct or indirect relationship to political matters.[13]

---

[11]*Re Uniform System of Accounts for Electric Utilities* (1957) 21 PUR 3d 412 (Wisconsin).

[12]*Re Alabama Power Co. et al.* (1959) 22 FPC 72, 29 PUR 3d 209 (Federal Power Commission). See also: a case concerning advertising of a political nature, *State of Missouri ex rel Nancy Corinne Dyer et al.* v. *Missouri Public Service Commission* (1961) ______ Mo ______, 37 PUR 3d 507, 341 SW2d 795 (Missouri); and cases promoting private over public power, *Re Pacific Power & Light Company* (1960) 34 PUR 3d 36 (Oregon), *Re Consumers Power Company* (1959) 29 PUR 3d 133 (Michigan), *Re Utah Power & Light Company* (1952) 95 PUR NS 390 (Utah).

[13]National Association of Regulatory Utility Commissioners, *Interpretations of Uniform System of Accounts for Electric, Gas, and Water Utilities*

Charitable Contributions and Donations

Like most other economic entities, public utility firms often are called upon to contribute to charitable, educational, and other non-profit institutions. If they do so, the question of proper accounting arises. Justification for including such expenditures above the line may be made in terms of maintaining good public relations, the educational and community benefit derived, and possible increased demands for service, the latter arising from contributions to the local chamber of commerce or community development surveys and projects.

Opposition to these items as legitimate expenses rests upon the question of forced or involuntary contributions being made by the rate payer. If charitable contributions are an above-the-line expense and are accounted for in this manner, they may become part of the rate paid by the consumer. A rate payer then is forced to contribute to certain organizations which in his mind may or may not be worthy of his support. The logical solution is that the rate payer should make contributions directly to those organizations which he feels worthwhile, and any utility expenditures for this purpose should be made by the utility owners and should be accounted for as below-the-line income deductions. This is not to say that accounting or regulation of accounting interferes with the utility's prerogatives to be community minded; rather, it is a regulatory and, subsequently, accounting obligation to make a proper interpretation and allocation of such expenditures.

Accordingly, the classifications of accounts make alternate provisions for charitable contributions and other donations. For example, the uniform system of accounts for Class A and B telephone companies provides, under "Other operating expenses," account 31.675, "Other expenses." This account, while not specifically authorizing

---

(Washington, D.C.: NARUC, October 1967 [hereafter cited as *Interpretations*]), question 58-EGW, p. 27.

Similar provisions for advertising expenses are made in the uniform system of accounts for Class A and B gas utilities; the uniform system of accounts for Class A and B telephone companies utilizes accounts 31.642, "Advertising," and 31.643, "Sales expenses," for legitimate operating expenses and 31.323, "Miscellaneous income charges," for below-the-line type advertising. Federal Communications Commission, *Rules and Regulations Part 31—Uniform System of Accounts for Class A and Class B Telephone Companies* (Washington, D.C.: U.S. Government Printing Office, September 1965 [hereafter cited as *Rules and Regulations—Part 31*]), vol. 8.

the inclusion of contributions and donations, would be the most logical category. In the case of telephone utilities, however, specific requirements state that contributions for charitable, social, or community welfare purposes should be charged to account 31.323, "Miscellaneous income charges," a below-the-line classification. In view of this the Federal Communications Commission in 1956 made specific note that the uniform system of accounts for telephone companies *should not be* amended to provide that these companies charge their contributions to organizations engaged in activities beneficial to the community to the operating expense account "Other expenses" (account 31.675), or to the appropriate operating departmental expense accounts, if directly related thereto, rather than to the below-the-line account, "Miscellaneous income charges" (account 323) as currently required.[14]

In 1963 the American Telephone and Telegraph Company again attempted to have these particular items reclassified as above-the-line expenses. The FCC replied: "An application for amendment of the uniform system of accounts for telephone companies to require 'contributions to organizations engaged in activities beneficial to the community, including educational activities' to be charged to operating expenses, in lieu of the present requirement that such items be charged to miscellaneous income charges, a below-the-line account, was denied."[15]

Although the uniform accounting systems which currently are authorized by regulatory bodies and used by the public utilities specify contributions and donations as below-the-line items, the commissions themselves are not always unanimous in their rulings. Those specifically following the uniform accounting classification are represented by the Public Service Commission of the District of Columbia, which said in 1964: "The allowance for charitable contributions as an operating expense of a utility amounts to an involuntary levy on ratepayers."[16] The Connecticut and New

---

[14]*Re Amendments of Part 31 of the Commissions Rules and Regulations* (1956) 13 PUR 3d 163 (Federal Communications Commission).

[15]*Re American Telephone & Telegraph Company,* 26 June 1963 (FCC).
Similar provisions are made for electric, gas, and water utilities in accounts 930, "Miscellaneous general expense," an above-the-line account, and account 426, "Other income deductions," a below-the-line account.

[16]*Re The Chesapeake & Potomac Telephone Company* (1964) 57 PUR 3d 1 (District of Columbia).

Jersey public service commissions also are of this opinion. "Donations and contributions should be charged to the account 'Miscellaneous Income Deductions,' which is not an operating expense."[17] "A contribution to a scholarship fund is not a proper expense for rate-making purposes and will be eliminated from operating expenses."[18]

On the other hand, the Florida Public Service Commission recognizes contributions above the line. "Charitable contributions in a reasonable amount are allowable as an operating expense for rate-making purposes."[19] "Charitable contributions in a reasonable amount are a part of a utility's cost of doing business and should be allowed as an operating expense."[20] The Federal Power Commission is in agreement: "Contributions of a reasonable amount to recognized and appropriate charitable institutions constitute a proper operating expense for rate-making purposes."[21]

Dues and Membership Fees

Closely allied to the topic of donations and charitable contributions is the question of utility payments for dues and professional memberships of its personnel. When dues or membership fees are paid by the utility for affiliation with state or local chambers of commerce or trade associations, such as the Edison Electric Institute and the American Gas Association, there seems to be little disagreement that payments are legitimate expenses of operation. For example, the Michigan Public Service Commission has said: "Cost of participation in state and local Chambers of Commerce should be allowed as an operating expense."[22]

The Kansas Supreme Court, in a decision of the Kansas State

---

[17]*Re Hartford Electric Light Company* (1960) 35 PUR 3d 64 (Connecticut).

[18]*Re New Jersey Water Company* (1963) 51 PUR 3d 224 (New Jersey).

[19]*Re Southern Bell Telephone & Telegraph Company* (1966) 66 PUR 3d 1 (Florida).

[20]*Re Florida Power and Light Company* (1966) 67 PUR 3d 113 (Florida).

[21]*Re United Gas & Pipe Line Company* (1964) 31 FPC 1180, 54 PUR 3d 285 (Federal Power Commission).

[22]*Re Michigan Consolidated Gas Company* (1960) 36 PUR 3d 289 (Michigan).

Corporation Commission contested by Southwestern Bell Telephone Company, essentially agreed with the Michigan decision but added an additional word of caution. Speaking for the majority, the court said: "The reasonable cost of meeting civic responsibilities such as Chamber of Commerce dues and charitable donations should be allowed as an operating expense in a rate investigation, but they are subject to close scrutiny as to reasonableness."[23] Further refinement was added by the New York Public Service Commission when it stressed the possibility of increased business through membership fees: "Membership dues in Chambers of Commerce paid by utility companies should be allowed as operating expenses rather than charged to income, since these organizations are dedicated to the improvement of business in, and attraction to, the communities involved, and their efforts result in added business for the utilities."[24]

On the other hand, dues paid to organizations which have doubtful benefit to the company or to service provided to customers usually are considered below-the-line income deductions. The Federal Communications Commission has said that "golf club dues, social club dues, service club dues, house charges, and entertainment of employees, and items of similar nature, are chargeable to Account 323, 'Miscellaneous Income Charges,' under the Uniform System of Accounts."[25] The interpretation by the National Association of Railroad and Utilities Commissioners of proper accounting under the uniform system of accounts for golf club dues and the like is that such expenditures are chargeable to account 426, "Other income deductions."[26] State commissions, such as the Michigan Public Service Commission, have taken similar views: "Dues in service clubs and Chambers of Commerce incurred by management but without any clear benefit in providing telephone service, should not be allowed as an expense to be charged against the customers."[27]

---

[23]*Southwestern Bell Telephone Company* v. *Kansas State Corporation Commission et al.* (1963) 192 Kan 39, 51 PUR 3d 113, 386 P2d 515 (Kansas Supreme Court).

[24]*Re Accounting Treatment for Donations, Dues, and Lobbying Expenditures* (1967) 71 PUR 3d 440 (New York).

[25]Ibid., 71 PUR 3d 446.

[26]Ibid., 71 PUR 3d 447.

[27]*Re Michigan Bell Telephone Company* (1960) 32 PUR 3d 395 (Michigan).

Accounting decisions with reference to dues and membership fees rest upon the eventual benefits to both the utility and the consumer. When benefits are apparent, both federal and state commissions have allowed these items to be accounted for above the line and interpreted as legitimate expenses for rate making. When such expenditures are of uncertain benefit to the public interest, they are best accounted for and interpreted for rate-making purposes as below-the-line income deductions.

Maintenance

The proper accounting procedures and regulatory requirements for maintenance expense involve ascertaining (1) that the expense is legitimate and reasonable; (2) that all items charged to maintenance, including materials and supplies and labor costs, actually have been incurred; and (3) that items expensed are properly interpreted as maintenance rather than improvements or replacements, which properly should be capitalized in the asset accounts. The question generally is not one of an above- or below-the-line expenditure, but of proper accounting for above-the-line items. Furthermore, expenditures incurred by the utility predicated on forces beyond the firm's full control must be allowed as legitimate expenses of operation. For example, labor costs determined in the marketplace are legitimate expense items. The Illinois Supreme Court concluded that "the commissioner is without authority arbitrarily to reduce an allowance for maintenance shown to have been actually paid, since amounts of operating expenses capable of definite proof may not be reduced by estimates of what the maintenance should have cost unless there is a further showing that for some reason the amount was improperly increased over a legitimate cost."[28]

The obligation of proof of expenditure for maintenance work is upon both the accounting utility and the commission. In a formal rate proceeding, the FPC evaluated the situation in this way.

> An expense allowance for maintenance of a natural gas pipe line company's compressor station equipment was reduced where the company had followed the improper accounting

[28]*Peoples Gas Light & Coke Company* v. *James M. Slattery et al.* (1939) 31 PUR (NS) 193, 373 Ill 31, 25 NE(2d) 482 (Illinois Supreme Court).

> practice of charging to such maintenance expense at the time, and as purchased, the cost of spare parts, materials and supplies regardless of whether such items were used for maintenance at the time of purchase or were retained in stock for future use, where the company had proffered no evidence to show the amount of such expense actually incurred during the past year, and where evidence supporting the downward adjustment of the expense allowance was unrefuted by the company, which merely contented itself with introducing certain calculations pertaining to unrelated maintenance expense accounts for which no adjustment was proposed.[29]

Likewise the utility must guard against expenditures which may have been incurred but were not properly classified as operating expenses. In a rate investigation the Public Service Commission of Wisconsin said that "expenditures for construction or replacement of plant are not chargeable to operating expenses."[30] The implication is that the items obviously should have been capitalized to the proper plant accounts chargeable to expenses of operation in future accounting periods through depreciation and amortization.

Merchandising Expense

Merchandising and jobbing are particularly relevant to electric and gas utilities. These firms often engage in the sale of appliances as a promotional activity. Although the sales themselves may not be extremely profitable for the utility, the ultimate objective is the promotional aspect of increasing future sales of utility services. The uniform classification of accounts is quite specific in instructing utilities on proper accounting for merchandising and jobbing expenses separately from expenses of operation. Specific expense items are discussed in greater detail in chapter 15, so at this point suffice it to say that merchandising and jobbing expenses may be categorized as above-the-line expenses or as below-the-line income deductions. Provisions for these items are made through accounts 914, "Revenues from merchandising, jobbing and contract work," and 915, "Costs and expenses of merchandising, jobbing and con-

---

[29] *Re Mississippi River Fuel Corporation* (1952) 95 PUR NS 435 (Federal Power Commission).

[30] *Re Browntown Telephone Company* (1949) 2-U-3072, 4 October 1949 (Wisconsin).

tract work," which are subclasses of "Operation and maintenance expense."

If commission requirements specify that merchandising, jobbing, and contract work are nonoperational activities, that is, activities concerning other than the utility's primary service function, they must be accounted for in income accounts 415 and 416. The former is entitled "Revenues from merchandising, jobbing and contract work," and the latter "Costs and expenses of merchandising, jobbing and contract work." These accounts are reflected below the line as net additions to or deductions from utility operating income.

Commodity or Supply Costs

Utilities may purchase their entire supply of the commodity or service dispensed or they may supplement their own producing facilities with outside purchases. The utility becomes, in part or in total, merely a distribution facility. In these circumstances, which are particularly evident in the electric, water, and gas utilities today, accounting procedures and commission scrutiny once again must ascertain the reasonableness for commodity and supply costs with reference to both water and electric energy supply. In the former case, the California Railroad Commission concluded that "if the price being paid for a water supply is excessive as compared with the cost of producing water independently, such price will not be considered as an element of cost in determining the rates of a water utility, which are based largely upon rates charged by other utilities operating under similar conditions."[31] With reference to electric utilities it concluded that "electric consumers should not be burdened, through the charge to operating expenses, by excessive rates for wholesale power supply paid by the electrical utility under contract, which are higher than obtainable from other sources at published rates."[32]

Natural gas distributors oftentimes purchase and store gas during low periods of demand to be used during periods of high consumption. As with any industry, regulated or unregulated, this inventory of gas must be properly expensed at the time it is sold.

---

[31]*Re Vidal Water Company* (1933) P.U.R. 1933A 50 (California).

[32]*Paul J. Hopper et al.* v. *Lassen Electric Company* (1933) P.U.R. 1933B 277 (California).

The Montana Public Service Commission expressed its opinion that "the last in–first out method was approved for use by a gas company in pricing withdrawals of gas from storage."[33] The point being made by the commission was probably twofold. In a physical sense the last gas placed in storage was undoubtedly the first gas removed; consequently, the price to be expensed for this product should be the last price paid by the distributing utility. Likewise, this expensed item more nearly parallels the cost of gas currently being supplied to the distributing firm.

Nonrecurring Items

Public utilities, like any other enterprise, incur certain expenditures of a nonrecurring nature. There is no regularity in their appearance as operating items and, consequently, they require individual attention as they arise. One problem often encountered in the regulated sector of the economy is the fact that nonrecurring items, if expensed at the time of their occurrence, greatly could distort the magnitude of operating expenses during any one accounting period. In nonregulated firms the problem is not as critical since such expenses usually are not directly involved with price determination, but since there is an unusually close relationship of cost and price in regulated utilities, this distortion must be evaluated carefully. Included among the expenses of a nonrecurring nature are acquisition adjustments amortized, expenditures for legal fees, unusual property losses due to storm damage and other acts of God, and expenses incurred in rate case proceedings.

Acquisition Adjustments. Acquisition adjustments arise when property or plant is purchased and sold among utilities. Chapter 9, "Accounting for Business Combinations," fully analyzes acquisition adjustments. Their amortization is a direct result of commission evaluation of purchase price at the time property is acquired. For example, a utility may purchase property which, in the eyes of the commission, involves an arm's-length transaction. The price paid for the property, although it exceeds the original cost thereof, may be reasonable, and benefits to the consumer are evident. Amortization of this property acquisition adjustment then would be in-

[33] *Re The Montana Power Company* (1962) 42 PUR 3d 241 (Montana).

terpreted as a legitimate above-the-line expense. Under these circumstances the amortization is charged to account 406, "Amortization of electric plant acquisition adjustments."

If, however, the commission interprets the purchase price as other than arm's length or reasonable, amortization would be made through account 425, "Miscellaneous amortization." This latter account represents an income deduction rather than an expense of operation and thus is chargeable below the line to the utility owners. The Virginia Supreme Court has commented on this topic: "The commission, in fixing rates, properly allowed for the periodical amortization of the amount paid at arm's length bargaining in excess of original cost when first devoted to public use."[34]

Legal evidence for treating plant acquisitions as below-the-line income deductions is available. According to the Pennsylvania Supreme Court, "payments in excess of the original cost of utility plant which an electric company makes in purchasing plant from another utility cannot be charged to operating expenses in a rate proceeding, since the excess amount represents strategic or preempted value in anticipation of increased earning power and if not realized should be charged to the stockholders."[35] That same court further elaborated: "Any amortization of excess amounts paid by an electric company in purchasing a plant of another company for more than its original cost should be as disposition of income, not an operating expense which would result in higher rates to consumers."[36]

LEGAL FEES. Nonrecurring legal fees are also part of a utility's operation. Commission interpretation of this particular item bears heavily on whether or not the incurred legal fee is a benefit to the consuming public. The California commission has said: "Where a water company would have litigation with a city, a reasonable

---

[34]*Board of Supervisors of Arlington County* v. *Virginia Electric and Power Company* (1955) 196 Va 1102, 8 PUR 3d 120, 87 SE2d 139 (Virginia Supreme Court). See also: *Re Alabama Gas Corporation* (1958) 25 PUR 3d 257 (Alabama); and *Re Southern California Edison Company* (1954) 6 PUR 3d 161 (California).

[35]*Harrisburg Steel Corporation* v. *Pennsylvania Public Utility Commission et al.* (1954) 176 Pa Super Ct 550, 7 PUR 3d 609, 109 A2d 719 (Pennsylvania Supreme Court).

[36] Ibid.

allowance was included in operating expenses for this cost, amortized over a period of three years."[37]

On the other hand, if the utility were in error and required legal consultation, or chose to defend a service complaint which it ultimately lost, commission interpretation seems to indicate that these expenses are not beneficial to the consuming public; the company owners would derive any advantage gained, and they should bear the cost. The California commission said that "legal expense incurred by a water company primarily as the result of errors and omissions in the design and construction of a water reservoir would not be charged against the company's customers."[38] The Pennsylvania Public Service Commission agreed: "A claim by a water company for the amortization of cost incurred in defending a service complaint where the utility was found to be at fault was denied, and the customers would not be compelled to bear such costs where the complaint was upheld."[39]

Extraordinary Losses to Property and Plant. From time to time most public utilities experience extraordinary losses to property and plant; they usually occur as the result of unforeseen circumstances against which the utility cannot protect itself beforehand with insurance, proper and full depreciation, or other reserves. The most prevalent causes for such losses are storm damage and technological and regulatory change. The Federal Power Commission interprets an extraordinary loss as one which exceeds approximately 5 percent of income computed before the loss.[40]

The uniform system of accounts recognizes that such events will arise and has provided techniques allowing the utility to account for their occurence. With commission approval a utility will account for extraordinary property losses as a deferred debit in account 182, "Extraordinary property losses."[41] Income taxes, positive or negative, which are reflected through accounting for extraordinary items must be separated into account 409.3. For tax purposes the utility

---

[37]*Re Park Water Company* (1963) Decision No. 65205, Case No. 7305, Application nos. 43659, 43685, 9 April 1963 (California).

[38]*Re Citizens Utilities Company of California* (1965) 58 PUR 3d 155 (California).

[39]*Township of Spring* v. *Citizens Utilities Water Company of Pennsylvania* (1966) 65 PUR 3d 134 (Pennsylvania).

[40]FPC, *Uniform System,* General Instruction no. 7, p. 101-3.

[41]Ibid., p. 101-31.

with adequate income normally will recognize the entire loss sustained during the year in which it occurs; to do the same for financial and rate-making functions could, and undoubtedly would, distort the utility's normal operating income. With commission approval the company is allowed to amortize these unusual losses recorded in accounts 182 through 407. The Wisconsin commission, recognizing that such unforeseen losses cannot be avoided, allowed "a telephone company . . . to amortize over a ten-year period a portion of the loss on property retirements occasioned by a dial conversion program where the company had not earned a fair return and had been unable to accumulate a sufficient depreciation reserve to cover its loss on abandoned property over its approximate life."[42]

The key issues in this decision obviously center around two considerations. First, since the utility under investigation was earning an insufficient return, it could not absorb any loss through net income. Second, since the telephone equipment was retired early, sufficient depreciation had not been accumulated to cover the cost of equipment. Under these circumstances, the amortization of the loss should be considered as an above-the-line expense. If the conditions are such that the utility is earning a sufficient return and the company has ample time to recover fully the cost of plant through depreciation, the company undoubtedly would be required to amortize the extraordinary loss through account 425 as a below-the-line deduction from utility income.

The Minnesota Supreme Court provides an excellent summary of the guiding principles for accounting as well as regulatory purposes. In *Minnesota Street Railway Co.* v. *City of Minneapolis*, the court said:

> The principle of law which should guide the discretion of the commission in determining whether the customer or investor should be charged with the amount of alleged loss due to obsolescence is twofold: (1) the future customer may not be charged for obsolescence through any method of accounting unless the investor has suffered an actual loss by not having fully recovered prudently invested funds, and (2) even if such loss has occurred, it is unreasonable to charge the customer if the investor has been compensated for assuming the risk of obsolescence.
>
> In proceedings before the railroad and warehouse commis-

---

[42]*Re Farmers Telephone Company* (1961) 2-U-5620, 21 December 1961 (Wisconsin).

sion involving determination of loss due to obsolescence, the company has the burden of proof to establish that book losses represent an actual loss of prudently invested funds and that such losses have not been compensated for by depreciation or by past rates which have included the risk of obsolescence.

In sustaining the burden of proof with reference to the issue of obsolescence the company must produce evidence including records which it should be reasonably expected to have, and in the absence of complete evidence, the commission may apply its experience and background of knowledge to reach a just result.

Where an actual loss has occurred due to obsolescence, the commission may, in the exercise of its judgment, apportion one-half of all such actual loss to the investor and charge the remaining one-half to future customers by amortization as an operating expense over a period of years.[43]

RATE CASE PROCEEDINGS. Since rate case expenditures are sporadic they generally are classified as nonrecurring items. Each time a public utility formally appears before the regulatory commission, whether voluntarily or by request, both the utility and the commission expend substantial sums. The utility incurs regulatory expenses directly, either by using internal personnel or by hiring outside legal and other expert advice. In addition, many jurisdictions assess utilities, generally by formula, for all regulatory work performed. These costs must be paid by the rate payer or the utility owners. If the commission decides that such expenses may be amortized above the line, account 928, "Regulatory commission expenses," of the uniform system of accounts is used. If the commission interprets regulatory expenses to be unnecessary or excessive and not properly chargeable to the rate payer, account 426, below the line, is used.

It is interesting to note one interpretation of commission assessment against the utility in a question posed to the National Association of Regulatory Utility Commisioners.

Question:

To what account shall be charged 'Remainder Assessments,' made on behalf of state regulatory bodies for general purposes of public utility regulation which are not identified with specific services performed in special or formal cases?

[43]*Minneapolis Street Railway Company* v. *City of Minneapolis* (1957) ______ Minn ______, 22 PUR 3d 223, 86 NW2d 657 (Minnesota Supreme Court).

Answer:

'Remainder Assessments' should be charged to account 408, Taxes Other Than Income Taxes.[44]

Since rate case expenses are sporadic and usually are nonrecurring, they are amortized over a period of time. If these expenses are found to be legitimate and reasonable, write-off takes place above the line. The Illinois Public Service Commission has maintained that "legitimate regulatory expense is a part of the cost of doing business and hence recoverable."[45] The Indiana Public Service Commission has said that "the amount necessarily paid for fees and expenses in connection with a rate case is properly charged as an operating expense for ratemaking purposes."[46] With regard to the particular time span involved in the amortization, the California and Vermont commissions authorized the write-off over three and five years respectively.[47]

On the other hand, if there is reason to believe that the expenses incurred were either excessive or unnecessary, the courts as well as the commissions generally have held such items to be below-the-line deductions. According to the North Carolina Public Service Commission, "although rate costs should be amortized to expenses when a proposed rate increase is approved, when a rate increase is not justified and there is no merit in the request, the stockholders, and not the rate payers, should bear the cost of the proceedings."[48] Likewise, the Kentucky Public Service Commission said: "Rate case expenses should be borne by the stockholders rather than the rate payers where proposed rates have not been justified and there is no merit for a request for a rate increase, particularly where claimed rate case expenses are completely out of proportion with the other factors in the case."[49] Finally, the Pennsylvania Superior Court said that "litigation expenses caused by a public utility's

[44]NARUC, *Interpretations,* question 4-EGW, p. 2.

[45]*Re Alton Water Company* (1957) 22 PUR 3d 358 (Illinois).

[46]*Re Indiana Gas & Water Company, Inc.* (1953) 2 PUR 3d 184 (Indiana).

[47]*Re California Water Service Co.* (1964) Decision No. 67262, Application no. 45452, 26 May 1964 (California); and *Henry C. Hastings* v. *Village of Stowe* (1965) 57 PUR 3d 200 (Vermont).

[48]*Re Carolina Water Company* (1960) 32 PUR 3d 462 (North Carolina).

[49]*Re Union Light, Heat & Power Company* (1953) 97 PUR NS 33 (Kentucky).

own unjust and unreasonable action in filing for increased rates should not be allowed as an operating expense."[50]

Payments to Affiliates

Many public utilities are affiliated with other economic enterprises; these provide the utility with materials and supplies, management talent, engineering and financial advice, and other products and services normally acquired from outside vendors. Accounting for such goods and services presents no unusual problems other than adequate assurance to the regulatory commission that all charges for these expenditures are just and reasonable. This prompted the New York Court of Appeals to state that "when operating expenses arise out of dealings between affiliates, the commission has not only the right but also the duty to scrutinize such transactions closely."[51]

When it is apparent that the materials purchased, whether from an affiliate or from other outside sources, are obtained at reasonable prices, the commissions view the expenditures as legitimate. The Florida Supreme Court, reviewing a case involving the city of Miami, concluded that "in a telephone rate proceeding, the commission did not err in allowing in the company's operating expenses the full cost of equipment purchases from a manufacturing affiliate where the commission made findings, presumably valid, that the prices paid were not excessive but were in fact less than would have been paid to similar suppliers, that the affiliate's profits were not unreasonable, and that the telephone customers had substantially benefited from the economies and efficiencies resulting from such purchases."[52] On the other hand, the California Supreme Court held differently when it ruled that "payments by a telephone company to an affiliated supplier for supplies and equipment were

[50]*Scranton-Spring Brook Water Service Company* v. *Public Service Commission* (1935) 14 P.U.R.(N.S.) 73, 119 Pa Super Ct 117, 181 Atl 77 (Pennsylvania Superior Court).

[51]*General Telephone Company of Upstate New York, Inc.* v. *James A. Lundy et al., Constituting New York Public Service Commission* (1966) 17 NY2d 373, 64 PUR 3d 302, 218 NE2d 274, 271 NYS2d 216 (New York Court of Appeals).

[52]*City of Miami* v. *Florida Public Service Commission* (1968) 73 PUR 3d 369, 208 So 2d 249 (Florida Supreme Court).

adjusted downward, for ratemaking purposes, so as to allow the supplier a rate of return no higher than that allowed the telephone company, notwithstanding the contention that the suppliers' prices were lower than those of nonaffiliated suppliers, where the company failed to prove that the prices actually paid to a supplier were reasonable for ratemaking purposes."[53]

In all fairness, the disallowance of profits or expenses simply on the grounds of affiliation is unreasonable.[54] However, payments to affiliates involve the type of expenditures which are best evaluated prior to performance. The cases cited above involve rate-making proceedings, yet their impact on accounting techniques is obvious.

Pensions and Labor Costs

Accounting for pensions, wages, and salaries is, in many respects, beyond commission control. The results of collective bargaining between labor and management are binding. On the other hand, executive salaries and pension costs, on occasion, have been challenged by the regulatory commission because such excess expenditures are, in fact, a form of concealed profits. As in other instances, these outlays are of the type which normally are questioned by regulatory commissions during formal rate hearings. Since public utilities are competing in the labor market for operation labor as well as executive talent, compensation must be commensurate with those offerings of unregulated firms. The capabilities of management talent are closely correlated with firm size. Commissions are aware of this situation and generally direct their criticism toward extraordinary salaries, bonuses, or pension plans which are unreasonable in view of the size of the company. For example, the New Mexico commission held that a salary of $25,000 for a nonresident proprietor of a gas utility was excessive when compared to the company's operating revenues of somewhat less than $700,000.[55] The Wisconsin Public Service Commission interpreted excess

[53]*Pacific Telephone and Telegraph Company* v. *California Public Utilities Commission* (1965) 62 Cal 2d 634, 58 PUR 3d 229, 44 Cal Rptr 1, 401 P2d 353 (California Supreme Court).

[54]*Re Southern Bell Telephone & Telegraph Company* (1966) 66 PUR 3d 1 (Florida).

[55]*Re Vernah S. Moyston, d/b/a Hobbs Gas Co.* (1963) 48 PUR 3d 459 (New Mexico).

salaries in this way: "A salary paid to a stockholder officer of a public utility company in excess of the reasonable value of the work performed is, in effect, disguised as a wage payment and should be disallowed as an operating expense for ratemaking purposes."[56]

Life insurance coverage of employees may name the employee's estate or the utility as beneficiary. Premiums paid for such coverage may be interpreted either as expenses of operation or income deductions. Commission rulings on proper accounting seem to vary. If insurance was acquired as a condition for meeting other company obligations, these premiums should be interpreted as legitimate expenses. For example, "premiums for life insurance on the manager of a water company were deemed a proper operating charge for ratemaking purposes where the insurance was taken out as a condition to the issuance of a mortgage note."[57] The above ruling is subject to further question since the ultimate reason for acquiring the insurance was of a financial rather than an operational nature. Likewise, commission rulings state that "if the utility is named beneficiary for income, the premium should be accounted for as legitimate expenses."[58] Other commissions have ruled for similar interpretations only if the employee's estate or the rate payers benefit.[59] In contrast, some commissions have ruled that if the utility benefits this must be interpreted as the owners benefiting, and premiums thus should be accounted for below the line.[60]

Bonuses to utility employees have been interpreted differently by various commissions. For example, the Alberta commission considers Christmas bonuses as merely supplementary wages that should be treated as operating expenses.[61] The Louisiana Public

---

[56]*Re Preston Telephone Company* (1965) 2-U-6233, 23 September 1965 (Wisconsin).

[57]*Re Colebrook Water Company* (1964) D-R4263, 20 March 1964 (New Hampshire).

[58]*Public Utility Commission* v. *Lewistown Transportation Company* (1945) Complaint Docket no. 13961, 19 February 1945 (Pennsylvania).

[59]*Re New England Telephone & Telegraph Company* (1960) 35 PUR 3d 100 (Vermont).

[60]*Re Commerce Teleph. Co.* (1960) File no. 19343, Docket no. 1580-U, 16 November 1960 (Georgia); and *Pennsylvania Public Utility Commission* v. *Scranton Steam Heat Company* (1960) 34 PUR 3d 322 (Pennsylvania).

[61]*Re Northwestern Utilities, Ltd.* (1951) File PU.2742, 26 July 1951 (Alberta, Canada).

Service Commission views Christmas gifts, including bonuses, as below-the-line income deductions.[62] Under this interpretation bonuses become a distribution of earnings and not compensation based on benefits to rate payers.

Duplicate Charges

Account 929 of the uniform system of accounts for Class A and B electric utilities is entitled "Duplicate charges—credit." The uniform system's explanation states that "this account shall include concurrent credits for charges which may be made to operating expenses or to other accounts for the use of utility service from its own supply. Include, also, offsetting credits for any other charges made to operating expenses for which there is no direct money outlay."[63]

Like any business enterprise, an electric utility requires the use of electric energy, a telephone utility requires the use of telephone services, and a water utility requires the use of water. For example, electricity used by the electric utility is metered and charged as an operating expense or is capitalized in a plant account accumulated through a work order. If the utility were to purchase such energy from an outside source, the seller would:

Dr. Accounts Receivable	xxx	
Cr. Operating Revenue		xxx

The purchasing utility would:

Dr. Operating Expenses or Construction Work in Progress	xxx	
Cr. Accounts Payable		xxx

Since the seller and the purchaser are the same (the utility), there is no sale for revenue, and the first entry is unnecessary. The utility does not owe anyone, so the credit portion of the second entry is unnecessary. While the utility must recognize the service

---

[62]*Ex Parte Breaux Bridge Telephone Co., Inc.* (1961) 41 PUR 3d 260 (Louisiana).

[63]FPC, *Uniform System,* p. 101-94.

utilized as an expense of operation to produce service for sale, it accounts for this as an operating expense. With no cash outlay involved, the credit entry is to "Duplicate charges—credit," account 929, and the entry becomes:

Dr.	*Operating Expenses or Construction Work in Progress*	xxx	
Cr.	*Duplicate Charges*		xxx

Without the duplicate charges account, the utility would be charging the rate payer twice for the same production input. In the first instance, the cost of the energy produced would be included in production expenditures. In the second instance, if the energy were metered and charged to the utility, and the utility added this charge to operating expenses or plant accounts, the charge to the rate payer would be doubled. The duplicate charge account eliminates a metered bill charge as a transaction involving operating revenues, but allows the cost of production of energy consumed to be included at cost to the rate payer.

The above examples illustrate the varying opinions for the accounting treatment of utility expenditures. To disallow legitimate, just, and reasonable expenses of operation would deny a utility and its owner the right to collect all costs of operations through consumer rates. On the other hand, to allow improvident expenses to slip into the costs of operations would be contrary to effective regulation in the public interest. Although the two goals need not conflict, decisions with respect to reasonable expenses may be products of effective compromise.

Selected References

See references listed for chapter 3, p. 55.

5

Accounting for Depreciation

Proper accounting for depreciation is important to any business enterprise, regulated or unregulated. Its importance to regulated industries is exceptionally critical because of the heavy investment in utility operating assets. As such, depreciation represents a substantial portion of total operating revenue.[1] This chapter deals with all phases of depreciation—its meaning, historical development, causes and methods of calculation. Included in this latter category will be a discussion of service lives and salvage values, accounting treatment, and variations in accounting required by taxing authorities as well as a discussion of the impact of inflation.

Depreciation Defined

One dictionary defines *depreciation* as "(1) decreasing value due to wear and tear, decay, decline in price, et cetera; (2) a decrease in the purchasing or exchange value of money; (3) a lowering in estimation; disparagement."[2] This interpretation stresses the notion of value and its decline. The American Institute of Certified

---

[1]In 1968 depreciation expense was 11.2 percent of total operating revenues for Class A and B electric utilities. U.S. Treasury Department, Internal Revenue Service, *Statistics of Income—1967–68, Corporation Tax Returns* (Washington, D.C.: U.S. Government Printing Office, 1972), pp. 20–25.

[2]*The American College Dictionary* (New York: Random House, Inc., 1961), p. 325 (emphasis added).

Public Accountants uses this definition: "Depreciation accounting is a system of accounting which aims to distribute cost or other basic value of tangible capital assets, less salvage (if any) over the estimated useful life of a unit (which may be a group of assets) in a systematic and rational manner. It is a process of allocation, not evaluation."[3]

According to the uniform system of accounts for Class A and B electric utilities, " 'Depreciation,' as applied to depreciable electric plant, means the loss in *service value* not restored by current maintenance, incurred in connection with the consumption or prospective retirement of electric plant in the course of service from causes which are known to be in current operation and against which the utility is not protected by insurance. Among the causes to be given consideration are wear and tear, decay, action of the elements, inadequacy, obsolescence, changes in the art, changes in demand and requirements of public authorities."[4] This same uniform classification defines *service value as* "the difference between *original cost* and the *net salvage* value of electric plant."[5]

Several points should be evident. An obvious one is the apparent conflict between terms within the various definitions. One discussion concerns value whereas another emphasizes cost. In a general interpretation, depreciation often is used to indicate value or, more particularly, loss in value. When an individual speaks of the depreciation of his automobile in a year, he is saying that the value of the car, if it were sold today, would be less than the initial purchase price. However, within the concept of value, items may not depreciate. After a period of time a car may have zero value and, indeed, one might have to pay to have it removed, but there are instances when increased age may cause an appreciation of value. Anyone owning an Edsel automobile, regardless of its serviceability, may find that it is worth more or valued higher today than when originally purchased.

Accounting has chosen to utilize a cost rather than a value concept when referring to depreciation. Any purchase of plant or

---

[3]American Institute of Certified Public Accountants, *Accounting Terminology Bulletin* no. 1 (New York: AICPA, Committee on Terminology, August 1953), p. 25.

[4]FPC, *Uniform System,* Definition no. 11, p. 1 (emphasis added).

[5]Ibid., Definition no. 26, p. 3 (emphasis added).

equipment which is known to be serviceable or useful for a period of time greater than one accounting period should have its cost apportioned over those several periods of time. Cost is interpreted as a prepayment; depreciation converts a cost into an expense as the cost is allocated over successive accounting periods. When one analyzes the definition of *depreciation* cited in the uniform system of accounts, that is, as a decline in service value based on original cost, one discovers that the apparent conflict between cost and value does not, in fact, exist. The special meaning given the word *value* is in the sense of *service value*, or original cost less net salvage dollars received at the time of disposal. The discussion actually is based on cost and not value.

Any item whose service life spans several accounting periods should have its cost or service value apportioned over those periods through the depreciation mechanism. At the end of the property's useful life, except for scrap value, the item should have depreciated to zero. At that point, what is the asset's value? Since depreciation is not a value concept, the answer is not clearly evident. Coincidentally, the value also may be zero or scrap value, although it is more likely to be either less or more than scrap value, as was illustrated by the Edsel example.

Historical Development

Most of the principles of accounting in use today have existed since before the birth of Christ, but depreciation accounting is relatively new. Although the depreciation factor was recognized in the late 1800s, it was not until the twentieth century that depreciation accounting was fully comprehended. The first legal views concerning depreciation as related to public utilities came in *Knoxville* v. *Knoxville Water Company* in 1909. In this landmark decision, the Supreme Court was recognizant of depreciation both as an item of expense and as a measure in decline of service value.

With respect to depreciation as an expense item, the court said:

> A water plant, with all its additions, begins to depreciate in value from the moment of its use. Before coming to the question of profit at all, the company is entitled to earn a sufficient sum annually to provide not only for current repairs, but for making good the depreciation and replacing the parts of the property when they come to the end of their life. The company

> is not bound to see its property gradually waste, without making provision out of the earnings the value of the property invested is kept unimpaired, so that, at the end of any given term of years, the original investment remains as it was at the beginning. It is not only the right of the company to make such a provision, but it is the duty to its bond and stockholders, and, in the case of a public service corporation, at least, its plain duty to the public. If a different course were pursued, the only method of providing for replacement of property which has ceased to be useful would be the investment of new capital in the issue of new bonds or stocks. This course would lead to a constantly increasing variance between present value and bond and stock capitalization—a tendency which would inevitably lead to disaster either to the stockholders or to the public, or both. If, however, a company fails to perform this plain duty and to exact sufficient returns to keep the investment unimpaired, whether this is the result of unwarranted dividends upon over-issues of securities, or of omission to exact proper prices for the output, the fault is its own. When, therefore, a public regulation of its prices comes under question, the true value of the property then employed for the purpose of earning a return cannot be enhanced by a consideration of the errors in management which have been committed in the past.[6]

Regarding the decline in service value, the court said:

> The cost of reproduction is not always a fair measure of the present value of a plant which has been in use for many years. The items composing the plant depreciate in value from year to year in a varying degree. Some pieces of property, like real estate for instance, depreciate not at all, and sometimes, on the other hand, appreciate in value. But the reservoirs, the mains, the service pipes, structures upon real estate, standpipes, pumps, boilers, meters, tools, and appliances of every kind begin to depreciate with more or less rapidity from the moment of their first use. It is not easy to fix at any given time the amount of depreciation of a plant whose component parts are of different ages with different expectations of life. But it is clear that some substantial allowance for depreciation ought to have been made in this case.[7]

This early case identifies clearly that depreciation based on original cost is designed to recapture the expenditure over an appropriate time period in order to keep the initial investment intact. The

---

[6]*Knoxville* v. *Knoxville Water Company* (1909) 212 U.S. 1 (U.S. Supreme Court).

[7]Ibid.

concept of the going concern is paramount. One also notices that mention is made of replacement, although the recaptured dollars are in no way identified with replacement of an item at the end of its service life. In fact, the item may never be replaced; even if it is, prices surely will have changed and the recaptured investment may be less than, equal to, or greater than the cost of a replacement item.

By the late 1920s and early 1930s regulatory rate-making policies were tending toward a reproduction or current cost standard, and the Supreme Court's thinking on depreciation also changed. In 1930, in *United Railways Electric Company* v. *West*, the court said that depreciation expense should be based upon present value, or reproduction cost, rather than original cost.[8] However, this decision was not long lived, and the same court, speaking in the *Lindheimer* case of 1934, stated: "In determining reasonable rates for supplying public service, it is proper to include in the operating expense —that is, in the cost of producing the service, an allowance for compensation of capital in order to maintain the integrity of the investment in the service rendered."[9] This decision appears to have overruled the *United Railways* case and to have reaffirmed early decisions which based depreciation on cost.

Cost-based depreciation was affirmed in 1944 and remains the landmark decision. In that year the Supreme Court, in a case involving the Federal Power Commission and Hope Natural Gas Company,[10] reaffirmed *Lindheimer*. It ruled that depreciation based on cost would best maintain the integrity of the investment which, after all, was the designated purpose of this accounting concept; no more or no less was required of depreciation. Although depreciation is anchored to the concept of cost, and cost is a known and certain parameter, the practice of depreciation remains an art. Many judgmental factors are used in depreciation calculations, and exact depreciation assessment is impossible.

---

[8]*United Railways & Electric Company* v. *West* (1930) 280 U.S. 234 (U.S. Supreme Court).

[9]*Lindheimer* v. *Illinois Bell Telephone Company* (1934) 292 U.S. 151 (U.S. Supreme Court).

[10]*Federal Power Commission* v. *Hope Natural Gas Company* (1944) 320 U.S. 591 (U.S. Supreme Court).

Causes and Significance

The many causes of depreciation may be outlined generally, although the tabulation may be subject to dispute and question. In an accounting sense, depreciation provides for a better matching of costs and revenues. Thus certain unexpired costs converted to expenses for the period under review are proper. The Federal Power Commission and the NARUC define *depreciation* as a loss in service value. An elaboration of this cause for depreciation might be considered in at least two ways.

Physical Factors

First, there are certain physical factors which justify depreciation as an operating expense. The Interstate Commerce Commission says that *depreciation* is the loss in value not restored by maintenance.[11] It is doubtful that the ICC is referring to deferred or improper maintenance but, rather, to the fact that even if property and plant are maintained in like new operating condition, deterioration not provided for in the maintenance scheduling will occur. Thus wear and tear from operation is one physical factor; others include time, action of the elements, and weathering.

Functional Factors

Second, functional factors are both apparent and real causes for depreciation. The very fact that a plant is expanding will render certain assets inadequate. This does not mean that they are physically worn out and require replacement, but that they are no longer satisfactory for a particular level of operation. Likewise, technological change renders many assets obsolete, and obsolescence is a crucial consideration when determining the timing of depreciation. Providing for regulatory requirements also is critical. Some of these requirements may be caused by inadequacy or obsolescence: specifying that water or gas mains must be made from specific materials and that telephone companies switch from manual to dial equipment are a few examples. Some of these require-

[11]For example, see Interstate Commerce Commission, *Uniform System of Accounts for Class I and Class II Common and Contract Motor Carriers of Property* (Washington, D.C.: ICC, 1965), p. 5.

ments are prompted by other circumstances: ruling that electric distribution lines be placed underground in areas already being served by overhead systems might be justifiable only on aesthetic grounds.

Contingencies

Finally, contingency factors, such as accidents or disease, may be important considerations. Possible reductions in the natural supply of gas or water should be provided for. Regularly occurring storm damage which can be calculated in determining the useful life of an asset also must be considered. The probability of occurrence of such phenomena can be measured and not merely speculated upon.

Determining Depreciation Expense

Providing for depreciation oftentimes is termed an accounting procedure as opposed to a cash expenditure. This is essentially true since the transaction does not involve the disposition of funds. Inasmuch as there is no cash outlay involved, the mere accounting entry serves to recognize a proper cost and prevent an improper distribution as dividends to equity holders or a transfer to the utility's retained earnings account. Regulators are vitally concerned with utility depreciation practices since control of these will be reflected in the rates charged to the consumer, and many commissions have the authority to prescribe depreciation methods and rates. Table 9 displays these policies and practices.

Tax authorities also are interested in depreciation, although their objectives may differ from those of either the commission or the utility. Nevertheless, it is imperative that the utility abide by the tax law. Oftentimes several methods of treating depreciation may be followed simultaneously. While this may necessitate the development and maintenance of additional accounting records, the time and effort is justified on an economic or legal basis. The extent to and manner in which depreciation effects taxes will be analyzed later in this chapter and in chapter 6.

Regardless of the purpose, the methods used, or the law being followed, the steps in determining depreciation expense are the same. These include (1) an estimate of the service lives of the depreciable assets; (2) an estimate of the net salvage value of the

TABLE 9. *Depreciation Policies and Practices*

State	The Commission has authority to[1] *Prescribe depreciation method*	*Prescribe depreciation rates*	*Require depreciation rate studies*	*Depreciation method prescribed*
FPC	X	X	X	Generally straight line
FCC	X	X	X	Straight line
Alabama	X	X	X	Straight line
Alaska	X	X	X	No opinion issued as yet
Arizona	X	X	X	Usually straight line
Arkansas	X	X	X	Straight line
California	X	X	X	Straight line remaining life
Colorado	X	X	X	Straight line unless otherwise ordered
Connecticut	X	X	X	None prescribed. Straight line generally used
Delaware	X	X	X	Generally reviews and approves method in effect
District of Columbia	X	X	X	Straight line
Florida	X	X	X	Straight line
Georgia	X	X	X	Straight line
Hawaii	X	X	X	Straight line and sinking fund
Idaho	X	X	X	Straight line and present worth
Illinois	X	X	X	Usually straight line
Indiana	X	X	X	Straight line
Iowa	X	X	X	None prescribed to date
Kansas	X	X	X	Straight line
Kentucky	X	X	X	Usually straight line
Louisiana	X	X[5]	X	Usually straight line
Maine	X	X	X	Usually straight line
Maryland	X	X	X	None prescribed (straight line encouraged)
Massachusetts	X	X	X	Straight line
Michigan	X	X	X	Straight line
Minnesota[2]	X	X	X	Straight line
Mississippi	X	X	X	Straight line
Missouri	X	X	X	Straight line
Montana	X	X	X	Straight line
Nebraska[2]	X	X	X	Straight line
Nevada	X	X	X	None prescribed
New Hampshire	X	X	X	Straight line
New Jersey	X	X	X	Any method if substantiated
New Mexico	X	X	X	None prescribed for gas or electric. Telephone in conjunction with FCC

TABLE 9.—*Continued*

State	The Commission has authority to[1] *Prescribe depreciation method*	*Prescribe depreciation rates*	*Require depreciation rate studies*	*Depreciation method prescribed*
New York		X[5]	X	None prescribed. Straight line generally used
North Carolina	X	X	X	Straight line
North Dakota	X	X	X	Straight line but other methods accepted when justifiable
Ohio	X	X	X	Straight line
Oklahoma	X	X[5]	X	Straight line
Oregon	X	X	X	Straight line (one sinking fund)
Pennsylvania	X	X	X	Straight line, but only in formal rate proceedings
Puerto Rico	X	X	X	Straight line
Rhode Island	X	X[5]	X	Straight line–age life
South Carolina	X	X	X	None prescribed
South Dakota[2]		X	X	None prescribed
Tennessee	X	X	X	None prescribed
Texas[3]	X	X	X	Straight line
Utah	X	X	X	Straight line generally
Vermont	X	X	X	None prescribed
Virginia	X	X	X	Straight line
Virgin Islands[4]	X	X	X	—[7]
Washington	X	X	X	Straight line
West Virginia	X	X	X	Straight line
Wisconsin	X	X	X	Straight line
Wyoming	X	X[6]	X	Straight line

SOURCE: Federal Power Commission, *Federal and State Commission Jurisdiction and Regulation, Electric, Gas and Telephone Utilities, 1967* (Washington, D.C.: the Commission, 1967), p. 13.

NOTE: X = "yes."

[1] Both for rate-making and for general accounting purposes.

[2] No commission regulation of electric or gas utilities.

[3] No commission regulation of electric or telephone utilities.

[4] Electric facilities are owned and operated by the government and are not regulated by the commission. No natural gas service in the Virgin Islands other than bottled gas, which is not regulated by the commission.

[5] "No" for general accounting purposes.

[6] Depreciation rates not prescribed unless required by public interest.

[7] Not reported.

assets;[12] (3) the selection of a depreciation method which will equitably distribute the cost of the asset over its estimated service life; and (4) the application of the selected method to the depreciable property.

Service Life Estimation

Determination of the service life of a single asset or group of assets requires an evaluation of the future effects of wear and tear, decay, action of the elements, and such functional causes as obsolescence, inadequacy, or regulatory requirements for plant relocation. Review of past retirement experience is perhaps the basic source of information, and this, in combination with engineering estimates of future service lives, will aid in the analysis. Service lives may be established on the basis of time—including hours, months, or years of use or operation—as well as vehicle miles or other similar units of output. Time measurements appear to be the most widely accepted for public utilities since the uncertainties of linking the past with the future and further speculation of functional causes make other approaches more difficult. Furthermore, there is no real assurance that past experience will be emulated in the future.

While past experience may not reflect the future, it does provide one of the best bases for estimates. Actuarial and plant turnover studies, such as the Iowa curves,[13] often provide the method of determination. Of the two, actuarial studies demand the most detailed data. They require retirement ages of individual items which can be plotted to develop a frequency curve to determine average service life, which information should be available from continuing property records. Plant turnover, on the other hand, is the method often used when detail of individual items is missing. Average service life determination is based on annual additions to and retirements from a group of assets. In those instances where the utility lacks past data on newer types of assets, reliance may have to be placed solely on engineering studies, manufacturer esti-

---

[12]Net salvage value is the price at which retired assets may be sold less any expenses involved in preparing the asset for sale, including cost of removal.

[13]NARUC, *Public Utility Depreciation Practices* (Washington, D.C.: NARUC, 1968), chap. 8, pp. 105–77.

mates, or on any data available from similar utilities or regulatory bodies.

Regardless of the source of past information, it always must be adjusted for expected future events. Since these considerations are conjectural and subjective, the result must be interpreted as the best available informed judgment.

Viewing depreciation as a tax deductible item, the magnitude of the deduction bears heavily upon the estimated service life of the depreciable property. Realizing that individual interpretations might produce dramatic variation in the anticipated lives of such property and, subsequently, tax deductions and liabilities, Congress has, over the years, provided guiding principles for estimating service lives when calculating the depreciation deduction. The specification of asset life, like accelerated depreciation rates, is used by the federal government to provide tax incentives for capital investment.

From the time the federal income tax law was enacted in 1913 until 1934, service life estimations were left up to the individual taxpayer. In 1934 certain modifications were introduced such that the taxpayer had to provide proof that appropriate lives were being used. In 1942 the Treasury issued Bulletin F specifying an item-by-item listing of useful lives for calculating depreciation.[14] In retrospect, these lives were considered too long, and, although the bulletin was only a guide, it was difficult for the taxpayer to prove that shorter lives were appropriate. To overcome the burden of reviewing service lives on the basis of individual items, Bulletin F was abandoned in 1962 in favor of new *guidelines* for depreciation arranged in broad industry classes of assets.[15] Some 75 asset groupings were adopted with lives about 30–40 percent shorter than Bulletin F lives. Incorporated in the guidelines were complicated reserve test ratios to provide a mechanical method or procedure to test whether the taxpayer's actual period of asset used conformed to the "useful life" used for tax purposes.[16] The complexities associated with these calculations led to their abandonment and

[14]U.S. Treasury Department, Internal Revenue Service, *Bulletin F* (Washington, D.C.: U.S. Government Printing Office, 1931 [revised 1942]).

[15]U.S. Treasury Department, Internal Revenue Service, *Depreciation Guidelines and Rules,* publication no. 456 (Washington, D.C.: U.S. Government Printing Office, July 1962 [revised August 1964]).

[16]Revenue Procedure 62-21.

replacement with the present Asset Depreciation Range (ADR) System in March 1971.[17] The ADR System may be adopted for tax purposes only or, as is most likely in the case of nonregulated firms, also may be used for financial reporting.

The Asset Depreciation Range System, like the 1962 guidelines, is based on broad industry classes of assets; however, rather than providing for a single life for a given class, a range of years is given. For each asset within an asset class, the taxpayer may select a depreciation period within the asset depreciation range prescribed for the class. These ranges are for a minimum of 20 percent below to a maximum of 20 percent above the *guidelines*. Also, the asset depreciation period may be shorter than the asset's useful life, although the period is the same as useful life for IRS purposes.[18]

If a public utility elects to use the ADR System, it must normalize the deferral for rate-making purposes. However, if accelerated depreciation and flow-through accounting are being used for assets for rate making, it appears that any deferred taxes resulting from the ADR election may also flow through since the regulations make no special requirements for such assets.

Salvage Value and Cost of Removal

Estimating net service value has a major impact on the determination of depreciation. Calculating cost of removal and salvage value thus will have an important effect on the final depreciation rate. Proper understanding requires the definition of certain terms. *Service value* means the difference between original cost and the net salvage value of electric plant. *Salvage value* means the amount received for property retired less any expenses incurred in connection with the sale or in preparing the property for sale, or, if retained, the amount at which the material recoverable is chargeable to materials and supplies or other appropriate accounts. *Net salvage value* means the salvage value of property retired less the cost of removal. *Cost of removal* means the cost of demolishing, dismantling, tearing down, or otherwise removing electric plant, in-

---

[17] 26 U.S.C.A. (IRC 1971), section 1.167(a)-11, Revenue Procedure 71-25, 12 July 1971.

[18] This is also the useful life to be used for investment tax credit purposes. See pp. 135–141.

cluding the cost of transportation and handling incidental thereto.[19]

As with estimation of service life, determination of salvage value and cost of removal probably are best based on past experience modified by future expectations, although even educated guesses should be avoided whenever possible. One other consideration is the governing commission's view on this matter. Some commissions prefer to use the net salvage concept; others have chosen to employ a gross salvage calculation. In the latter, cost of removal is recognized as an expense in the year the asset is retired. Under a variety of circumstances utilities often experience negative service value.

Selecting a Method of Depreciation

In the past utilities have used a number of techniques identified as depreciation accounting methods, but today perhaps only two basic approaches and several variations remain. These two are the retirement reserve accounting and age-life methods. Within the latter, utilities use straight-line and variations of the sinking fund methods. Furthermore, tax depreciation allows the use of double-declining balance or sum-of-the-year's-digits methods.

Retirement and Replacement

Retirement and/or replacement methods of depreciation or amortization are used today only in selected isolated applications. In general, their use is obsolete and not generally accepted. When employed, their application often is connected with extraordinary obsolescence, abandoned or superseded plant, and with certain bond indentures.[20] Retirement accounting simply carries all assets at original cost until they are retired. The full original cost then is charged as an operating expense. In this form the method fails to match costs and revenues adequately, and it often has been described as something other than a depreciation method.

Replacement accounting, somewhat similar to the retirement approach, charges all new additions to the plant accounts, but any

---

[19]FPC, *Uniform System,* pp. 1–3.

[20]In the latter, bonding requirements relating to net income and interest charges provide a minimum level on amounts of depreciation to be charged. This minimum, in effect, assures that provision is made for retirements and replacements.

replacements or retirements without replacement are expensed as under the retirement method. Again, there is a wide fluctuation in expenses, and no adequate assurance is given of a proper matching of costs and revenues.

A slight modification of the above has been termed retirement-reserve accounting. An effort is made to avoid wide fluctuations in retirement charges and the utility accumulates a type of reserve. There is no attempt, however, to match the reserve accumulations with true costs for the period. The reserve usually is maintained at a percentage of plant and is designed to cope with any excess retirements which will be effected within the next year or two. Thus normal retirements are expensed as above, but any retirements greater than normal are charged to the reserve.

Age-Life

Several forms of age-life depreciation are employed by utilities. Among these are the sinking fund, straight-line, and accelerated methods, including double-declining balance and sum-of-the-year's-digits.

SINKING FUND. The sinking fund method enjoys little use today. The sinking fund or annuity approach to depreciation accumulation is so designed that periodic accumulations to the sinking fund earn interest at a specified compounded rate which will produce an amount to cover the cost of an asset at the end of its service life.

This method assumes that the periodic deposits into the fund are, in fact, reinvested in new utility operating property and plant; the sinking fund earns interest at the same rate as the utility's allowed rate of return. For the utility to earn at this rate requires the use of a gross or undepreciated rate base, and the accumulated provisions for depreciation, in effect, are allowed to earn interest. Accounting for sinking fund depreciation is illustrated in Table 10. It should be noticed that using the sinking fund results in an above-the-line depreciation expense and an interest expense (the return on the sinking fund) which is a below-the-line income deduction.

The other age-life methods of depreciation used by utilities include straight-line and accelerated methods. These are illustrated in Table 11.

TABLE 10. ***Sinking Fund (Age-Life) Depreciation Method***

Year	*Annual contribution to sinking fund*	*Assumed interest earned on sinking fund*	*Accumulated depreciation*
1	$ 532.19	$ 0	$ 532.19
2	532.19	31.93	1096.31
3	532.19	65.78	1694.28
4	532.19	101.67	2328.14
5	532.19	139.67	3000.00

NOTE: Assumptions: Original cost, $3,200; estimated service life, five years; estimated net salvage value, $200; and interest rate on sinking fund, 6 percent.

TABLE 11. ***Age-Life Methods of Calculating Depreciation***

Year	*Depreciation rate (in percentage)*	*Annual depreciation expense (in dollars)*	*Accumulated provision for depreciation (in dollars)*	*Book value (in dollars)*
		Straight-line method		
0	—	—	—	3200
1	20.00	600	600	2600
2	20.00	600	1200	2000
3	20.00	600	1800	1400
4	20.00	600	2400	800
5	20.00	600	3000	200
		Sum-of-the-year's-digits method		
0	—	—	—	3200
1	33.33	1000	1000	2200
2	26.67	800	1800	1400
3	20.00	600	2400	800
4	13.33	400	2800	400
5	6.67	200	3000	200
		Double-declining balance method		
0	—	—	—	3200.00
1	40.00	1280.00	1280.00	1920.00
2	40.00	768.00	2048.00	1152.00
3	40.00	460.80	2508.80	691.20
4	40.00	276.48	2785.28	414.72
5	40.00	165.89	2951.17	248.83

NOTE: Assumptions: Original cost of asset, $3200; net salvage value, $200; and estimated service life, five years.

STRAIGHT-LINE. The straight-line method is designed to distribute the depreciable cost of an asset in equal amounts over its useful life. The periodic depreciation charge is calculated by

$$\frac{\text{Original cost} - \text{net salvage value}}{\text{Estimated service life}}.$$

Dividing the periodic depreciation by the gross original cost of the asset produces a percentage rate of depreciation expressed in increments of time or output (months, years, vehicle hours, output, and so forth). Straight line is the predominant method used by utilities and sanctioned by most regulatory bodies. Table 9 details the approved methods to be used by the utilities under various state and federal regulatory control.

ACCELERATED METHODS. As has been noted, the Internal Revenue Service authorizes both regulated and nonregulated firms to use rapid or accelerated methods when calculating depreciation expense as a tax deduction. The two most common formulas used are the sum-of-the-year's-digits and the double-declining balance methods. In the former, annual depreciation expense is determined by

$$\frac{\text{Number of years remaining at begining of current year}}{\text{Total of digits of years of life}} \times (\text{Original cost} - \text{salvage}).$$

The double-declining balance method produces an annual depreciation rate which is 200 percent of the straight-line method ignoring salvage value.[21] Thus, if the straight-line method provides for depreciation at a 20 percent rate, the rate for the double-declining balance method is 40 percent. The calculated rate is then applied to the undepreciated balance at the beginning of the current period, which has been reduced by the depreciation expense for the prior periods. The use of the declining-balance approach also will leave an unexpired cost which is not to be interpreted as salvage value. To overcome having an unexpired amount, tax law allows the firm to switch to a straight-line method in order to fully depreciate the asset. Since the initial calculation ignores salvage value when the

[21] Salvage value does not enter into the calculation of depreciation expense under the declining-balance method. 26 U.S.C.A. (IRC 1954), section 1.167, (b)-2(a).

double-declining rate is applied, salvage value must be deducted before dividing the undepreciated balance among the remaining years of the asset's life.[22]

Both accelerated methods affect depreciation expense by weighting the early years of the asset's life with greater cost. Depreciation expense is greater and depreciation accumulation grows more rapidly during that time. The assumptions are that an asset makes a greater contribution to revenues during the earlier part of its life and that service value expires more rapidly in the early years. Both assumptions are subject to question, but the method is arbitrary. A comparison of results of using different age-life methods of depreciation is shown in Table 12. Further discussion of the accelerated methods of depreciation as related to taxes is reserved until later in this chapter.

Application of Depreciation Formulas

Applying the selected depreciation method to the depreciable assets may be done in a number of ways. Depreciation expense and the accumulated provisions for depreciation may be accounted for on an individual item basis, by groups of like property items, by functional groups of plant accounts, or by utility plant as a whole.

Individual Property Items

Accounting for depreciation on an item-by-item basis provides the greatest amount of detail but involves an unusually large amount of work in the capital-intensive utility industries. Except for certain large assets this method is seldom used for most utility property. When it is used and when an asset is sold or retired, the utility usually finds it necessary to cope with a gain or loss on the disposal of the item.

Group Depreciation

On the other hand, public utilities are well adaptable to the uses of group depreciation plans due to the large number of similar units. Furthermore, regulatory commissions often require group methods.

---

[22] 26 U.S.C.A. (IRC 1954), section 1.167(e)-1b.

TABLE 12. *Comparison of Results Using Different Age-Life Depreciating Methods*

Method	*Year 1*	*Year 2*	*Year 3*	*Year 4*	*Year 5*	*Total*
			Annual depreciation			
Straight line	$ 600.00	$600.00	$600.00	$600.00	$600.00	$3000.00
Sinking fund	532.19	564.12	597.97	633.86	671.86	3000.00
Declining balance	1280.00	768.00	460.80	276.48	165.89	2951.17
Sum of the years' digits	1000.00	800.00	600.00	400.00	200.00	3000.00
			Percentage of annual depreciation rate			
Straight line	20.00	20.00	20.00	20.00	20.00	
Sinking fund	17.74	17.74	17.74	17.74	17.74	
Declining balance	40.00	24.00	14.40	8.64	5.18	
Sum of the years' digits	33.33	26.67	20.00	13.33	6.67	

NOTE: Assumptions: Original cost, $3,200; estimated service life, five years; estimated net salvage value, $200; and interest rate on sinking fund, 6 percent.

For example, the *Uniform System of Accounts for Class A and B Telephone Companies*, as prescribed by the FCC, states:

> a. Depreciation charges shall be computed by applying the composite annual percentage rate considered applicable to the original cost of each class of depreciable telephone plant owned or used by the company. These percentage rates shall be based upon the estimated service values and service lives developed by a study of the company's history and experience and such engineering and other information as may be available with respect to prospective future conditions. These percentage rates shall be computed in conformity with the group plan of accounting for depreciation and shall be such that the loss in service value of the property, except for losses excluded under the definition for depreciation, may be distributed under the straight-line method during the service life of the property. Such percentage rates shall not include any allowance for loss of service value of property expected to be installed in the future. The percentage rates shall, for each primary account comprised of more than one class of property, produce a charge to operating expenses for that account equal to the sum of the amounts that would otherwise be chargeable for each of the various classes of property included in the account.
>
> b. In the event any composite percentage rate becomes no longer applicable, revised composite percentage rates shall be computed in accordance with Paragraph (a) of this section.
>
> c. The company shall keep such records of property and property retirements as will reflect the service life of property which has been retired, or will permit the determination of service-life indications by mortality, turnover, or other appropriate methods, and also such records as will reflect the percentage of service value, or net salvage value, as appropriate, for property retired from each class of depreciable telephone plant.[23]

Grouping of Like Items. Classes of property consisting of meters, poles, transformers, and so forth which have similar service-life expectancies generally are accounted for by groups. Each group is considered as a single asset represented by the balance in that control account. Under this method it is necessary to derive an average service life for the group. Using the example of poles, the group undoubtedly will contain a substantial number of units which will have an average service life. At the same time, there will be a number of poles which will survive longer than average because of unusual and ideal conditions such as shelter from the elements and certain destructive factors. On the other hand, a number of units'

[23]FCC, *Rules and Regulations—Part 31,* p. 12.

service lives will be cut short by unusual action of the elements, be it rapid decay, storm damage, destruction by mankind, or technological and regulatory requirements. Average service life takes on those characteristics of mortality tables used by life insurance companies. Once the group of physical assets is identified, a depreciation rate must be established based upon one of the acceptable depreciation methods.

When units are retired from the group, the full cost of the items retired is charged against the accumulated depreciation account. This is true whether the item is retired early, at the calculated average service life, or well beyond the average. No gain or loss on the retirement is recognized. Theory states that if the average service life is estimated correctly, even though all items do not die at an average point in time, those items that live longer will be compensated for by those items which are retired earlier than average. At the end of the lives of the entire group of assets, all lives will average to the initial estimate; charges to depreciation expense over the entire group's life will be no more or no less than the cost incurred.

Unit Summation Method. Another approach which utilizes the group depreciation plan has become known as the unit summation method.[24] It is based on the anticipated lives of functional groups of assets, such as distribution facilities or the whole utility plant, regardless of the assets' characteristics. Those which have much shorter lives are grouped together, and those which are much longer lived are included in another group. This particular approach has not been employed extensively, but it has enjoyed considerable use when commissions require a single depreciation rate for the utility's entire property. For example, the overwhelming majority of a water utility's entire property is long lived with the possible exception of trucks, automobiles, or similar conveyances. A depreciation rate can be established for the long-lived assets and a separate, much more rapid rate of depreciation can be used for the shorter lived trucks and cars. Establishment of a composite straight-line depreciation rate for grouped assets is illustrated in Table 13.

Once a rate is determined, the advantage of group depreciation is its ease in application. In addition, it once was thought that the vast quantity of like items made it virtually impossible to depre-

---

[24]NARUC, *Depreciation Practices*, p. 27.

TABLE 13. *Computation of a Composite Depreciation Rate*

Asset	*Cost*	*Net salvage value*	*Cost to be depreciated*	*Years of estimated service life*	*Annual depreciation expense*
1	$200,000	$50,000	$150,000	25	$ 6,000
2	50,000	—	50,000	5	10,000
3	100,000	5,000	95,000	10	9,500
4	150,000	10,000	140,000	14	10,000
5	25,000	1,000	24,000	12	2,000
	$525,000	$66,000	$459,000		$37,500

NOTE: The composite depreciation rate is based on original cost: $37,500 ÷ $525,000 = 7.14%.

ciate them on an item-by-item basis. It is doubtful that such reasoning is as valid today, since methods and tools are available which allow the utility to do this. Electronic data processing equipment can perform the necessary calculations required for unit depreciation with very little effort. The question that must be asked, however, is how much more accurate is unit depreciation versus a group method. The point should be clear: If accuracy is not sacrificed under a group method and may, in fact, be greater than under a single unit method, the use of group depreciation is not only proper and expedient, but also almost a requirement. Whether or not group depreciation is used is certainly a management decision. The utility manager, however, must be aware of the shortcomings as well as the advantages of the method to ensure that within the legal confines and uniform accounting systems prescribed no more or less than the cost of the assets should be reflected through depreciation accounting.

Accounting for Depreciation

The procedure of accounting for depreciation involves a systematic converting of unexpired asset costs into periodic expenses. Expressed another way, it is the appropriate matching of revenues with expenses—depreciation expense representing the extinguishing of an asset's useful life to produce revenues for the particular accounting period. Accounting for depreciation expense recognizes that: (1) the cost of the asset less salvage value is the amount to be systematically allocated as depreciation; (2) no more nor no less than the cost of the asset is depreciable; and (3) by considering this cost only depreciation will keep the initial investment of nominal dollars intact. The asset remains on the utility's accounting records until it is either retired or replaced, and only then are the accounting records relieved of a particular item.

The journal entries involved in the life of an asset are presented below.

(1) To record the asset placed into utility service:

Dr. Electric Plant in Service
Cr. Accounts Payable, Cash, Construction Work in Process, or Materials and Supplies

Explanation: Either one or a combination of the credit entries will be used depending upon the financial arrangements made to pay for these assets as well as whether it was constructed by the utility or purchased complete.

(2) To record periodic depreciation expense and accruals of depreciation:

Dr. *Depreciation Expense, Operating Expenses, Clearing Accounts, or*
Cost and Expenses of Merchandising, Jobbing and Contract Work
Cr. *Accumulated Provision for Depreciation of Electric Plant in Service or other appropriate fixed asset depreciation accumulation accounts*

Explanation: Depreciation is an operating item and is an above-the-line expense. Depreciation of nonutility assets which concern other utility activities and property used for this work should be charged to depreciation expense designated for such purposes. Most uniform accounting systems also provide for the use of clearing accounts. These serve as a means of distributing various items that subsequently affect more than one account or class of accounts but whose distribution is awkward as it is incurred. The clearing account acts as a collection center from which a distribution can be made in lump-sum segments at a designated time in the future.

The Federal Communications Commission's *Uniform System of Accounts for Class A and B Telephone Companies* requires the use of certain clearing accounts.[25] Most other uniform accounting systems permit their use as the utility finds it convenient to employ them.[26] If Entry 2 were rewritten using clearing accounts, it might look as follows:

Dr. *Depreciation Expense, Operating Expenses, Vehicles and Other Work Equipment, or Supply Expense*

---

[25]FCC, *Rules and Regulations—Part 31,* pp. 9, 58, 59.

[26]FPC, *Uniform System,* p. 101-1.

Cr. Accumulated Provision for Depreciation of Electric Plant in Service

EXPLANATION: This procedure allows for the separation of expenses of operation and investment costs. For example, the "Vehicles and other work equipment" account and "Supply expense" may be cleared subsequently into "Work in progress" accounts.

(3) To record costs of removal for items retired from service:

Dr. Accumulated Provision for Depreciation of Electric Plant in Service
Cr. Cash or Accounts Payable

EXPLANATION: When an asset is retired, a company may incur additional expense in removing the asset from operations, such as labor, machinery, or other outside contract work expenses. These additional costs are a debit to the "Provision for depreciation" account.

(4) To realize gross salvage on units retired from service:[27]

Dr. Cash, Materials and Supplies, or Accounts Receivable
Cr. Accumulated Provision for Depreciation of Electric Plant in Service

EXPLANATION: Gross salvage value refers to any amount received for material or equipment which was disposed of. Original cost or some variant thereof is used for calculating a value on any material which is retained by the utility as reusable and is placed in the "Materials and supplies" account.

(5) To retire an asset from service:

Dr. Accumulated Provision for Depreciation of Electric Plant in Service
Cr. Electric Plant in Service

---

[27]Sometimes net salvage value only is recorded. This is the difference between the gross salvage value and the cost of removal.

EXPLANATION: This removes the original cost of the item from the utility's accounting records.

These examples give one the impression that throughout an asset's life the accountant has been able to accurately predict cost of removal and/or salvage value so that net salvage value plus accumulated depreciation equals the historic or book cost of the asset. Unfortunately, we do not live in a world so neatly arranged. When an asset is removed and disposed of, the accumulated depreciation and net salvage value probably will be more or less than the original cost. When an individual asset is considered, if net salvage is greater than anticipated, the utility enjoys a gain or profit; if the net salvage is less than predicted or estimated, the utility suffers a loss. Such gains or losses are recognized in the "Other income and deductions" section of the income statement.

In those instances where utilities utilize group depreciation, (1) assets are depreciated on an estimated average service life of the group; (2) when an asset is retired, whether at the average, early, or late life of the group, the retirement is still calculated on the basis of the asset reaching its average retirement age, and the entire original cost of that item is debited to the accumulative provision for depreciation; (3) as long as an asset continues to live, even though its life exceeds the average life of the group, depreciation expense continues to be accumulated for that particular item until such time as the asset finally dies. At that time it is removed from the group as if it had been retired at an average age; and (4) under group depreciation, there is no recognition of gains or losses on the sale or removal of any one asset from the group. Theory would indicate that, on the average, gains and losses will be neutralized.

Accumulative Provisions

For many years accumulative provisions for depreciation were referred to as *depreciation reserves*, and one still finds mention of them today. The term *depreciation reserves* connotes the establishment of a fund to be expended for some purpose(s). Since depreciation accounting does not involve actual dollar expenditures or the allocation of dollars, such a reserve in the form of a fund is nonexistent. If a utility is profitable, depreciation accounting essentially is designed to keep the initial investment intact by recognizing a decline in service value and preventing the initial investment from being paid out as dividends. While accumulated depreciation may represent segregated cash initially, one cannot identify the cash as a fund. These monies may have been reinvested in other utility property, thus returning them to a fixed asset account, or they may have been used for other expenditures requiring money outlays.

Depreciation Fund

The above represents the normal situation. However, certain commissions are required by statute to instruct public utilities under their jurisdiction to maintain a depreciation fund. The state of Indiana is one such example. Their public utility statute states that:

> All money thus provided [by depreciation] shall be set aside out of the earnings and carried in a separate depreciation fund. The money in this fund shall be applied first to depreciation expenses, may be invested by the public utility or expended temporarily by it for new construction, extensions or additions to its utility property. This fund shall be used for no other purpose. If invested, the income from the investment shall be carried into and become part of the depreciation fund. Any balance, not applied to depreciation expenses, shall always remain a part of the depreciation fund. In no event shall monies, temporarily expended from this fund for new construction, extensions or additions to the property, be carried into or considered a part of the capital account of such public utility. Upon the sale of any public utility property, to continue in operation as such, the balance in the depreciation fund, unexpended for depreciation expenses, shall be transferred to the purchaser and by the purchaser shall be held, administered and used as herein authorized and required.[28]

In compliance therewith the *Uniform System of Accounts Prescribed for Public Utilities and Licensees* as well as accounting systems for gas and water utilities designate balance sheet account 126, "Depreciation fund." The classification defines account 126 in this way: "'This account shall include the amount of cash and the book cost of investments which have been segregated in a

---

[28]*Burns' Indiana Statutes Annotated,* vol. 10, Part II, p. 723. [*Acts 1913,* Ch. 76, 25, p. 167; 1925, Ch. 64, 2, p. 210.]

special fund for the purpose of identifying such assets with the accumulated provisions for depreciation."[29] Account 126, a type of sinking fund, is categorized as other property and investments of a nonutility nature and is not a part of utility plant used and useful.

ACCOUNTING FOR THE FUND. Those utilities which use account 126 must make an additional entry at the time they account for depreciation expense.

(1) To account for depreciation expense:

Dr. Depreciation Expense
Cr. Accumulative Provision for Depreciation

EXPLANATION: To record depreciation expense for the period.

(2) To account for the depreciation fund:

Dr. Depreciation Fund
Cr. Cash

EXPLANATION: To establish the fund and segregate dollars to be expended in accordance with the depreciation fund statute.

If a utility, by requirement or choice, uses account 126, subsidiary records are necessary to show the expenditures from this fund. Additional utility property may be purchased with the monies, investments may be made outside the utility, or the cash may be held in an idle state. If utility plant is purchased from the fund, one cannot merely debit the "Utility plant in service" account and credit the "Depreciation fund." Under the Indiana statute, a utility accounting system must be set up in microcosm to account for utility property financed by depreciation funds.[30]

THE FUND AND RATE MAKING. Under such circumstances very critical questions arise when the regulator must consider the calculation of the utility's rate base. The net investment rate base normally has been interpreted as a net amount identifying property

---

[29]FPC, *Uniform System,* p. 101-25.

[30]By commission ruling, the statute is interpreted as an alternative and not a requirement.

and plant used and useful; it is determined by taking an established gross value and deducting accumulative provisions for depreciation. Under this theory, when a utility does not utilize a depreciation fund the deduction for the accumulated depreciation is, in effect, designed to do two things. First, it reflects recaptured investment contributed by the rate payer through depreciation expense. Since this investment has been returned, the rate payer should not be required to pay a return the second time, and the accumulated depreciation is deducted. Second, the theory implies that monies segregated by allocating net income between depreciation and earnings available for common equity holders does, in fact, generate funds which are reinvested in utility assets. The rate payer, under this assumption, is not expected to pay for invested plant which he contributed. At the same time, it is fair to assume that the original investor expects and is entitled to a return on the funds which he initially invested—the gross expenditure for property and plant.

Under the two conditions just stated, the deduction of the depreciation reserve satisfies both the investor and the rate payer. One actually is analyzing the problem from two different points of view, those of the investor and the rate payer, using identical assumptions: The utility is a profitable organization, and allocations of income through depreciation accounting are reinvested in property and plant. In fact, the last assumption might even be relaxed. One might ask the question, what if the utility does not fully reinvest funds provided through depreciation? Is the rate payer or the investor being harmed? The answer is negative. Deducting the full accumulation of depreciation removes the plant purchased by depreciation funds from the rate base, thus eliminating the requirement that the rate payer pay a return on his contributed capital and, at the same time, throws the burden on management to account to investors for the fact that it did not reinvest all of this fund allocation.

If management reinvests in outside activities, the rate payer and the investor are content. However, if management finds it impossible to invest in outside activities and economic conditions are such that the plant is not expanded, the accumulated depreciation probably is retained by the utility in idle cash. Under these conditions, management is responsible and must answer to the stockholders. However, as far as utility functions are concerned, all parties are receiving their just reward through good regulatory and accounting procedures.

USES FOR THE FUND. When a utility establishes a depreciation fund and a statute declares that property acquired from this fund be so segregated and identified, rate-making procedures make one of two requirements. First, the amounts recorded in Account 101, "Utility plant in service," must be considered as the rate base in the gross amount without consideration of accumulated depreciation, or, second, if a net rate base is calculated, utility plant purchased under the depreciation fund must be included within the rate base. The commission, however, cannot use gross rate base and depreciation fund or net rate base and eliminate the depreciation fund. Although the fund was provided by the rate payers, it is part of the investor's capital on which he must be allowed to earn a return.

The depreciation fund is little used today. It serves no useful purpose other than perhaps representing a throwback to the time when reserve for depreciation was thought of as a separate fund. Consequently, it might be wise for the commissions to eliminate this account from the uniform classifications.

Depletion Accounting

The natural gas industry, which utilizes a wasting natural resource, must account for the depletion of the natural gas fields. This usually is done on a unit-of-production basis for each leasehold or field. A cost for the period is arrived at by applying a predetermined unit rate to the total number of units produced during the period. Several different methods may be used to determine the unit rate. One is to divide the net book cost of depletable plant by the estimated number of units to be recovered; a second is to divide the gross book cost by the total past plus estimated future units to be extracted.

The depletable base usually includes the leasehold (geological and geophysical) costs plus the intangible drilling and development costs. Thus

$$\text{Depletion rate} = \frac{\text{Acquisition cost} - \text{Residual value}}{\text{Estimated life in production units}}.$$

An example will illustrate the concept. Assume a natural gas producer acquires a natural gas field whose net acquisition cost is

$100,000 and whose estimated life in production units is 400,000 Mcf. The cost per Mcf is 25 cents. If 75,000 Mcf of gas are withdrawn during the year, the total depletion allowance is $18,750 (75,000 × 25¢). This will be recorded as

Dr. *Amortization and Depletion of Producing Natural Gas Land and Land Rights*	$18,750
Cr. *Accumulated Provision for Amortization and Depletion of Purchasing Natural Gas Land and Land Rights*	$18,750

Depreciation and Taxes

The uniform systems of accounts as well as commission interpretation provide for depreciation on a straight-line basis for financial and rate-making purposes. An asset or group of assets is retired based upon a fixed proportion of the invested asset's cost being recaptured in equal increments each accounting period over the service life of the asset. Depreciation expense, like other expenses of operation, is tax deductible. Tax legislation administered by the Internal Revenue Service may be at variance with regulatory legislation administered by the various public service commissions at federal and state levels. When the two conflict, differences must be recognized and accounted for.

The Tax Law

The Internal Revenue Code of 1954, 68A Stat. 3, allowed for the use of several accelerated methods of depreciation and amortization for tax purposes. Of particular interest to public utilities are Sections 167 and 168.

§ 167. *Depreciation*
(*a*) *General rule.*—There shall be allowed as a depreciation deduction a reasonable allowance for the exhaustion, wear and tear (including a reasonable allowance for obsolescence)—
(1) of property used in the trade or business, or
(2) of property held for the production of income.

(*b*) *Use of certain methods and rates.*—For taxable years ending after December 31, 1953, the term "reasonable allowance" as used in subsection (a) shall include (but shall not be limited to) an allowance computed in accordance with regula-

> tions prescribed by the Secretary or his delegate, under any of the following methods:
>
> (1) the straight line method,
>
> (2) the declining balance method, using a rate not exceeding twice the rate which would have been used had the annual allowance been computed under the method described in paragraph (1),
>
> (3) the sum of the years-digits method, and
>
> (4) any other consistent method productive of an annual allowance which, when added to all allowances for the period commencing with the taxpayer's use of the property and including the taxable year, does not, during the first two-thirds of the useful life of the property, exceed the total of such allowances which would have been used had such allowances been computed under the method described in paragraph (2).
>
> Nothing in this subsection shall be construed to limit or reduce an allowance otherwise allowable under subsection (a).[31]

Section 168, "Amortization of emergency facilities," was a tax provision for a sixty-month write-off period for any facilities which were purchased for emergency production during the Korean conflict.[32] This provision was terminated 31 December 1959.

Tax and Book Depreciation

Accelerated depreciation assumes higher depreciation charges in the earlier years of an asset's life than does straight-line depreciation; it also assumes lower depreciation charges during later years of an asset's life than does the straight-line method. Therefore, when an asset is newer, depreciation expense is greater, taxable income is lower, and income tax is less. As assets age, depreciation expense declines, taxable income increases, and income taxes rise. The discrepancy which must be accounted for arises because of differing net taxable income. Regulatory commissions have authorized two approaches for reconciling or eliminating the tax discrepancy. These have become known as the normalization and the flow-through methods. While the former reconciles, the latter eliminates the need for reconciliation. As reported to the FPC, Table 14 indicates which method is authorized by various commissions and which a utility must follow in that jurisdiction.

---

[31]26 U.S.C.A. (IRC 1954), sections 167 and 168.

[32]Ibid.

TABLE 14. *Commission Treatment of Tax Effects Caused by Provision of Income Tax Law Before 1 January 1970*

State	Accounting treatment: flow through or deferral[1]		
	Investment tax credit	*Accelerated amortization*	*Liberalized depreciation*
FPC	Either	Deferral	Either[12]
FCC	Either	—[10]	—[13]
Alabama	Not decided	Not decided	Not decided
Alaska	Deferral	Not decided	Deferral
Arizona	Either	Either	Either
Arkansas	Deferral	Deferral	Deferral
California	Flow through[6]	Deferral	Flow through
Colorado	Either	Either	Either
Connecticut	Flow through	Flow through	Flow through
Delaware	Flow through	Flow through	Flow through
District of Columbia	Either	Not used	Flow through
Florida	Deferral	Deferral	Deferral
Georgia	Deferral	Deferral	Deferral
Hawaii	Either	Deferral	Deferral
Idaho	Deferral	Deferral	Either
Illinois	Deferral	Deferral	Deferral
Indiana	Deferral	Deferral	Deferral
Iowa	Not decided	Not decided	Not decided
Kansas	Deferral	Deferral	Deferral
Kentucky	Either	Either	Either
Louisiana	Deferral	Deferral	Deferral
Maine	Flow through	Deferral	Flow through
Maryland	Either	Either	Either
Massachusetts	Deferral	Deferral	Deferral
Michigan	Deferral	Deferral	Deferral
Minnesota	Deferral	Not used	Not used
Mississippi	Deferral	Deferral	Deferral
Missouri	Either	Deferral	Flow through
Montana	Deferral	Either	Either
Nebraska[2]	Deferral	Deferral	Deferral
Nevada	Deferral	Flow through	Flow through
New Hampshire	Either	Deferral	Flow through
New Jersey	Either	Deferral	Flow through
New Mexico	Either[7]	Deferral	Deferral
New York	Flow through[8]	Deferral	Flow through
North Carolina	Deferral	Deferral	Deferral
North Dakota	Deferral	Deferral	Deferral
Ohio	Either	Deferral	Flow through
Oklahoma	Deferral	Deferral	Deferral

TABLE 14.—*Continued*

State	Accounting treatment: flow through or deferral[1]		
	Investment tax credit	*Accelerated amortization*	*Liberalized depreciation*
Oregon	Flow through[9]	Deferral	Flow through
Pennsylvania	Deferral	Deferral	Flow through
Puerto Rico[3]			
Rhode Island	Not decided	Not decided	Flow through
South Carolina	Deferral	Deferral	Deferral
South Dakota[2]	Deferral	Not decided	Not decided
Tennessee	Either	Deferral	Deferral
Texas[4]	Deferral	—[11]	Deferral
Utah	Either	Deferral	Not decided
Vermont	Flow through	Flow through	Flow through
Virginia	Deferral	Deferral	Deferral
Virgin Islands[5]	Not decided	Not decided	Not decided
Washington	Either	Flow through	Flow through
West Virginia	Flow through	Deferral	Flow through
Wisconsin	Flow through	Flow through	Flow through[14]
Wyoming	Deferral	Deferral	Deferral

SOURCE: Federal Power Commission, *Federal and State Commission Jurisdiction and Regulation of Electric, Gas, and Telephone Utilities* (Washington, D.C.: U.S. Government Printing Office, 1967), pp. 38–39.

[1]Flow through: Only actual taxes to be paid for the period are included in the income statement. Deferral: Actual taxes plus deferred taxes are included in the income statement.

[2]No commission regulation of electric or gas utilities.

[3]U.S. revenue provisions not applicable to Puerto Rico.

[4]No commission regulation of electric or telephone utilities.

[5]Electric facilities are owned and operated by the government and are not regulated by the commission. No natural gas service in the Virgin Islands other than bottled gas, which is not regulated by the commission.

[6]Usually on an average basis.

[7]For telephone, deferral.

[8]Except for New York Telephone Co., for which service-life flow through is permitted.

[9]Deferral permitted if amount materially would distort income.

[10]Question never arose.

[11]Not reported.

[12]Depends upon date asset purchased.

[13]No final decision to date; however, FCC order no. 45115 adopted 26 February 1970 permits deferral accounting.

[14]Income tax expense includes only taxes currenly payable, but depreciation expense includes the tax saving due to the use of liberalized depreciation.

NORMALIZATION ACCOUNTING. Those states in which a utility must normalize the tax discrepancy require that the company reflect in its financial accounting income statement a deferred tax so that the entire federal income tax expense is equal to that which the utility normally would have had to pay if it had chosen to use straight-line depreciation for tax purposes as well as for financial accounting. The utility's entry to record tax expense under the normalization procedure is as follows:

Dr. Income Tax Expense (for current tax liability) and	xxx	
Provision for Deferred Income Tax	xxx	
Cr. Taxes Accrued (for current tax liability) and		xxx
Accumulated Deferred Income Tax		xxx

The *Uniform System of Accounts Prescribed for Public Utilities and Licensees* specifies that only current tax liabilities incurred during that period may be included in the "Income tax expense" account. Utilities using tax normalization therefore will set up subaccounts as illustrated in the entry above to record both the liability and the deferral.

The building up of the deferred tax account during the first years of an asset's life is designed to compensate for the fact that tax expense will be greater in the later years of an asset's life. Over the entire life of the asset, taxes will be normal, that is, "as if" the utility had used straight-line depreciation for both tax and financial accounting. Accounting for taxes in later years is as follows:

Dr. Income Tax Expense (for actual current liability) and	xxx	
Accumulated Deferred Income Tax	xxx	
Cr. Taxes Accrued (for actual current liability) and		xxx
Income Tax Deferred in Prior Years		xxx

TAX REFORM ACT OF 1969. The Tax Reform Act of 1969 produced certain fundamental and important changes in accounting for accelerated depreciation and its attendant tax liability.[33] These changes are designed to freeze what the Treasury viewed as a double loss in tax revenue—one loss caused by increased depreciation expense, and a second by lower tax revenues engendered by reduced utility rates (prices).

Under the pre-1969 law, utilities had an opportunity to select either the straight-line or one of the accelerated methods of depreciation for tax purposes. If the utility used an accelerated method it was told by the jurisdictional regulatory authority whether it could normalize as a tax deferral or whether the saving had to be flowed through. For example, from 1956–1964 the Federal Power Commission required utilities under its control to use a normalization method of deferred taxes. Amounts which accrued in the deferred tax reserve were included in the utility's capitalization and earned a return of 1.5 percent.

From 1964–1969, following their opinion in the Alabama-Tennessee Natural Gas Company of Florence, Alabama, case[34] the FPC required electric and gas utilities using liberalized depreciation to flow through the tax savings to their customers.

> Under the new rules, in general, the utility must continue to use the depreciation method which it used in its last accounting period ended prior to August 1, 1969. Different rules are provided for public utility property owned prior to January 1, 1970 and property acquired on or after that date. For pre-1970 public utility property (owned at January 1, 1970), the rules can be summarized as follows:
>
> 1. If the taxpayer has been using a straight-line method (or any method other than a declining balance method or a sum of the years-digits method), it must continue to use such method.
> 2. If the taxpayer used an accelerated method for its latest taxable year for which a return was filed prior to August 1, 1969, together with the normalization method of accounting, it may continue this method.
> 3. If the taxpayer used an accelerated method of depreciation for its latest accounting period ending before August 1, 1969, together with a flow-through method of accounting, the taxpayer may continue to use the accelerated method.

---

[33] Tax Reform Act of 1969, Subtitle E—Depreciation Allowed Regulated Industries Earnings and Profit Adjustment for Depreciation, Act Sec. 441 (IRC 1954), section 167(1), p. 193.

[34] *Re Alabama-Tennessee Natural Gas Company* (1964) 31 FPC 208, 52 PUR 3d 118 (Federal Power Commission).

For post-1969 public utility property (acquired after 1969), the available methods may be summarized as follows:

1. The straight-line method (or any method other than a declining balance method or sum of the years-digits method).
2. An accelerated method, if the normalization method of accounting is employed.
3. An accelerated method of depreciation, although the flow-through method of accounting is used, if the same depreciation method was used for pre-1970 public utility property of the same (or similar) type most recently placed in service and the flow-through method of accounting was used for its latest accounting period ending before August 1, 1969.

For taxable years beginning after December 31, 1970, a taxpayer using the flow-through method of accounting may elect to change to a straight-line method; or if normalization accounting is permitted by the regulatory agency, an accelerated depreciation method with respect to property which increased its productive or operational capacity. The election is not available for replacement property. The election must be made within 180 days of enactment of the new law, that is, no later than June 28, 1970.[35]

Under the Tax Reform Act, the FPC now allows utilities—electric and gas—to continue whatever form of tax depreciation they were using on all new properties. If they used the straight-line method, they must continue to do so, or switch to a normalization method with commission approval. If the utility was using flow through, the 1969 act provides that the company *may* change to straight-line methods to account for post-1969 property or, with FPC approval, to a normalization method if new property represents an expansion. However, "the Tax Reform Act of 1969 permitting an election as to the treatment of liberalized depreciation does not diminish the authority of the Federal Power Commission to determine whether a company may abandon flow-through and use liberalized depreciation with normalization for property not subject to the statutory election, that is, the pre-1970 property and the post-1969 property which does not represent an expansion."[36]

Flow-Through Accounting. When a utility is required by commission dicta to flow through the tax savings which the utility enjoys

[35]Forest W. Brown, "Depreciation and Amortization," in *Analysis of the Tax Reform Act of 1969,* ed. Gilbert Simonetti, Jr. (New York: AICPA, 1971), pp. 341–42.

[36]*Re Texas Gas Transmission Corporation* (1970) 84 PUR 3d 193 (Federal Power Commission).

with the use of accelerated depreciation, the financial statements of the utility reflect straight-line depreciation and actual taxes paid. The result is an increase in net income after taxes. In a rate-making situation this will mean a higher rate of return. The flow-through concept not only advocates flowing through the actual tax savings and, subsequently, higher income on the income statement, but also anticipates a flowing onward to the rate payer in the form of lower rates since the rate of return has now increased and the savings, in fact, belong to the rate payer.[37]

Of interest is the philosophy of the American Telephone and Telegraph Company regarding accelerated depreciation. For fifteen years, 1954–1969, AT&T selected the continued use of straight-line depreciation for both taxes and financial reporting. The FCC, in its decision of Phase 1-a, Docket 16258, while formally postponing a firm decision on the future course they would follow regarding accelerated depreciation, did, nevertheless, consider the variation in risk when determining the rate of return.[38] By using accelerated depreciation, "the company *could* increase its cash flows and thus obtain interest-free capital in the form of deferred taxes. By refusing to use accelerated depreciation, the company is refusing to accept this capital contribution. Thus, the model lends support to the thesis that neither the customer nor the stockholders benefit from straight-line depreciation. Until evidence to the contrary has been evaluated, there is reason to question whether it is advisable for a utility commission to permit a company under its jurisdiction to disregard the tax savings afforded by liberalized depreciation."[39]

---

[37]Eugene F. Brigham and James L. Pappas, *Liberalized Depreciation and the Cost of Capital* (East Lansing: M.S.U. Public Utilities Studies, 1969), chap. 3.

[38]*Re American Telephone and Telegraph Company et al.* (1967) 70 PUR 3d 194 (Federal Communications Commission); and *Re South Central Bell Telephone Company* (1970) 83 PUR 3d 317 (Federal Communications Commission). In this latter case the commission said: "As a result of Congress' enactment of the Tax Reform Act of 1969, public utilities may now take advantage of accelerated depreciation provided that they are not required to flow through the resulting tax deferrals to their respective customers in the form of rate reductions; and in response to the enactment of the law the Federal Communications Commission has issued a waiver of its rule in connection with accounting for deferred taxes resulting from the use of accelerated depreciation for income tax purposes so as to permit normalization, retroactive to January 1, 1970."

[39]Brigham and Pappas, *Liberalized Depreciation,* p. 92.

While the accountant may be satisfied that he has faithfully executed the proper accounting entries based upon regulatory requirements, he cannot ignore the further economic impact which such action produces when reported to the company's shareholders. The basic question which arises concerns the deferred tax account when normalization procedures are followed. Deferred taxes arise from an increased expense which, if not paid, restricts earnings and provides management with additional funds. The accountant must satisfy himself that in reporting to shareholders he adequately explains whether the deferred tax benefits the consumer, the rate payers, neither, or both.[40]

The Impact of Inflation

As stated earlier, depreciation is calculated on the basis of the original cost of the asset less net salvage value, and this net depreciable figure is systematically allocated over the expected life of the asset. In general, accounting assumes a stable dollar; utility accounting assumes the same. However, there is one important difference between depreciation expense and other expenses which require cash outlays. Depreciation expense is covered with dollars of current value, but it is repaying a cost which actually was expended with "historical" dollars. For at least twenty years the U.S. economy has been in an inflationary spiral. The question thus arises as to whether or not an adjustment should be made in depreciation expense to compensate investors for the declining value of the dollar. If not, one might argue, the investor's initially contributed value is not being retained—the integrity of the original capital is threatened. If dollars provided through the depreciation technique are reinvested in new plant, and if this plant is of a more modern technology which can produce service at a cost low enough to compensate for the decline in the value of the dollar, then integrity is maintained. However, during periods of rapid inflation (or deflation) such maintenance is extremely difficult.

Two things must be made extremely clear. First, the utility is depreciating the original dollar investment regardless; second, the purpose of depreciation is just that, and not that the utility will provide funds for asset replacement. Inflation adjustments there-

---

[40]Ibid., chaps. 4, 5, and 6.

fore are not designed to provide enough money for new assets as might be implied. New assets may never be purchased, or, if they are, no one is able to specify the replacements which a utility actually will acquire. Chances are very good, however, that these replacements will be substantially different technologically from current facilities. The only thing that would be maintained with inflation dollar value adjustment would be the purchasing power of that initial investment.

To summarize, the NARUC Committee on Depreciation reached the following conclusion in its 1954 report: "This committee's reexamination of the question as to what is the proper depreciation base, leads firmly to the conclusion that the claims advanced in support of economic depreciation are lacking in probative force. The committee is convinced that the long-established cost basis is sound, practical, and equitable and should be continued."[41]

Selected References

Brigham, Eugene F., and Pappas, James L. *Liberalized Depreciation and the Cost of Capital.* East Lansing: MSU Public Utilities Studies, 1969.

Garfield, Paul J., and Lovejoy, Wallace F. *Public Utility Economics.* Englewood Cliffs, N.J.: Prentice-Hall, Inc., 1964, chap. 8.

National Association of Regulatory Utility Commissions. *Public Utility Depreciation Practices.* Washington, D.C.: NARUC, 1968.

[41]NARUC, *Report of Committee on Depreciation* (Washington, D.C.: NARUC, 1954).

6

Accounting for Taxes

Public utilities have been referred to as the tax collector par excellence. In fact, in 1968 total taxes paid by electric, gas, and telephone utilities amounted to approximately $8.3 billion. Since utilities are allowed to include all taxes resulting from operations, including income tax, as legitimate above-the-line expenses, the effect on the rate payer is substantially one of a sales tax.[1] In order to arrive at the proper amount of taxes to be included above the line, the accountant must provide records which substantiate an allocation of taxes by type of taxing district. Furthermore, a number of transactions within which a utility becomes involved may be interpreted differently and, depending upon the interpretation given, may have substantial effects on the amount of taxes allocated and eventually paid.

Under current economic conditions tax increases probably are unavoidable, and the importance of effective tax accounting cannot be overemphasized. While it is true that the tax accountant will keep records in accordance with good accounting principles, his concern should extend beyond mere record keeping. The primary and secondary impact of taxes is felt throughout the economy, and, inasmuch as our discussion evolves around public utilities, social and economic implications are particularly evident. In any business

---

[1]*Department of Public Works of Washington* v. *Seattle Gas Company* (1934) 3 P.U.R.(N.S.) 479 (Washington).

the tax accountant struggles to identify all tax deductible items to produce a low tax base, but in the utility industry that struggle must be intensified. The utility supplying a necessary service has the legal as well as social obligation to incur tax bills in the lowest amounts possible. Only then can the utility supply service at its lowest cost to the greatest number of consumers.

It is interesting to note that because of tax obligations each additional dollar of net income earned by the utility requires approximately $2.50 of increased revenues. The following example is illustrative. Assume that the combined rate for federal and state income taxes is 55 percent, gross revenue tax is 5 percent, and excise tax is 10 percent. What is the required increase in revenue for each after-tax dollar of net income? The solution is calculated by: $\$1.000 \div 45.0\% = \$2.222$; $\$2.222 \div 95\% = \$2.338$; plus 10 percent excise tax of $0.234. The required increase in revenue from customers is $2.572.

Shifting the Tax Incidence

One often hears discussion on shifting the tax incidence. The above equations indicate that the incidence of utility taxes is shifted to the rate payer, and essentially this is correct. From a legal viewpoint there is little quarrel that utilities are allowed to collect all tax payments from the rate payer; unregulated business may attempt to shift taxes, but Supreme Court dicta have legally sanctioned utilities to do so. In 1922 the Supreme Court decided in *Galveston Electric Company* that "in calculating . . . a proper return, it is necessary to deduct from gross revenue the expenses and charges; and all taxes which would be payable if their return were earned are appropriate deductions. There is no difference in this respect between state and federal taxes, or between income taxes and others."[2] From that date little question has remained as to the legal incidence of utility taxation. Like many other expense items, however, while taxes may be classified as above-the-line items, they often are paid for by consumers' dollars designated for the utility owners.

The practical matter of shifting the incidence may not be as

[2]*Galveston Electric Company* v. *Galveston* (1922) 258 U.S. 388, 399, 400 (U.S. Supreme Court).

straightforward as it appears. When a utility has a rate hearing before a regulatory commission, the commission determines the general rate level at which the utility should attempt to operate; test year expenses—including taxes—are adjusted and used to determine the amount of dollars to be allocated for such items in the future. Added to the expense dollars are amounts to pay reasonable or normal returns on the various forms of invested capital. Predicting the future based upon the past will be only as reliable and accurate as the degree to which the future emulates the past. If tax rates increase after the general rate level is set and other expense elements are held constant, the return to equity capital declines and full tax incidence is not shifted forward to the rate payer.

Types of Taxes

All investor-owned utilities are subject to many forms of taxation, although these may vary in number and amount depending upon the firm's location. Generally, a utility is subject to both federal and state net income taxes, property or ad valorem taxes, gross revenue taxes assessed in addition to or in lieu of property taxes, and a franchise tax assessed against the utility in return for its right to operate. Utilities also must account for employers' and employees' shares of withholding and unemployment taxes. The utility is a true tax collector for its employees' shares withheld from wage payments. Likewise, under certain economic conditions, excise taxes are collected from the consumer, although they are not reflected in the utility rates charged.

The utility's large tax incidence, amounting to approximately 18–25 cents of every revenue dollar, is accounted for by a number of factors. The sheer physical size of a utility's revenue-generating capacity will produce revenues and, subsequently, taxable income of considerable magnitude. Furthermore, if a utility is a declining-cost operation and if rates do not parallel the cost declines, more taxable revenue is generated as output rises.

The widespread geographical location of public utility property creates a substantial tax base for ad valorem or property taxes. In a capital-intensive industry such as a utility, property extends into many taxing districts, including local, state, and interstate territories. For this reason, as noted in the discussion of continuing property records, utility property generally is identified by taxing districts.[3]

These numerous taxing districts often have wide discrepancies in property values and imported property values from other areas. To aid in overcoming this problem many states utilize the unit rule of property assessment: The utility is valued as a single entity (unit) by a central assessment board or committee. The total assessment is then apportioned among the various districts on the basis of identifiable physical values, service units of output, or gross revenue for the district. Establishing an acceptable tax rate also is required, and this may be a local or an average state rate. If the state collects the tax revenue it must be returned to the property taxing districts. While central assessment is the better approach, a number of states still rely upon local assessors for this work. Under such conditions unreal assessments or double taxation are likely.

Accounting for Taxes

The various uniform systems of accounts illustrate two types of tax expense control accounts. For Class A and B electric utilities these are accounts 408, "Taxes other than income taxes," and 409, "Income taxes." Account 408 controls two subaccounts, 408.1 and 408.2, which separate those taxes applicable to utility functions and those attributable to nonutility activities. Account 409 controls three subaccounts: "Utility income taxes," "Non-utility income taxes," and "Income taxes" (both positive and negative on extraordinary items). Companion liability accounts to which items are credited are account 236, "Taxes accrued," based on estimates and adjusted periodically to reflect reality as facts become available, and account 165, "Prepayments," which is used to record prepayment of taxes applicable to the period subsequent to the balance sheet. These prepayments represent actual payments in excess of the current liability for the present accounting period. For example, real estate taxes often are filed and paid for in advance. Payroll tax deductions and sales taxes collected by utilities are not part of a utility's tax liability; they are interpreted as an accounts payable

[3]See chapter 7.

and thus are recorded in the current liabilities account 241, "Tax collections payable."

One must remember that these accounts are used in conjunction with operating expenses peculiar to utility and nonutility functions. Those taxes which apply to plant construction must be charged to work in progress and closed into the proper asset account. Such taxes will be expensed in future account periods through periodic depreciation charges. Thus, taxes may be distributed to certain maintenance, clearing, materials and supplies,[4] nonoperating, and reserve accounts as well as the appropriate construction work in progress accounts.[5]

Consolidated Tax Returns

A particularly thorny issue arises in tax allocation when a utility files consolidated income tax returns for federal and, possibly, state obligations. Utilities may perform other than utility functions through their subsidiaries or separate departments within the

---

[4]For example, in response to the following question regarding sales tax on materials, the NARUC stated:

Question No. 30:

Note E under Account 408, Taxes Other Than Income Taxes, provides that sales taxes shall be charged, as far as practicable, to the same account as the materials on which the tax is levied. Is it permissible under this provision to include such taxes in Account 163, Stores Expense, and clear that account each month through loading charges on issues during the month?

Answer:

Where it is impracticable to charge sales taxes to each item of material purchased for stock because of the large number of items, it is permissible to charge sales taxes to Account 163, Stores Expense, and to clear the charges in the latter account through loading charges to stores issued during the month, provided that sales taxes on large, readily identifiable items are included in the unit cost of such items and are not included in the clearing account mentioned.

This interpretation applies to electric, gas, and water utilities. NARUC, *Interpretations,* question 30-EGW, p. 13.

[5]With reference to payroll taxes (social security and unemployment benefit taxes), the interpretation of the NARUC is: "Social security, unemployment benefit and other forms of payroll taxes, to the extent applicable to operating payrolls, should be included in Account 408, Taxes Other Than Income Taxes, and not distributed over the various expense accounts to which the payroll was charged. Such portions of these classes of taxes as are applicable to construction work should be distributed directly or through clearing accounts to the appropriate utility plant accounts. Likewise, any such taxes applicable to nonutility operations should be charged to the appropriate nonutility expense account." Ibid., question 2-EGW, p. 1.

utility, or may be part of a larger holding company organization; if so, they usually file consolidated federal tax returns to take advantage of lower total tax payments. The problems of consolidation center around three areas: (1) allocation of consolidated return income tax liability; (2) allocation of corporation income taxes by functions or departments; and (3) accounting classifications of tax effects of unusual deductions from taxable income. All raise questions regarding tax reporting versus tax accounting. In this regard the Wisconsin Circuit Court was quite definite when it said: "The allocation of consolidated income taxes for tax purposes is not controlling for accounting purposes."[6]

Allocation of Consolidated Tax Liabilities

Under certain conditions some departments, functional areas, or separate entities within the consolidated organization may have suffered losses and, consequently, experienced no income tax liability. In filing a consolidated return, the loss reduces the consolidated taxable income. A problem arises as to the allocation of the taxes paid back to the contributing members of the consolidation; in effect, it becomes one of allocating federal income taxes in such a way that negative amounts are shown with offsetting normalizing amounts charged to income tax expense. If a subsidiary should sustain a loss that results in an allocation of negative tax to the subsidiary, correspondingly higher taxes will be allocated to the profitable subsidiaries. Negative amounts may be indicated in an income tax expense account or in a deferred charge, plant, or surplus account.

An alternative might be that the company sustaining the loss have nothing allocated to it and that the profitable firms bear the entire tax burden. Yet, reviewing the interpretation found in the uniform system of accounts under account 409, it clearly appears that this account should contain charges solely for accruals for the actual liability for income taxes.[7] If interpretation is correct, taxes

[6]*General Telephone Company of Wisconsin* v. *Wisconsin Public Service Commission* (1962) 46 PUR 3d 1 (Wisconsin Circuit Court).

[7]"A water company which participated in a consolidated federal income tax return with its parent corporation was allowed, for rate-making purposes, only that tax liability which it actually incurred under the consolidated return." *Re Davenport Water Company* (1968) 76 PUR 3d 209 (Iowa).

should be allocated among those corporations within the group that had taxable income without allocating negative taxes to those entities suffering losses or charging higher than actual taxes to those entities having taxable income. The Securities and Exchange Commission and the Internal Revenue Code generally concur with this interpretation.[8]

One logically might argue for negative taxation inasmuch as the company or entity sustaining the loss in fact reduced the total consolidated tax payable. The unprofitable company should be compensated for this loss while the companies having taxable income should concurrently be charged an extra tax expense. This amount still should be less than that which would have been assessed under the filing of separate returns. Yet, the Supreme Court said:

> A gas company's consolidated income tax was properly allowed in the cost of service under a formula which first applied the losses of unregulated companies in the group to the gains of other unregulated companies, which also provided that if a net taxable income remained in the unregulated group the regulated companies would not share in the savings from the consolidated return and would be deemed to have paid the full 52 per cent tax rate, and which further provided that if losses of the unregulated companies exceed their net income and hence reduce the taxes of the regulated group below what they would have paid had they filed separate returns, the consolidated tax paid would be allocated among the regulated companies in proportion to their taxable incomes.[9]

Negative income taxes have been interpreted as donated capital to the loss sustaining company and recognized as investment on the part of the contributor. Logic states that the contributor purchased certain property rights of the loss sustaining entity thereby increasing the contributed investments. However, to treat consolidated tax savings as revenue or as an asset violates generally accepted accounting principles. Furthermore, since income taxes never can be less than zero, the recording of negative taxes implies a fictitious

[8] 26 U.S.C.A. (IRC 1954), section 1552, subparagraphs (a)(1) and (a)(2); and 15 U.S.C.A. 79, SEC ruling U45(b)6.

[9] *Federal Power Commission* v. *United Gas Pipe Line Company et al.* (1967) 386 US 237, 68 PUR 3d 321, 18 L ed 2d 18, 87 S Ct 1003 (U.S. Supreme Court).

tax expense and might be viewed as financial distortion.[10] Table 15 illustrates tax allocations among a holding company and two subsidiaries, first filing separate returns, then filing a consolidated return.

Allocation of Taxes Among Departments

Allocation of taxes among departments of a single utility, for example, electric, gas, merchandising, and other nonutility functions, requires the same general approach as used among separate entities filing a consolidated return. The utility should accord no different accounting treatment to tax allocations among departments than occurred with separate operating corporations. Two alternatives exist: (1) all departments should be allocated taxes, whether positive or negative; and (2) those departments that contributed no taxable income should not be allocated negative taxes.

In 1968 a Kentucky Public Service Commission rate hearing concluded: "A saving of 6 percent on federal income taxes by reason of a consolidated return with affiliated corporations was reflected in the taxes allowable to a water company as an expense for rate-making purposes."[11] The Connecticut commission took a somewhat drastic view when it said in the *Connecticut Company* case: "No income tax expense was allowed for a transit company even though it would have net income, where its parent company, with which the transit company would make a consolidated return, would incur no income tax liability because of deficits."[12] However, the U.S. Court of Appeals stated:

> In determining the federal income tax allowance in the cost of service of a natural gas pipeline company which is a mixed company having both regulated and unregulated sources of income, and which has joined with affiliates in filing consolidated tax returns, the Federal Power Commission must divide the income of the company into regulated and unregulated

[10]The telephone *Separations Manual* published jointly by the NARUC and the FCC makes provision for the allowance of negative tax allocation. NARUC-FCC Cooperative Committee on Communications, *Separations Manual* (Washington, D.C.: FCC, February 1971).

[11]*Re Lexington Water Company* (1968) 72 PUR 3d 253 (Kentucky).

[12]*Re Connecticut Company* (1963) Docket no. 10163, 22 March 1963 (Connecticut).

TABLE 15. *Allocation of Consolidated Federal Income Taxes, in Dollars*

	Holding company	Subsidiary A	Subsidiary B	Consolidated return
Assumptions				
Total capitalization	20,000,000	15,000,000	15,000,000	30,000,000
Debt capital 5 percent	15,000,000	10,000,000	—	25,000,000
Equity capital	5,000,000	5,000,000	15,000,000	5,000,000
Income before interest and income taxes	1,400,000	2,000,000	2,000,000	
Interest expenses	750,000	500,000	—	
Intercompany dividends		500,000	900,000	
Dividends received—cr.	(1,190,000)			
Taxes based on separate returns				
Taxable income	(540,000)	1,500,000	2,000,000	
Tax at 50 percent		750,000	1,000,000	
Tax on a consolidated basis				
Taxable income	(750,000)	1,500,000	2,000,000	2,750,000
Tax at 50 percent				1,375,000
Allocation of consolidated taxes				
Based on income of those companies in the consolidation which had taxable income	—	589,286	786,714	1,375,000
Based on contribution of each company to taxable returns	(375,000)	750,000	1,000,000	1,375,000

components where there is evidence of record by which these components may be calculated, and must then set off net losses and net income from unregulated sources against each other, and if the unregulated component is sufficient to absorb all such net losses, and no excess remains to reduce the regulated taxable income of the company, the company must be allowed the full statutory income tax rate.[13]

Table 16 illustrates the allocation of consolidated income taxes for a single company with departments of electric, gas, merchandising, and nonutility investment.

Interperiod Tax Allocations

A related problem involves interperiod tax allocations. These arise from transactions that affect the determination of net income for financial accounting purposes in one reporting period and the computation of taxable income in a different reporting period. The American Institute of Certified Public Accountants (AICPA) Accounting Research Study No. 9 classified these timing differences.

Reported for income taxes after recognized for accounting income

(A) Revenues or gains are taxed after accrued for accounting purposes. These differences usually result from voluntary elections of the taxpayer.

(B) Expenses or losses are deducted for tax purposes after accrued for accounting purposes. These differences usually result from requirements and interpretations of the tax laws.

Reported for income taxes before recognized for accounting income

(C) Revenues or gains are taxed before accrued for accounting purposes. These differences result from requirements and interpretations of the tax laws.

(D) Expenses or losses are deducted for tax purposes before accrued for accounting purposes. Some of these differences result from voluntary elections of the taxpayer; others may result from requirements and interpretations of the tax laws.[14]

The study emphasizes that such allocation is not intended to remove fluctuations in income or expenditures, nor is it a normaliza-

---

[13] *United Gas Pipe Line Company* v. *Federal Power Commission* (1968) 72 PUR 3d 391, 388 F2d 385 (U.S. Court of Appeals).

[14] Homer A. Black, *Interperiod Allocation of Corporate Income Taxes,* Accounting Research Study no. 9 (New York: AICPA, 1966), p. 3.

TABLE 16. *Allocation of Income Taxes Among Departments of a Utility, in Dollars*

	Department			*Common stock in subsidiary company*	*Total Company*
	Electric	*Gas*	*Merchandising*		
Assumptions					
Total capitalization	600,000	350,000	50,000	200,000	1,200,000
Debt capital at 5 percent[a]	300,000	175,000	25,000	—	500,000
Equity capital	300,000	175,000	25,000	200,000	700,000
Taxable income					
Income before interest and income taxes	90,000	8,000	(5,000)	20,000	113,000
Interest expense	15,000	8,750	1,250	—	25,000
Dividend received—cr.[b]				(17,000)	(71,000)
Taxable income	75,000	(750)	(6,250)	3,000	71,000
Income tax at 50 percent					35,500
Allocation of income tax					
Based on contribution to total corporate taxable income	37,000	(375)	(3,125)	1,500	35,500
Based on departments having taxable income	34,135	—	—	1,365	35,500

[a] Allocated on basis of bondable property in each department.
[b] To eliminate intracompany payments.

tion, the artificial smoothing of income. Rather, its intention is to provide a better matching of expenses and revenues.

In this regard the Federal Power Commission seems to be moving in the same direction. The *Uniform System of Accounts Prescribed for Public Utilities and Licensees*, account 283, "Accumulated deferred income taxes—other," illustrates the point. Instructions A and B for this account state:

> A. This account, when its use has been authorized by the Commission for specific types of tax deferrals shall be credited and account 410, Provision for Deferred Income Taxes, shall be debited with the amount equal to that by which taxes on income payable for the year are lower because of the current use of deductions other than accelerated amortization or liberalized depreciation in the computation of income taxes, which deductions for general accounting purposes will not be fully reflected in the utility's determination of annual net income until subsequent years.
> B. [Likewise] . . . account 411, Income Taxes Deferred in Prior Years—Credit, shall be credited with an amount equal to that by which taxes on income payable for the year are greater because of deferral of taxes on income in previous years, as provided by paragraph A, above, because of difference in timing for tax purposes of particular income deductions from that recognized by the utility for general accounting purposes, other than with respect to accelerated amortization or liberalized depreciation.[15]

Specific Tax Deductions

Regardless of the extent of regulation, few corporations report the same net income for tax purposes as they report for financial purposes to stockholders or regulatory commissions. Thus operating income for a public utility may vary considerably from taxable income. These variations exist because of differences between the legal rules and administrative regulations which control the determination of net taxable income and the uniform system rules and accounting conventions that control determination of income or return on investment.

Deductions of Bond Interest

One such cause for variation is the treatment of bond interest, a tax deductible item, which generally is displayed in the utility

[15] FPC, *Uniform System,* p. 101-40.

income statement following net operating income. Since a utility has a substantial portion of its invested capital in the form of debt securities, and the related cost is not deducted in arriving at net operating income, a substantial difference exists between taxable income and net operating income.

A number of additional variations exist between taxing rules and the uniform accounting systems.

Interest Income

Interest income received on tax-free securities, such as state and municipal obligations, is excluded as part of taxable income but included in financial income under accounting regulations.

Sale or Exchange of Property

Gains and losses on a sale or exchange of property may be reflected in the income statement for that accounting period, may be prorated over several periods, or may be charged to retained earnings. The accounting method depends upon the type of income statement used by the corporation.[16] For tax purposes, however, the gain or loss must be recognized during that taxable year, subject to carry-back and carry-forward provisions.

Sections 1231, 1245, and 1250 of the Internal Revenue Code are pertinent to this discussion.[17] Property subject to these sections include real and depreciable property held for more than six months either sold, exchanged, or subjected to involuntary conversion. All gains and losses must be aggregated. If aggregation produces a net gain, all gains and losses are treated as *net long-term capital gains and losses*. However, if losses exceed gains, all gains and losses are treated as *ordinary gains and losses*. In addition, the calculation must exclude recaptured income through depreciation. If any part of the gain is represented by recaptured depreciation,

---

[16]To conform with the Accounting Principles Board's *Opinion No. 9—Reporting the Results of Operations,* issued 9 October 1966, the FPC (Docket R-344, Order No. 389) and FCC (Docket No. 18477) have adopted an "all inclusive income statement" concept.

[17]26 U.S.C.A. (IRC 1954). Section 1231 of the Code describes sales of property used in a trade or business; sections 1245 and 1250 outline rules on the recapture of depreciation on sales, exchange, or involuntary conversion of property.

all other prior year deductions from income must be deducted before applying the above rules. Such recaptured depreciation is taxed as ordinary income.

Involuntary conversions through losses due to storm damages occur at infrequent intervals during a utility's life. Financial accounting requires that the utility recognize the tax savings on the loss that year, but prorate the balance of the loss over a period of years in order to smooth expenses for rate making.[18]

Depreciation Expense

Depreciation expense as a tax deductible item may vary considerably depending upon the utility's use of accelerated depreciation for tax purposes versus straight-line depreciation for financial statements. Use of the former will show substantially more depreciation for tax than for financial purposes (see chapter 5). The financial statements of those utilities which must normalize accelerated depreciation require additional expense and liability accounts which aid in identifying these differences.

Two examples of providing for these accounts include decisions by the state commissions of Oregon and New York. The former said: "Because of a conflict between Commission orders and the manner in which the surviving company of a merger reported to federal agencies, the survivor was required to establish new accounts No. 410, 'Provision for Deferred Taxes on Income;' 411, 'Income Taxes Deferred in Prior Year—Credit;' and 281, 'Accumulative Deferred Income Taxes—Accelerated Amortization' and

---

[18]*Question:*
What treatment should be accorded the income tax effect of gains or losses from transactions which involve unusual or general nonrecurring charges or credits that are so large as to require special treatment in the accounts, such as by direct entries to surplus or by deferrment over a period of years?
Answer:
The income tax effect of such charges or credits to surplus shall also be charged or credited to surplus. Large or unusual charges, which are deferred in the accounts and amortized over a future period, shall be amortized net; that is, after being reduced by the income tax effect of the item.
Note: This interpretation may be subject to modification in the event changes in the systems of accounts become necessary to accommodate the all-inclusive income statement theory (APB Opinion No. 9).
NARUC, *Interpretations,* question 80-EGW, p. 41.

an existing account, 'Earned Surplus Restricted for Deferred Income Taxes Resulting from Accelerated Amortization' was required to be transferred to the new Account 281."[19] It also said: "In order to avoid misleading financial statements as a result of the abnormalities occasioned by accelerated amortization, four accounts may be used, depending upon the circumstances affecting a particular utility: Account 538, 'Miscellaneous Income Deductions;' Account 540, 'Miscellaneous Reservations of Net Income;' Account 413, 'Miscellaneous Reservations of Surplus;' and Account 414, 'Miscellaneous Debits to Surplus;' but no tax deferrals occasioned by accelerated amortization should be charged or credited to Account 539, 'Income Taxes.' "[20]

The difference between the two depreciation methods—straight line and accelerated—is not evident if the regulatory commission requires flow-through procedures. In this instance actual taxes are shown as they are recorded in the tax return.

Refunding Long-Term Debt

Refunding bond issues often raises questions of tax accounting. The NARUC gives the following advice:

> *Question:*
> Several utilities which have refunded bond issues, have had substantial tax savings in the year the refunding occurred, because the unamortized debt discount, expense and call premium associated with the refunding securities is permitted as an income tax deduction during the year redeemed. Instead of showing the actual taxes paid or accrued in the tax account, the utilities in question have also included therein the amount of the tax saving due to the refunding operation with an offsetting credit usually to Account 181, Unamortized Debt Discount and Expense. Is this permissible?
> *Answer:*
> No. The tax Account 409 should include only provisions for actual taxes and the account should not be increased by the amount which would have been paid had the refunding transaction not occurred. In other words, there was an actual saving in taxes and this saving should be reflected in the income statement because it is a fact. It is believed, too, that

[19]*Re Pacific Power & Light Company* (1961) 39 PUR 3d 142 (Oregon).

[20]*Re Niagara Mohawk Power Corporation* (1959) 28 PUR 3d 171 (New York).

the text of Account 409 does not permit the accounting practice resorted to by the utilities in the illustration cited. (See also paragraph E of Account 181, Unamortized Debt Discount and Expense.)[21]

Interest During Construction

Interest during construction is recognized for tax purposes only to the extent of the interest accrued or paid. Imputed interest on equity funds is not recognized for taxation, although it may be reflected in the financial accounts.

Investment Tax Credit

From time to time Congress finds it necessary to stimulate general economic activity. This may be done through various monetary and/or fiscal policies. Examples of the latter include reductions in income tax liabilities. One such illustration was given in chapter 4, pages 110–18, in the discussion of accelerated depreciation. Another method available is through the use of investment tax credits.

Investment Credit Legislation

As an incentive to increase investment in fixed production facilities through the use of the *fiscal* technique, Congress passed several pieces of legislation pertinent to the investment tax credit.

REVENUE ACT OF 1962. The Revenue Act of 1962 provided for an investment tax credit which was equal to a certain percentage of the cost of qualifying depreciable assets acquired and put in service after 1961.[22] The investment credit was applied as a reduction from the income tax liability for the year in which the property was put into service. Section 38 of the 1962 Revenue Act describes that property which qualifies for the investment credit.[23]

The percentage of asset cost that was allowed as investment credit was graduated up to 7 percent of the cost for nonregulated industries and regulated transportation companies, such as natural gas pipelines, railroads, and airlines. For regulated utilities, such

---

[21]NARUC, *Interpretations,* question 41-EGW, pp. 17–18.

[22]26 U.S.C.A. (IRC 1962), sections 1.46–1.48.

[23]Ibid., section 38.

as electric, gas, water, telegraph, and telephone companies, the investment credit percentage was $3/7$ of what it was for the above mentioned firms—in other words, a graduation up to 3 percent. The graduation of these percentages was based upon the useful life of the depreciable property which was estimated by the taxpayer at the time he placed the property into service. The full credit was available only on those assets having a life of more than seven years.

Furthermore, the 1962 act stated that the investment credit was to be realized through a direct reduction of income tax liability. Because the taxpayer had to have taxable income to realize the benefit of the credit, the act allowed any unused portion of the credit to be carried back three years or carried forward five years to ensure that the taxpayer would be able to fully realize the credit. It also placed a limitation of $25,000 plus 25 percent of the liability for income taxes in excess of $25,000 on the investment credits taken in any one year.

The investment credit provision in the original act required that the basis of the property on which the investment credit was taken must be reduced by an amount equal to the 7 percent or 3 percent (whichever was applicable) of the qualified investment. This reduced basis had to be taken into account for depreciation purposes and all other purposes except for computing the qualified investment and for computing additional first year depreciation. Therefore, if an electric utility were to construct a plant at a cost of $1,000,000 with a useful life of 25 years, the basis for depreciation, for tax purposes, would be $970,000 ($1,000,000 minus the 3 percent investment credit).

Revenue Act of 1964. The Revenue Act of 1964 modified several provisions of the 1962 act.[24] One change concerned the definition of property in Section 38. Another stated that a lessee's qualified investment was to be based on fair market value of property in all cases except where property was leased by a corporation which was a member of an affiliated group. In the 1962 act the basis to the lessee was the same as the basis of the property in the hands of the lessor.

A more significant change of special interest to utilities was

[24] 26 U.S.C.A. (IRC 1964).

contained in Section 203 (e) of the 1964 act.[25] Stated briefly, this change prevented any federal regulatory agency (such as the Federal Communications Commission or the Federal Power Commission) from interfering with a taxpaying public utility's treatment of its investment credit in such a way as to spread the benefit over the life of the property which created the tax credit. The purpose of the change was to prevent utilities from being forced to treat the investment credit as a reduction in expenses for rate-making purposes. Section 203(e) applied to federal agencies only.

Finally, an important change both from a theoretical as well as a practical viewpoint in the 1964 act was that the taxpayer did not have to deduct the amount of the investment credit from the cost of the property to arrive at the basis for depreciation. Cost now became the basis for depreciation, and this applied to property put into service between 1 January 1962 and the passage of the 1964 act as well as to that put into service after the passage.

THE 1969 AND 1971 ACTS. The investment tax credit remained in effect until 1969. On 30 December of that year President Nixon signed into law the Tax Reform Act of 1969. Section 703 of the act and Section 49 of the Internal Revenue Code terminated the investment credit for most property acquired or built after 18 April 1969. Subsequent changes by the 1971 Revenue Act restored the investment credit as Section 50 of the Code,[26] and contained similar provisions as provided and modified during the 1960s to certain properties acquired, built, or rebuilt after various specified dates in 1971. In general, the credit was restored at the 7 percent rate for nonregulated and transportation companies; however, the rate for regulated public utilities was increased from 3 to 4 percent. Further modification stated that, in general, no credit is to be allowed that reduces a utility's cost of service for rate-making purposes or its base for rate making.[27] Some special flow-through rules are provided; for example, rates may be reduced for certain property acquired after certain 1971 dates, but the savings must be spread over the useful life of the asset.[28]

---

[25]Ibid., section 203(e).

[26]U.S.C.A. (IRC 1971), section 50

[27]Ibid., paragraph 5981.

[28]Ibid., paragraph 5928.

The limit on amounts for qualifying Section 38 property is $4/7$ of the cost of the asset or 4 percent for property having a service life of more than seven years. As in the original act, the rate also diminishes for property with lives down to three years. Property with a service life of less than three years does not qualify for credit treatment. The total reduction in current liability which a utility may take is not more than $25,000, plus 25 percent of any amount in excess of $25,000 for property acquired before suspension, and 50 percent of any excess for the years after suspension.

Accounting for Investment Tax Credit

Determining the proper method of accounting for the investment credit depends upon one's interpretation of congressional intent as well as acceptable accounting principles. Interpretation of proper accounting depends upon the interpretation of the real substance of the investment credit. The two major and most popular concepts concerning the basic nature of the credit are the tax reduction (flow-through) and the cost reduction (normalization) concepts. The former essentially says that the investment credit is a selective reduction in income taxes related to the taxable income of the year in which the credit arises. The latter concept, on the other hand, argues that the credit should be a reduction in or offset against a cost otherwise chargeable in a greater amount to future accounting periods.

Over the years specific ways have been used to account for the investment credit. These include the 100 percent flow-through method and the 100 percent deferral method. The following example and illustrative journal entries may be helpful. Assume an acquired utility property at a cost of $5,000,000 with a twenty-year life, just put into service; the company's federal income tax expense for the current year is $400,000, and the applicable investment credit is 4 percent, or $160,000.

The 100 percent flow-through method is the accounting treatment prescribed by those that believe the investment credit is a tax reduction. The amount of the tax credit is used to reduce the income tax expense in the year the property is put into service. The full effect of the credit is allowed to flow through to net income, and plant remains at cost. The journal entry would be:

Dr. Tax Expense	$240,000	
Cr. Taxes Accrued		$240,000

Advocates of this method say that it accounts for the investment credit just as the law calls for it—as a reduction in federal income taxes. As a result of the above, the federal income tax expense for the year is reduced $160,000, to $240,000. The net income will be increased by $160,000 because the tax credit is allowed to flow through the income statement.

The 100 percent deferral or normalization method is based on the cost reduction concept of the investment credit. This method spreads the tax savings of the investment over the life of the property that qualified for the credit. Advocates of this method believe that increase in earnings due to the tax savings should not be realized fully in the year property was put into service. Rather, they believe it is better to set up a separate credit account to be amortized over the life of the property. An appropriate journal entry would be:

Dr. Tax Expense	$240,000	
Investment Tax Credit Adjustment	160,000	
Cr. Taxes Accrued		$240,000
Accrued Deferred Investment Tax Credit		160,000

As a result the tax liability is reduced by the full amount of the investment credit, while the total income tax expense for the current year remains at $400,000. The investment credit becomes a deferred credit, balance sheet item to be spread over the life of the property rather than an income statement item as it was in the flow-through method.[29]

While these methods are quite different in the way they account for the investment credit, they do have one thing in common. The investment credit eventually is realized as income. The approaches are distinguished by the timing of the realization. Specifically, the

[29]Another way that has been set forth is to make a direct credit to the depreciable asset rather than to the deferred credit account. This, however, essentially was eliminated as a possibility by the Revenue Act of 1964, which no longer required that the credit be deducted from the cost of the qualifying property.

flow-through method realizes as income the full investment credit (provided there are sufficient federal income tax liabilities to realize the tax credit) in the year property is put into service. The normalization method does so through amortization of the deferred credit over the life of the qualified investment.

The Accounting Principles Board of the AICPA has issued *Opinions No. 2* and *No. 4* concerning accounting for the investment credit—the former in December 1962, the latter in March 1964. Paragraph 9 of *Opinion No. 2* explains what the board considers is the real substance of the investment tax credit: "We believe that the interpretation of the investment credit as a reduction in or offset against a cost otherwise chargeable in a greater amount to future accounting periods is supported by the weight of the pertinent factors and is based upon existing accounting principles."[30] In Paragraph 13 of the same opinion, the board explains what they believe is the proper accounting for the investment credit: "We conclude that the allowable investment credit should be reflected in net income over the productive life of acquired property and not in the year in which it is placed in service."[31]

In supporting these views the board says that the investment credit is merely an administrative device to allow the taxpayer to withhold the cash equivalent of the credit from taxes otherwise payable, and that it is not an element to enter into income determination. It is also their opinion that earnings do not arise from the acquisition of property, but rather from its use. Finally, they say that the ultimate realization of the investment credit depends to some degree on future developments; therefore, the entire amount of investment credit should not be realized as income at the earliest possible point.

When accounting for the investment credit in regulated industries, the board said it is possible that some other procedure than the one they prescribed might be acceptable. Whatever method is used, it should be based on generally accepted accounting principles with due recognition given the rate-making process of utilities.

Opinion No. 4, in line with the Revenue Act of 1964, while not overruling *Opinion No. 2*, merely stated that an acceptable alterna-

---

[30]Accounting Principles Board, *Opinion No. 2—Accounting for the Investment Credit* (New York: AICPA, December 1962), p. 6.

[31]Ibid., p. 7.

tive was to treat the investment credit as a reduction in tax expenses of the year in which the credit arises as well as to defer it. However, full disclosure is essential.

Reviewing the stands taken by various commissions, the FPC and FCC allow either flow-through or normalization methods both for rate making and accounting. The various state regulatory bodies still have the power to prescribe accounting treatment of the investment credit to those utilities in their jurisdiction. In 1967 the FPC reported that 9 state commissions required utilities under their jurisdiction to account for the investment credit by using flow through; 25 states allowed for deferral; 14 provided for either method; and 4 were undecided. For rate-making purposes, 12 states required the use of actual tax as an operating expense; 26 allowed normalized tax; 5 allowed either; and 8 were undecided. Table 14, chapter 5, pages 112-13, details this breakdown.

When necessary, the tax accountant must be prepared to reconcile the differences between financial and taxable income. The important thing for him to remember, however, is his particular role as a public utility accountant and the subsequent effect accounting techniques may have on rates assessed against consumers.

7

Continuing Property Records and Work Order Systems

Adequate property records and a detailed work order system are prerequisite to the maintenance of complete and up-to-date utility property and plant accounts. These records are primary sources of information necessary in recording both additions to and retirements from plant in service accounts.

Continuing Property Records

Many firms, regardless of their regulatory status, maintain continuous or perpetual inventory records of items on hand. In the nonregulated sector of economic activity these records are used primarily for current assets such as raw materials and semifinished and finished goods inventories. Similar records may be kept for fixed property items. While the maintenance of such records is imperative for a regulated public utility, the emphasis is on fixed assets rather than current, short-lived inventories. This is true for several reasons. First, utilities provide a service rather than a product. Second, because of the service aspects there are few current asset inventory items. Third, a utility is endowed with an unusually large investment in fixed property and plant. Fourth, many of these assets are scattered over a wide geographic area. Finally, return on investment as authorized and approved by the regulatory commission is based upon the dollars invested in these assets. Thus continuing property records (CPRs) are of vital importance not only to utility management but also to the regulatory authorities.

CPRs appropriately might be considered subsidiary or auxiliary records used to support plant accounts 310 through 399, which in turn are summarized in account 101—"Utility plant in service."[1] The continuing property record supports the ledger accounts by providing necessary details. Each entry on the CPR indicates that portion of the total plant cost associated with the particular retirement units being enumerated.

Although one might rightly assume that utilities maintained inventory records of property retirement units for many years, it was not until the era of utility accounting reform, the 1930s and 1940s, that the continuing property record and the detailed work order system became prominent and virtually were required by regulatory commissions. Table 17 indicates those commissions which have prescribed specific rules for the maintenance of continuing property records. The Federal Power Commission, the Federal Communications Commission, and a majority of state commissions have instituted such rules on their own or through the NARUC.

The uniform system of accounts for Class A and B electric corporations prescribed by the State of New York Public Service Commission and as contained in the *Official Compilation of Codes, Rules, and Regulations of the State of New York*, Title 16, Section 165.0–172.7 is typical of the rules set forth by commissions.

> 168.11 *Work order and property record system required.* (a) Each utility shall record all construction and retirements of electric plant by means of work orders or job orders. Separate work orders may be opened for additions to and retirements of electric plant or the retirements may be included with the construction work order, provided, however, that all items related to the retirements shall be kept separate from those relating to construction and provided, further, that any maintenance cost involved in the work shall likewise be segregated.

---

[1]Account numbers and titles refer to those accounts as they apply to Class A and B electric, gas, and water utilities and as found in the uniform systems. A similar classification, but numbered differently, applies to telephone utilities.

TABLE 17. *Commission Jurisdiction Over Utility Property Records*

State	The commission has: *Prescribed rules for*			*Authority to prescribe units of property for*					
				Electric			*Gas*		
	Maintenance of continuing property records	*Preservation of records*	*Units of property to be used in accounts*	Private	Public	Cooperative	Private	Public	*Telephone*
FPC	×	×	FPC	×[13]	—[17]		×[13]		
FCC	×	×	FCC						×
Alabama	×	×	NARUC, FCC	×			×		×
Alaska			No	×		×	×		×
Arizona			No	×		×	×		×
Arkansas		×	FPC,[5] FCC[5]	×			×		×
California	×	×	FPC, FCC	×		×	×		×
Colorado	×	×	NARUC, FCC	×	—[18]	×	×	—[18]	×
Connecticut	×	×	NARUC, FCC	×	×	—[15]	×	×	×
Delaware			NARUC	×		×	×		×
District of Columbia	×	×	FPC, FCC	×	—[15]	—[15]	×	—[15]	×
Florida	×	×	NARUC	×			×		
Georgia	×		NARUC,[6] FCC[6]	×			×		×
Hawaii	×	×	NARUC, FCC		—[15]	—[15]		—[15]	
Idaho	×	×	FPC, FCC	×			×		×
Illinois	×	×	NARUC[7]	×			×		×
Indiana	×	×	NARUC, FCC	×	×	×	×	×	×

Iowa		X	No	X			X		X[22]
Kansas	X	X	FPC,[4] FCC,[4] REA[4]	X		X	X		X
Kentucky	X	X	FPC, FCC	X		X	X		X
Louisiana			No	X			X		X
Maine	—[1]		No	X	X		X	X	X
Maryland	X	X	FPC	X	X	X	X	X	X
Massachusetts	X	X	No	X	X	—[15]	X	X	X
Michigan	X	X	NARUC,[8] FCC[8]	X		X	X		X
Minnesota		X	No	—[14]	—[14]	—[14]	—[14]		X
Mississippi			No	X			X		X
Missouri	X	X[4]	FPC,[4] FCC[4]	X			X		—[23]
Montana	X	X	NARUC, FCC	X	X		X	X	X
Nebraska		X	FCC[9]	—[15]	—[14]	—[15]	—[14]	—[15]	X
Nevada	X	X	No						
New Hampshire	X	X	OWN	X	X	X	X	—[15]	X
New Jersey	X	X	No	X	X	X	X	—[15]	X
New Mexico	X[2]	X[2]	NARUC[2]	X	—[19]	X	X	X	X
New York	X	X	No[10]	X	X	—[20]	X	X	X
North Carolina	X	X	NARUC, FCC	X			X		X
North Dakota			NARUC	X			X		X
Ohio		X	FPC,[11] FCC[11]	X			X		X
Oklahoma	X	X	No	X			X		X
Oregon	X	X	No	X			X		X
Pennsylvania	X	X	OWN	X			X		X
Puerto Rico	X	X	NARUC, FCC	—[15]		—[15]	X	—[15]	X
Rhode Island	X	X	NARUC, FCC	X	X	—[15]	X	—[15]	X
South Carolina			No	X			X		X
South Dakota			No	—[14]	—[14]	—[14]	—[14]	—[14]	X
Tennessee	X		No				X		X
Texas	—[3]	—[3]	—[3]	—[14]	—[14]	—[14]	X		—[14]

TABLE 17.—*Continued*

State	The commission has								
	Prescribed rules for			*Authority to prescribe units of property for*					
				Electric			*Gas*		
	Maintenance of continuing property records	*Preservation of records*	*Units of property to be used in accounts*	Private	Public	Cooperative	Private	Public	*Telephone*
Utah	×	×	NARUC, FCC	×		×	×		×
Vermont	×	×	No	×	×		×	×	×
Virginia		×	NARUC	×		×	×		×
Virgin Islands			No	—[16]	—[16]	—[16]	—[21]	—[21]	×
Washington	×	×	No	×			×		×
West Virginia	×	×	—[12]	×	×	×	×	×	×
Wisconsin	×	×	NARUC[6]	×	×		×	×	×
Wyoming	×	×	FPC, FCC	×	—[18]	×	×	—[18]	×

SOURCE: Federal Power Commission, *Federal and State Commission Jurisdiction and Regulation of Electric, Gas, and Telephone Utilities* (Washington, D.C.: U.S. Government Printing Office, 1967), pp. 16, 17, 18.

NOTE: X = "Yes."

[1]This has been encouraged in isolated cases.
[2]"No" for telephone.
[3]Not reported.
[4]Informally.
[5]Modified to require state of Arkansas property to be segregated.
[6]With modifications.
[7]Adaptation of NARUC.

[8]Generally.
[9]FCC, but not prescribed.
[10]"Yes" for telephone. State lists used.
[11]For interstate companies.
[12]NARUC electric; FPC gas; FCC telephone.
[13]For interstate companies and licensees other than state of municipal licensees.
[14]Not regulated by state commission.
[15]No such system of ownership.
[16]Electric facilities are government owned and operated and are not regulated by the commission.
[17]U.S. agencies must follow FPC accounting.
[18]"No," except outside corporate limits of municipalities.
[19]"No," unless authorized by municipal election.
[20]"No," annual statistical report only.
[21]No natural gas service in the Virgin Islands other than bottled gas, which is not regulated by the commission.
[22]Required for privately owned utilities with more than 2,000 stations.
[23]"Yes" for all utilities except mutuals.

> (b) Each utility shall keep its work order systems so as to show the nature of each addition to or retirement of electric plant, the total cost thereof, the source or sources of costs, and electric plant account or accounts to which charges are credited. Work orders covering jobs of short duration may be cleared monthly.
>
> (c) Each utility shall maintain records in which, for each plant account, the amounts of the annual additions and retirements, subsequent to the effective date of this system of accounts, are classified so as to show the number and cost of the various record units or retirement units.[2]

The extent to which a utility elaborates on CPRs beyond minimum requirements will depend on a number of factors: the size of the utility; geographic dispersion of property; budgetary constraints; and a determination of that point where costs exceed benefits.

Information Provided by a CPR System

Every system of continuing property records must provide certain fundamental data: (1) name of item(s), manufacturer's description, code or serial numbers, or, if fabricated by utility personnel, description of major items' size and other characteristics, including engineering drawings and details of materials; (2) location of property unit(s) and department or subdivision which is responsible for its custody; (3) date acquired and from whom (source of manufacture); (4) cost of the asset(s); (5) an estimate of service life and salvage value; (6) other factors pertinent to depreciation accounting such as monthly and yearly rate (percent) and actual dollar deduction; (7) recorded depreciation accumulation; (8) whether depreciation is calculated on a unit or group basis; (9) all additions, modifications, and retirements including physical count and cost as recorded on the CPR; (10) taxing district in which property is located; and (11) asset control account and numbers to which property is charged.

The displaying of this data on any continuing property record will vary among utilities, depending on the individual utility's

[2] 16 NYCRR, *Uniform System of Accounts for Electric Corporations, Classes A and B* (New York: New York Public Service Commission, 1 January 1969), section 168.11, p. 33.

needs. In fact, those firms using computer data processing equipment may have little, if any, visible evidence of CPRs.

Establishing a CPR System

If a utility does not have or is contemplating revision of its continuing property records system, a number of decisions must be made. First, selection of the CPR unit is basic. This will depend on the size of the item, its cost, how it is identified, and the cost of maintaining the record. For example, a CPR unit could be all outside property of the utility, an individual substation, transformers in the substation, or the land on which the substation is located, or it could be one or more retirement units. All utility retirement units are identified by the NARUC or individual regulatory commissions (see Table 17).

Second, in addition to identifying the CPR unit, the accounting area must be defined by city, county, state, or other political subdivisions. Whatever the area decided upon, it should be practical for as many uses as possible. Property tax districts generally provide good clues to accounting areas. Crossing state lines usually is unwise. The accounting area or areas often provide reasonable subdivisions for rate making, divisions of responsibility, and so forth.

Finally, costs must be established. If the property was purchased, bills of sale and invoices can provide the desired data; if the property was constructed, cost data can be obtained from the construction work order. If neither source is available, estimates of original cost may be necessary. From this information depreciation data and rates also can be determined.

All property must be accounted for, whether on one CPR or on many. Individual records may be established for every pole and meter if the utility believes that it would be beneficial. Records may be summarized as feasible while still maintaining required details.

Uses for CPRs

The Federal Communications Commission's *Uniform System of Accounts for Class A and B Telephone Companies* states the basic objectives of continuing property records: "(1) An inventory of property-record units which may be readily spot-checked for proof of physical existence, (2) The association of costs with such property-record units to assure accurate accounting for retirement, and (3) The determination of dates of installation and removal of plant retired to provide data for use in connection with depreciation studies."[3]

More specifically, the CPR makes information available for use both within and outside the utility. It provides for cost data—original, average, or other basis—to be fully explained for summary in the utility plant accounts. These costs may be derived from work orders or from purchase invoices, and they are extremely useful in planning the capital expenditures budget; they also may provide data on the cost of property retired. Rate proceedings will utilize this cost information for rate base determinations. If the regulatory commission requires actual (original) cost data, it is readily available; if the regulator utilizes fair value or reproduction cost standards, the CPR provides basic information so that properly developed index numbers may be applied to individual retirement units or groups of units in order to arrive at a current cost rate base.

Among its other uses, the continuing property record is a detailed history of identified property units. Because the record shows all additions and retirements, it provides data on asset lives, which information is invaluable in depreciation studies. In addition, as a form of internal control the CPR is fundamental. These records will substantiate and must agree with the data shown in the utility plant control accounts as well as the balance sheet summaries. Furthermore, maintenance work by the utility is readily facilitated. Maintenance crews must be knowledgeable regarding the types of property requiring attention, and the continuing property record is a ready source of information as to materials and components used in the initial property construction. When the repair or maintenance crew is dispatched, it will be able to requisition and have available proper replacement parts. Finally, CPR data are useful for outside interests. Taxing authorities might use them for ad valorem purposes; insurance underwriters will utilize the information related to location, cost, and materials used in construction for insurance valuations; long-term creditors are able to establish values for mortgage security purposes.

---

[3]FCC, *Rules and Regulations—Part 31,* paragraph 31.2–26, pp. 29–30.

Cost of Installing CPRs

Continuing property records, whether developed and maintained merely to facilitate managerial functions or as a regulatory requirement, are costly to install. Past experience indicates that expenditures range from $8 to $10 per $1,000 of plant in service. Obviously, the more detail incorporated in the CPR, the more costly the installation. Thus, consideration must be given to the benefits to be derived. With reference to accounting for these costs the NARUC has stated:

> *Question:*
> To what accounts should the cost of installing a system of continuing property records be charged? The principal items under this question are:
> A. Cost of making maps to be used in connection with plant records.
> B. Cost of labor involved in spotting property on maps as well as other pertinent information.
> C. Cost of cards and first cost of labor involved in recording information on such cards.
> D. Cost of labor and expense in making inventory of property.
> E. Cost of ledgers and ledger sheets (first cost) used in connection with the installation of the record system, also labor involved (first cost).
>
> *Answer:*
> The cost of installing continuing property records should be charged to Account 930, Miscellaneous General Expenses, except that the compensation and expenses of regular officers and employees who incidentally work on continuing property records should be charged to the accounts appropriate for the normal functions of such individuals.[4]

Regulatory rate decisions regarding these costs, which are, in effect, extraordinary or at least nonrecurring, suggest that they are properly chargeable to operations over some time period. For example, the Pennsylvania Public Utilities Commission reasoned that "the amortization of the cost of establishing continuing property records will be based on a 10-year amortization period where the amount involved is large enough to warrant amortization."[5] The Indiana Public Service Commission has had similar thoughts:

---

[4]NARUC, *Interpretations,* question 11-EGW, pp. 4–5.

[5]*Pennsylvania Public Utility Commission* v. *Uniontown Water Company* (1954) 5 PUR 3d 232 (Pennsylvania).

"The expense of establishing and maintaining continuing property records as required by the Commission is a proper operating charge for rate-making purposes, and where a special expense is incurred with regard to the establishment of such records, they may be properly amortized over a period of years."[6]

Yet, such pronouncements by commissions are not without reservation, particularly if the utility has neglected such record keeping in the past. Speaking on this point, the New York Public Service Commission said: "All the cost of establishing continuing property records which should have been maintained from the beginning cannot fairly be included in current operating expenses."[7] It also said: "The expense of a public utility company of installing continuing property records is not a recurrent item, and the allowance of the total amount in the computation of annual income would be excessive."[8] Finally, the same commission said: "The cost of preparing continuing property records, nonrecurring in nature, should not be considered in fixing rates for the future except to the extent that costs will be incurred to keep them up to date."[9]

The evidence is clear. Whether the utility is allowed to amortize the costs of establishing continuing property records over a reasonable period of time, or whether management must bear the expense from its net income, the contributions to both utility and regulatory operations appear to be worthwhile. Today, electronic data processing equipment not only facilitates the establishment of such records but also makes updating a relatively simple task.

Work Order Systems

A utility's work order system is the virtual heartbeat of information about the firm's operating assets. The work order both initiates and controls all additions to and retirements from the property and plant accounts. Before any change is undertaken which in-

---

[6]*Re Terre Haute Water Works Corporation* (1958) No. 27381, 25 April 1958 (Indiana).

[7]*Re Yonkers Electric Light and Power Company* (1936) Case No. 7606, 12 August 1936 (New York).

[8]*Re Syracuse Lighting Company* (1938) Case No. 8490, 8 February 1938 (New York).

[9]*Re Orange and Rockland Electric Company* (1943) 49 PUR (NS) 257 (New York).

volves utility assets, a work order must be issued. Likewise, the information requested by and contained on this work order presents budget cost data which can be compared with actual cost information and serves as a management control over expenditures.

The work order system serves as a focal point to which all investment or construction costs are charged, regardless of whether the item is purchased intact and merely installed or whether the utility contracts for or constructs the asset from raw materials. The collection of all costs are transferred to work in progress accounts and, finally, to one of the primary electric plant accounts as well as the appropriate asset control account. In this respect, the work order aids management in budgeting funds and identifying expenditures so that work is performed in the most economical manner.

The work order system as a primary accounting document is so important to the public utility that the uniform systems of accounts specifically require that all additions to or retirements from utility plant be recorded initially through a work order arrangement.[10] While the Federal Communications Commission does not refer specifically to a work or job order system, it does say the following: "There shall be shown by appropriate reference the source of all entries. All drawings, computations, and other detailed records which support either the quantity or the costs included in the continuing property record shall be retained as a part or in support of the continuing property record."[11]

Work orders usually are issued for each project requiring capital expenditures and, therefore, can serve as a control device. Thus the document must provide sufficient detail to identify these capital outlays when transferred to the company's continuing property records. Figure 3 is a sample work order.

Work Order Content

Like the CPR, the style and arrangement of the work order may vary among utilities. Regardless of its appearance, every work order must contain the following information: name and number

---

[10]See pages 143 and 148 of this chapter for the full text of the requirement as stated in the New York State *Statutes* and system of accounts.

[11]FCC, *Rules and Regulations—Part 31,* Appendix B, paragraph 8, "References to Sources of Information," p. 67.

Work Order No. 341 | Date October 1, 197-

Name of Job Relocation of distribution line along Fox River

Taxing District Boone Township Department Electric Location Happy Hollow Budget Item 4206

Work to be started December 1, 197- Work to be completed February 28, 197-

Work to be performed by I.S.E. Co. Crews ☒ Contractor ☐

Name ______

Reason for work: To relocate 75 poles and attendent line along 15 miles of Country Road 15 between Happy Hollow and Stoney Lonesome. This work is necessary because of the rebuilding and relocation of Highway 15.

Summary of Estimated Cost		Budgeted Cost	Actual Cost
Distribution Construction	$2,600		
Retirements	900		
Cost of Removal	250		
Salvage	650		
Total Net Expenditures	$2,200		

Submitted by: Imin A. Hurry October 1, 197-

Approved by: G. O. A'Head October 10, 197-

FIGURE 3. *Instant Service Electric Company Work Order*

of project; location of project and taxing district; department or division having custodial responsibility; budget item number (this may be the same as the project number); description of work to be performed; reason for work (justification); account numbers involved; and an estimate of costs, quantities, and description of materials and labor needed. The work order also must include a cost summary detailing direct costs (labor, materials and supplies, contract costs, and transportation); overheads (including construction, supervision, engineering, and administrative items); interest and taxes charged to construction; customer contributions in aid of construction; costs of removal (including overheads); salvage values; and net expenditures. Finally, the order must show the date and name of person(s) preparing the work order and the date and name of person(s) approving the work order. Any maps, engineering drawings, or other diagrams to be used by construction personnel should be attached to the order.

Initiating the Work Order

The work order in its initial stages is a mechanism for alerting those departments or individuals involved in the project. The drawings, for example, would have to be prepared by the engineering department, which, if the work is being done internally, would generate bills of material to be used in the actual performance of the job. The work order, through the engineering department, then would trigger action by the stores or stock department to make the proper materials available. If they are not in stock, the purchasing department would have to be notified to order the needed items. If the job were to be performed by an outside contractor, the purchasing department would have received the original work order and would have been asked to solicit bids for the work from outside vendors.

Closing Out the Work Order

As construction progresses, the work order will accumulate information relative to new materials and supplies used, units retired, expenditures represented in terms of hours required to remove old units, and items or units salvaged from removal. This basic data is needed by the cost accounting department in order to make proper entries in the temporary work in progress accounts. In the cost accounting analysis prior to the distribution of work in progress to permanent asset accounts, overhead items—including construction, supervision, engineering, and administrative costs (referred to as CSE&A), and interest and taxes during construction—and, where appropriate, tool expense should be accounted for. These costs, identified on some predetermined basis, also would be charged to the temporary work in progress account and credited to the indirect expense accounts involved.

Upon completion of the particular project or subtotaling of a blanket or standing work order, the accountant will analyze and distribute from the work in progress clearing accounts to the appropriate plant accounts and update the continuing property records. A comparison also must be made between the estimated and actual costs with the proper explanation of variances which, in turn, serve as a check between budgeted and actual expenditures.

The graphic and verbal illustrations given above concern a combination construction and retirement work order. This is not to say that separate documents might not be produced by certain utilities. The point to be made, however, is that if construction work and retirements are combined into one work order unit, it is important to clearly distinguish between each operation. This is necessary both in summary as well as in supporting detailed subsidiary forms. The size of the utility as well as the complexity of the job will aid in determining the detail required.

Minor Versus Major Changes of Plant

One readily can see that the accounting burden created by an enormous number of work orders would be unmanageable. Consequently, projects generally are divided into those of a major and a minor nature. Minor recurring changes in plant might be performed, with regulatory commission authorization, on a standing or annual work order basis.

MINOR ITEMS. Use of this timesaving approach requires a definition of minor changes or additions, and these generally are determined by the number of dollars expended. A commission may approve annual work orders for changes of less than, for example, $1,000, $2,000, or $5,000. Minor changes usually include replacement of those parts which make up a retirement property unit. Minor items of property retired and not replaced should be credited to the proper plant account. Cost less salvage value recovered should be debited to the appropriate accumulated depreciation account. If the minor property item is part of a retirement unit to be accounted for at some future point in time, the minor item will be held in suspension until that future date. If minor property items are replaced, this is a maintenance procedure and the cost is expensed accordingly. If, however, the replacement of the minor item results in an improvement or betterment of the retirement unit, the cost must be capitalized. The item retired should be treated as described above. Utilities, like other business enterprises, usually set minimums on items to be expensed versus items to be capitalized, for example, $50 or $100.

Changes in outside plant generally consist of minor items, the classic example being distribution facilities. These include electric poles, attendant wires and fixtures, conductors, mains, service drops, and meters. While the items may be of small unit cost in absolute dollars, the total amount may be substantial. From a budgetary point of view, there is an annual standing allotment for such work, which is charged to a blanket work order. Depending on utility size, this work order may be closed annually, semiannually, or monthly. A new work order need not be processed and completed for each new job; costs merely are subtotaled and apportioned at points in time judged to be appropriate.

The question arises of when the blanket or annual work order is to be replaced by an individual one. While it is difficult to make even a general statement, the dollar amounts cited earlier can serve as a guide. Another guideline may be the impact of the project itself. It is one thing to replace minor outside plant, but it is quite different to install transmission facilities between two distribution points; both may be easily distinguished, but both are described as outside plant. The transmission facilities undoubtedly would require a separate cost accounting evaluation. Other than the accountant, management and regulators also would be interested in a lump-sum cost of this particular installation. When such information is desirous, a separate work order obviously is recommended.

Major Items. Inside plant, including building, structures, and most production and central office facilities, are classed as major property units. While outside plant often is located on public or other individual's private property, inside plant usually means property specifically located on land owned by the utility. Furthermore, such structures or equipment not only are of substantial size but also involve substantial dollar amounts. Thus, separate cost analysis has distinct advantages, and, when construction or retirement of inside plant is authorized, it generally is accepted that separate work orders be provided for each project.

Summary

It may be helpful to restate certain functions performed and advantages gained through the use of a work order system as it applies to a public utility. While the work order is a mechanism to initiate action by other departments and subfunctional areas, it also furnishes information to management for comparison of actual and budgeted expenditures and facilitates the apportionment of specific construction costs by providing the detailed data needed in such work. It is a key to other clearing accounts which the work order itself generates, such as work in progress. Furthermore, it is a method of gathering information on additions to and retirements of plant and, finally, provides the data needed by management and regulatory commissions in setting general rate levels based upon identified investment costs. Consequently, it is not unusual for commissions to review or audit work orders of a utility and, as indicated in the system of accounts, check for evidence that proper accounting procedures have been followed. While the work order system provides a summary of rather broad accounting transactions, it is the only means by which management and regulators can authorize construction projects, be apprized of the anticipated expenditures of these projects, and maintain control over those expenditures.

8

Accounting for Utility Property and Plant

Economic regulation of public utilities serves the consumer by providing the utilities with guidelines for charging just and reasonable rates. These same regulations fulfill the commission's obligation of enabling the utility to earn a fair return on its investment. The genesis of this dual oversight evolves from the rule of rate making, sometimes referred to as revenue requirements.[1] The rule provides that consumer payments, when aggregated, will produce sufficient revenues to cover the utility's expenses of operation, including depreciation, income taxes, and all other taxes such as property (ad valorem), gross revenue, employment, and excise, and allow the firm to earn a fair return on its rate base. While one might quarrel over legitimate and reasonable expenses of operation, the commission's duty to determine a proper rate base is even more difficult. In fact, most statutes under which commissions operate find it sufficiently important to detail instructions regarding rate base determination. For example, the Wisconsin statute concerning regulation of public utilities says: "196.05 *Utility property; valuation; revaluation.* (1) Whenever the commison shall deem it

[1]Other synonyms for the *rule of rate making* include: cost of service, gross operating revenue, revenue requirements, and general level of rates. This concept was first expressed in the landmark Supreme Court decision, *Smyth* v. *Ames* (1898) 169 U.S. 466 (U.S. Supreme Court).

either proper or necessary in the interest of effective regulation, the commission shall *value* or *revalue* all the property of every public utility *actually used and useful* for the convenience of the public" [emphasis added].[2]

Utility Property and Plant

Utility property and plant consists of both tangible and intangible items. The former include land and land rights, easements, and structures and improvements functionally classified as production, transmission, distribution, and general plant. The latter consists of expenses of organization, legal fees, franchises, consents, licenses, patents, and other miscellaneous expenditures, all of which have been properly capitalized as part of the utility's property and plant.

The general rule for asset capitalization is that the expenditure have a life of over one year. Most utility plant is composed of long-lived items, many of which survive for 25, 50, or, in the case of underground water mains, 100 to 200 years. This is not to say, however, that certain items which survive longer than one year necessarily will be capitalized. Most accounting systems and management directives indicate that expenditures of less than $50 be expensed immediately. Likewise, certain small items such as tools, while they have inherent physical characteristics which would allow them to live for long periods of time, generally are expensed since their value to the utility is of rather short duration due to their unexplained loss or disappearance.

Because of the importance of utility plant accounting in maintaining the utility's financial well-being, proper recognition of all capitalized costs is imperative. The system of work orders discussed in chapter 7 and the continuing property records resulting from the work order provide the basis for this meticulous and detailed evaluation. The *Uniform System of Accounts Prescribed for Public Utilities and Licensees* issued by the Federal Power Commission provides a concise explanation of all cost components which must

---

[2] *1961 Wisconsin Statutes Administered by or Related to the Public Service Commission of Wisconsin* (Madison: compiled by the Public Service Commission of Wisconsin, July 1962), chap. 196, p. 2698.

be recognized and included in the utility plant accounts. This covers both direct as well as overhead cost items.

(1) "Contract work" includes amounts paid for work performed under contract by other companies, firms, or individuals, costs incident to the reward of such contracts, and the inspection of such work.

(2) "Labor" includes the pay and expenses of employees of the utility engaged on construction work, and related workmen's compensation insurance, payroll taxes and similar items of expense. It does not include the pay and expenses of employees which are distributed to construction through clearing accounts nor the pay and expenses included in other items hereunder.

(3) "Materials and Supplies" includes the purchase price at the point of free delivery plus customs duties, excise taxes, the cost of inspection, loading and transportation, the related stores expenses, and the cost of fabricated materials from the utility's shop. In determining the cost of materials and supplies used for construction, proper allowance should be made for unused materials and supplies, for materials recovered from temporary structures used in performing the work involved, and for discounts allowed and realized in the purchase of materials and supplies. . . .

(4) "Transportation" includes the cost of transporting employees, materials and supplies, tools, purchased equipment, and other work equipment (when not under own power) to and from points of construction. It includes amounts paid to others as well as the cost of operating the utility's own transportation equipment. (See item 5 following.)

(5) "Special machine service" includes the cost of labor (optional), materials and supplies, depreciation, and other expenses incurred in the maintenance, operation and use of special machines, such as steam shovels, pile drivers, derricks, ditchers, scrapers, material unloaders, and other labor-saving machines; also expenditures for rental, maintenance and operation of machines of others. It does not include the cost of small tools and other individual items of small value or short life which are included in the cost of material and supplies. (See item 3 above.) When a particular construction job requires the use for an extended period of time of special machines, transportation and other equipment, the net book cost thereof less the appraised or salvage value at time of release from the job, shall be included in the cost of construction.

(6) "Shop service" includes the proportion of the expense of the utility's shop department assignable to construction work except that the cost of fabricated materials from the utility's shop shall be included in "materials and supplies."

(7) "Protection" includes the cost of protecting the utility's property from fire or other casualties and the cost of preventing damages to others, or to the property of others, including payments for discovery or extinguishment of fires, cost of apprehending and prosecuting incendiaries, witness fees in relation thereto, amounts paid to municipalities and others for fire protection, and other analogous items of expenditures in connection with construction work.

(8) "Injuries and damages" includes the expenditures or losses in connection with construction work on account of injuries to persons and damages to the property of others; also the cost of investigation of and defense against actions for such injuries and damages. Insurance recovered or recoverable on account of compensation paid for injuries to persons incident to construction shall be credited to the account or accounts to which such compensation is charged. Insurance recovered or recoverable on account of property damages incident to construction shall be credited to the account or accounts charged with the cost of the damages.

(9) "Privileges and permits" includes payments for and expenses incurred in securing temporary privileges, permits or rights in connection with construction work, such as for the use of private or public property, streets, or highways, but it does not include rents, or amounts chargeable as franchises and consents. . . .

(10) "Rents" includes amounts paid for the use of construction quarters and office space occupied by construction forces and amounts properly includable in construction costs for such facilities jointly used.

(11) "Engineering and supervision" includes the portion of the pay and expenses of engineers, surveyors, draftsmen, inspectors, superintendents and their assistants applicable to construction work.

(12) "General administration" includes the portion of the pay and expenses of the general officers and administrative and general expenses applicable to construction work.

(13) "Engineering services" includes amounts paid to other companies, firms, or individuals engaged by the utility to plan, design, prepare estimates, supervise, inspect, or give general advice and assistance in connection with construction work.

(14) "Insurance" includes premiums paid or amounts provided or reserved as self-insurance for the protection against loss and damages in connection with construction, by fire or other casualty, injuries to or death of persons other than employees, damages to property of others, defalcation of em-

ployees and agents, and the nonperformance of contractual obligations of others. . . . [Also see item 2 above.]

(15) "Law expenditures" includes the general law expenditures incurred in connection with construction and the court and legal costs directly related thereto. . . . [Also see items 7 and 8 above.]

(16) "Taxes" includes taxes on physical property (including land) during the period of construction and other taxes properly includable in construction costs before the facilities become available for service.

(17) "Interest during construction" includes the net cost for the period of construction of borrowed funds used for construction purposes and a reasonable rate on other funds when so used. . . .

(18) "Earnings and expenses during construction". The earnings and expenses during construction shall constitute a component of construction costs.[3]

Each new construction project may include all or a few of the above items. The decision to include will be based on the type and magnitude of the project as well as the expenditures involved. The important point is to see that all expenditures are accounted for properly in the construction work order and, subsequently, are allocated to the correct utility property and plant accounts.

Control Accounts

The uniform systems provide for the segregation of the cost of the utility property into several control or summary accounts. These include four temporary accounts, "Construction work in progress," "Completed construction not yet classified—electric," "Electric plant in process of reclassification," and "Electric plant purchased and sold," and three permanent plant accounts, "Electric plant in service," "Electric plant leased to others," and "Plant held for future use."

Temporary Plant Accounts

There are a number of plant accounts contained in the uniform systems which provide temporary storage of fixed asset costs until

[3]FPC, *Uniform System,* pp. 6–7.

such costs can be identified permanently. These accounts, as listed above, require explanation.

CONSTRUCTION WORK IN PROGRESS. "Construction work in progress" includes the balances of all work orders for utility plant in the process of construction. It is a clearing account, and as soon as work is completed it should be allocated properly to permanent control accounts.

COMPLETED CONSTRUCTION NOT YET CLASSIFIED. "Completed construction not yet classified" is a clearing account generally of short duration. It is designed to accept those completed construction projects which have not been classified for transfer to a permanent plant account. It is a convenience to aid the utility on any particular date when financial statements are due, but at which time proper plant classifications of finished construction work have not been made.

ELECTRIC PLANT IN PROCESS OF RECLASSIFICATION. Another temporary account is "Electric plant in process of reclassification." It includes balances of the cost of utility plant which have not yet been classified to conform with changes in the uniform system classification. The importance of this account has diminished.

ELECTRIC PLANT PURCHASED OR SOLD. Finally, "Electric plant purchased or sold," also a clearing account, is temporary in that it includes only those costs of plant which as yet have not been permanently classified in accordance with the uniform system. This account is important in utility mergers and consolidations and will be discussed in further detail in chapter 10.

Permanent Plant Accounts

The permanent accounts identified with utility property and plant include "Electric plant in service," which is all property and plant used to provide a utility's primary service function; "Electric plant leased to others"; and "Plant held for future use." The latter includes property and plant formerly in service, or that which is not as yet used and useful in providing the utility service function but which will be used in the future. Often it is necessary for a utility to purchase facilities or acquire property in excess of that which actually is needed. This may be done for a number of reasons, including cost considerations, planning for future needs, or, under certain circumstances, acquisition of property may be contingent on a larger purchase. In any of these situations property so acquired must be allocated to reflect that which is used and useful (property and plant in service) and property and plant held for future use.[4]

Of these several accounts, probably the most important from a regulatory and a utility's point of view is the plant account "Electric plant in service." This is account 101 as identified by the *Uniform System of Accounts Prescribed for Public Utilities and Licensees*. The account is subdivided into several functional categories of utility plant identified by accounts 301–399 and includes "Intangible plant," "Production plant," "Transmission plant," "Distribution plant," and "General plant." This functional approach lends itself particularly to the electric utility's cost accounting system. Further discussion of the functional classification is reserved for chapter 13.

Electric Plant in Service. "Electric plant in service" is the control account identifying the plant used to produce utility service and is the summary account appearing in a utility's balance sheet. Instructions pertinent to it state:

> A. This account shall include the original cost of electric plant, included in accounts 309 to 399 prescribed herein, owned and used by the utility in its electric utility operations, and having an expectation of life in service of more than one year from date of installation, including such property owned by the utility but held by nominees.
>
> B. The cost of additions to and betterments of property leased from others, which are includable in this account, shall be recorded in subdivisions separate and distinct from those related to owned property.[5]

Note that the account specifies the *original cost* of utility plant. Definition 18 in the uniform system identifies *original cost* as "the cost of such property to the person first devoting it to public service."[6] The special meaning of this term requires further explanation. Property that was placed in service through construction is

---

[4]Such purchases of property also may include items which never will be part of property and plant used and useful. These costs must be accounted for under nonutility functions and must not be included in property held for future use.

[5]FPC, *Uniform System*, p. 101-20.

[6]Ibid., p. 2.

recorded at original construction cost, and it is that cost which is given consideration when a regulatory commission determines the rate base. At some future date the property may be sold in part or intact to another public utility. For example, utility A sells property which it constructed and placed in public service to utility B at a price greater than original cost. Utility B will continue utilizing this property in service to the public. The latter must record in its "Electric plant in service" account(s) that cost of construction incurred by utility A, regardless of the price paid for the property. Account 101 of utility B must indicate the "original cost." Any difference between purchase price and original cost will be recorded in utility B's acquisition adjustment accounts.

Another example may be helpful. Utility B in the previous illustration purchased utility type property—a generator—from a nonutility. The nonutility had been producing its own utility service but now desired to dispose of its generating plant. The private enterprise had not, in effect, placed the property in public service, so in this particular case it is utility B which is the "first person" devoting the property to public use. In accounting for the original cost of the property, utility B would record the purchase price regardless of the construction cost or purchase price expended when the private enterprise first acquired the facilities.

The rationale for what might seem to the nonregulated industry accountant an unusual interpretation of cost has its roots in utility investment problems of the pre-1935 period. At that time it was common practice for utilities to operate through holding companies; a company in the lower echelons of the holding company pyramid would sell property to companies at higher levels. These properties would be sold at prices greater than those paid for property when it initially was constructed or acquired. As a result, the mere selling of property within the holding company system—intracompany sales—could inflate property prices and greatly enhance the rate base figures. The important point is that this property already had been devoted to the public service; it was supplying the rate payers with a utility type service. The exchanges of property among the various sectors of the holding company were merely financial transactions. Since no improvements were made, service was not bettered—all that transpired was an accounting entry. As a result of this type of rate base "inflation," Congress passed the Public Utility Holding Company Act as Title

I of the Federal Power Act.[7] This legislation indicated that the property and plant in the "Electric plant in service" account and its subaccounts should reflect original cost and that original cost should be identified as cost to the first owner placing the property in public use.

One might be inclined to question the relevance of this requirement today since financial bungling of the pre-1935 period supposedly has been corrected. When the economy is in an inflationary spiral, plant devoted to public service some years ago, if sold today, obviously would command a price greater than original cost. One eminent authority on the subject expresses his views in the following way:

> Subject to a qualification to be noted presently, I think that this contention is without merit and that the relevant cost datum is the . . . depreciated original cost. True, the . . . transfer price [greater than original cost] was also an actual cost—in fact, the only cost actually incurred by "the present accounting company." But this cost does not represent a contribution of capital to the public service. Instead, it represents a mere purchase by the present company of whatever legal interests in the properties were possessed by the vendor. Even under an actual cost [original cost] standard of rate control, investors are not compensated for *buying* utility enterprises from their previous owners any more than they are compensated for the prices at which they may have bought public utility securities on the stock market. Instead, they are compensated for devoting capital to the public service. The only capital so devoted was the original [expenditure]. . . . The present company's claim is therefore merely a claim to be standing in the vendor company's shoes. This conclusion would be equally valid if . . . the acquisition cost were [less than] . . . the depreciated original cost.
>
> The foregoing conclusion is subject to revision if the transfer of the properties to their present corporate owner was an essential, or at least a desirable, part of a program of integration, justified in the public interest for the purpose of securing operating efficiencies that would offset any unavoidable excess in acquisition costs over original costs. In such a situation, and in view of the failure of our prevailing public utility laws to provide for compulsory mergers, a claim by the present company that its purchase price of the acquired properties was, in effect, a devotion of capital to the public service, cannot be dismissed without merit.[8]

---

[7]15 U.S.C.A. 79, 49 Stat. 803 (1935) Title I, Public Utility Holding Company Act of Public Utility Act, 1935.

[8]Bonbright, *Principles,* pp. 176–77.

Under certain conditions, one easily might conclude that we have become a slave to a requirement so necessary some years ago but which today may have outlived its usefulness.

OTHER ELECTRIC PLANT ACCOUNTS. The two utility plant accounts (other than temporary clearing accounts) which must be mentioned are number 104, "Electric plant leased to others," and number 105, "Plant held for future use." The former refers to utility property and plant but, unlike account 101, this property has been leased to another utility as an operating unit, and the lessor possesses no authority to utilize the facility. Thus, it is excluded from rate base considerations. The same interpretation also might be true for account 105, although the FPC and several states currently allow this property as part of the rate base.

Both accounts 105 and 121, "Nonutility property," are summary accounts of investment in property and plant which currently is not used by the utility in producing its service. Items in the former are so classified because their use in public utility service will be forthcoming. At times the line between the two accounts may be rather dim. For example, the Pennsylvania Public Service Commission said: "The value of land purchased by a transportation company for a new office building to be constructed when building costs are lower and materials more available should be charged to the nonoperating property account until the building is constructed."[9] Those amounts held in account 121 generally are felt to be property and plant for which there is no intention of public service. Like the utility plant in service account, accounts 104 and 105 should be subdivided into the necessary functional utility plant categories. In the electric system these include intangible, production, transmission, distribution, and general plant facilities.

Utility Plant No Longer Used

There are times when certain units of utility property cease to be used and useful. This may be caused by changes in technology,[10]

[9]*Montgomery-Chester County's Industrial Union Council* v. *Schuylkill Valley Lines* (1949) Complaint Docket No. 14376, 1 February 1949 (Pennsylvania).

[10]"A telephone company which retired considerable property as obsolete before depreciation of such property was complete, as part of a planned improvement program, was permitted to amortize the difference between the

by installing more economical plant, or perhaps by regulatory requirement. Accounting for this type of property which remains on the utility records may prove troublesome. One solution is to eliminate the property completely from accounting records. In fact, this was advocated in a gas company case when the New York Public Service Commission stated: "Property no longer in service should be eliminated completely from a gas company's balance sheet by charging it to depreciation reserve, subject to the depreciation reserves being made adequate, rather than being placed in the account 'Other Deferred Debits.' "[11] In this particular example the utility appears to have been using group depreciation for the property involved. Thus there was no need to consider a property gain or loss.

However, if the company were retiring an asset accounted for individually, the loss on retirement either could be handled with commission approval by a direct charge to the retained earnings account or to some expense account representing extraordinary or nonrecurring property losses. The account chosen would depend on whether or not the commission advocated and the utility followed an all-inclusive or clean surplus method of income determination. Nonregulated accounting would follow the accepted all-inclusive accounting principle and recognize the loss when it occurred; however, such treatment of extraordinary losses by utilities might cause rather dramatic fluctuations in revenue requirements.[12] Thus utility accounting might sacrifice this accounting principle and allow the loss to be amortized over a future period of time ranging from five to ten years, or for the remaining useful life of the asset as initially determined for depreciation purposes.

The Wisconsin and Florida commissions represent both of these

---

[11]*Re Iroquois Gas Corporation* (1948) Case No. 9694, 1 July 1948 (New York).

[12]See Accounting Principles Board, *Opinion No. 9—Reporting the Results of Operations* (New York: AICPA, 9 October 1966); Federal Power Commission, Docket No. R-344, Order No. 389; and Federal Communications Commission, Docket No. 18477.

---

bounds in the company's reserve for depreciation applicable to such property and the property's original cost, as a retirement loss, less income tax, by charges to operating expenses over a period of fifteen years." *Re Farmers' Union Telephone Company* (1965) Docket No. 6411, 810, 26 March 1965 (New Jersey).

views. The former authorized an amortization over a ten-year period,[13] the latter over the remaining useful life.[14] The effect allows for the continuation of an operating expense, but at the same time removes the prematurely retired or abandoned property from the plant account. In both cases the asset would be transferred from account 102 to account 182, "Extraordinary property losses." The explanation of this account states that "when authorized or directed by the Commission, this account shall include extraordinary losses on property abandoned or otherwise retired from service which are not provided for by the accumulative provisions for depreciation or amortization and which could not reasonably have been foreseen and provided for."[15] Good accounting principles might be at variance with this definition as well as with the maintenance of such an account. The root problem is not that depreciation was deficient, but the reason for this deficiency, which rests upon the fact that initially anticipated service life was incorrect.

Interest During Construction

Determining the full cost of utility plant as provided in the work order system requires that various overhead items be allocated to the plant account. Other than the costs of construction which are added to the work order and subsequently transferred from "Work in progress" to the "Electric plant in service" account, there is an item commonly called interest during construction. This overhead cost obviously is not limited to the regulated sector of the economy. Capitalizing interest as part of construction cost is a common practice in most business enterprises. The peculiarity in the regu-

---

[13] "The commission authorized a gas company, for accounting purposes only, to amortize over a 10-year period the extraordinary property loss from retirement of plant occasioned by the substitution of natural gas for liquified petroleum." *Re Northern States Power Company* (1959) 30 PUR 3d 248 (Wisconsin).

[14] "When property is retired prematurely for causes not factors in depreciation, the proper course to pursue is to charge only the estimated portion that has been provided through depreciation of the retired plant to the depreciation reserve; the balance, after deduction of salvage value, should be charged to extraordinary retirement reserve and amortized over the remaining estimated life that would have obtained had the plant remained in service for its full useful life." *Re Peninsular Telephone Company* (1956) 17 PUR 3d 109 (Florida).

[15] FPC, *Uniform System,* p. 101-31.

lated sector, however, is that while all enterprises, regulated and unregulated, might capitalize actual interest charges incurred upon debt capital, the regulated sector also imputes "interest" on equity funds. Thus *interest* is a misleading term.[16]

Although the term itself may be a misnomer, a more serious issue is its role. It is apparent that investors have supplied funds, long-term debt, equity capital, or both, and that the construction period of most utility property is unusually long; consequently, invested capital remains unproductive for a considerable period of time. Sentiment has been with those investors who have foregone alternative opportunities or sources of investment which would have been productive immediately and thus earned an acceptable return.

Any discussion of interest during construction raises several fundamental questions. First, what is interest during construction? Second, what is it supposed to do? Third, if the concept is accepted, on what funds should it be applied? Fourth, what is the interest rate? Fifth, what is the base on which the cost is calculated?

Definition

The utility plant instructions in the uniform system defines *interest during construction* as "the net cost for the period of construction of borrowed funds used for construction purposes and a reasonable rate on other funds when so used. No interest charges shall be included in these accounts upon expenditures for construction projects which have been abandoned."[17] A similar definition, although somewhat more detailed, is found in the rules and regulations supplied by the Federal Communications Commission in the *Uniform System of Accounts for Class A and B Telephone Companies*. The FCC's classification specifies interest during construction to include "the amount of interest upon all monies, including the company's own funds, used in the acquisition or construction of telephone property."[18]

[16]Better titles for this account might include "Returns on funds devoted to construction" or "Allowance for funds used during construction." The latter was adopted by the Federal Power Commission in their rule-making Docket No. R-416, Order No. 436, 9 August 1971.

[17]FPC, *Uniform System,* p. 101-7.

[18]FCC, *Rules and Regulations—Part 31,* paragraph 31.2–22, p. 27.

Purpose and Funds to Which Applied

No one quarrels with capitalizing interest expenditures on funds provided by long-term debt; however, imputing interest on equity funds is a different matter. Generally, return on this capital is available only when the plant is in operation and profitable, but such is not the case during a period of construction. Yet, it is difficult to argue against the cost of money, real or implied, during the construction period. Ignoring the misnaming of the concept, one is, in effect, speaking of fund costs regardless of source. In the case of equity capital, it is an opportunity cost foregone during the lengthy construction period and not compensated for in the usual risks attributed to this type of financing.

A Fair and Reasonable Interest Rate

Determination of the applicable rate for capitalizing interest is subject to debate. If funds involve only debt capital, the rate of interest on the debenture provides the answer; however, rate determination is more difficult when equity capital, which has no contractual return, is employed. Since the rate must be fair and reasonable, an acceptable definition would be the cost of the money or the foregone opportunity cost of alternative investments of equal risk.

Some commissions, usually without full explanation, have interpreted the rate on general funds to be 6 percent.[19] Still others have used the company's rate of return as a guide, reasoning that the mixture of funds is similar in composition (bonds and stock) to the overall financial structure and thus should earn the same composite return. For lack of positive capital identification, this method seems to be the best alternative. Table 18 identifies those commissions which have defined the proper period and rate for interest during construction.

Applying an agreed upon interest rate to some inventory of construction work is the final step in the process of interest calculation. Inventory undergoes constant change; completed projects are reviewed and become part of "Utility plant in service" or some

---

[19]See, for example, *South Carolina Generating Company* v. *Federal Power Commission* (1957) 249 F2d 755, 22 PUR 3d 86 (U.S. Court of Appeals).

other asset classification; other projects are started and become part of the construction inventory. While it is an agreed fact that interest should be charged only during the period of construction, not before or after, calculating the amounts involved may not be an easy task. Some commissions allow utilities to progressively close out construction work as it comes on line.[20] In other cases the actual physical closing of the construction work order signals the end of interest during construction. The method used by the utility may depend on commission dicta, or, lacking that, the utility should evaluate methods which are both feasible and economically sound (see Table 18).

Alternatives

Interest during construction has been part of the regulated utilities' accounting systems for many years. There are a number of alternatives which might be used by a utility in identifying and subsequently recording interest during construction.[21]

NO INTEREST CAPITALIZATION. A utility may choose not to capitalize interest on its construction work. The utility merely records a liability for interest on debt capital (assuming this is the particular form of financing used) by:

Dr. Interest Expense	xxx	
Cr. Interest Payable		xxx

CAPITALIZATION ON DEBT CAPITAL ONLY. The utility may choose to capitalize only that expenditure incurred for interest on debt capital. If so, the preceding entry is required plus another:

Dr. Construction Work in Progress	xxx	
Cr. Interest Charged to Construction—Cr.		xxx

[20]"The uniform systems of accounts do not require a universal application of the physical method of closing under all circumstances, and a gas company's progressive accounting method of closing interest during construction was held to be a permissible method and was found to be fairly conceived and reasonably appropriate in a rate case." *Re Southwest Gas Corporation* (1967) 69 PUR 3d 348 (Nevada).

[21]A further alternative for rate making would be to allow the utility to include construction work in progress, or some part thereof, in the rate base and eliminate all consideration of capitalized interest.

TABLE 18. ***Regulation of Contributions in Aid of and Interest During Construction, 1967***

State	*The commission allows*	*The commission has defined the*	
	Transfers from contributions in aid of construction account	*Proper period for capitalization of interest during construction*	*Proper interest rate for the capitalization of interest during construction*
FPC	—[4]	×	
FCC	—[5]	×	
Alabama	×[6]		
Alaska	—[7]		
Arizona	×[6]		×
Arkansas	×[6]	×	
California			
Colorado			
Connecticut	×[8]		
Delaware			
District of Columbia	×[6]	×	
Florida			
Georgia			
Hawaii	×[9]		
Idaho			
Illinois		×	
Indiana			
Iowa	—[7]		
Kansas		×	×
Kentucky			
Louisiana			
Maine	—[10]	×	×
Maryland	×[6]		
Massachusetts	—[11]	×	
Michigan			
Minnesota[1]			
Mississippi			
Missouri	×[6, 12]	×	×
Montana		×	×
Nebraska[1]			
Nevada			
New Hampshire		×	×
New Jersey		×	
New Mexico		×[17]	
New York	×[13]	×	×
North Carolina			
North Dakota			

TABLE 18.—*Continued*

State	*The commission allows* *Transfers from contributions in aid of construction account*	*The commission has defined the* *Proper period for capitalization of interest during construction*	*Proper interest rate for the capitalization of interest during construction*
Ohio			
Oklahoma			
Oregon	X[14]	X	X
Pennsylvania	X[15]	X	X
Puerto Rico	X[16]	X	X
Rhode Island		X	X
South Carolina			
South Dakota[1]			
Tennessee	X[6]		
Texas[2]			
Utah	—[7]		
Vermont		X	X
Virginia			
Virgin Islands[3]	—[7]		
Washington	X[6]	X	
West Virginia			
Wisconsin		X	X
Wyoming		X[18]	X[18]

SOURCE: Federal Power Commission, *Federal and State Jurisdiction and Regulation of Electric, Gas, and Telephone Utilities* (Washington, D.C.: U.S. Government Printing Office, 1967), p. 19.

NOTE: X = "Yes."

[1]No commission regulation of electric or gas utilities.
[2]No commission regulation of electric or telephone utilities.
[3]Electric facilities are owned and operated by the government and are not regulated by the commission. No natural gas service in the Virgin Islands other than bottled gas, which is not regulated by the commission.
[4]Generally "no." In rare cases, and only with commission approval, transfers allowed to the accumulated provision for depreciation.
[5]FCC requires contributions in aid of construction to be credited directly to the plant accounts.
[6]To the accumulated provision for depreciation.
[7]Not decided.
[8]To account 242, "Miscellaneous current and accrued liabilities."
[9]To retained earnings.
[10]Normally "no."
[11]"No," except for highway reimbursements if separately accounted for.
[12]Rarely approved.
[13]To the related plant account where identifiable. Others on a case-by-case basis.

[14]Normally to the accumulated provision for depreciation or to retained earnings.
[15]To plant or retained earnings with commission approval.
[16]Donated plant.
[17]"No" for telephone.
[18]Defined on a case-by-case basis of criteria presented by petitioner.

If long-term debt is supplying all construction capital, the result is an offsetting of interest expense in the first entry with interest during construction recorded in the second. Regardless of the fact that equity capital, accumulated depreciation, or funds generated through retained earnings may have been used, no accounting entry is required as long as interest is not capitalized. The liability, interest payable, is relieved when a debit is made to the account and a credit to cash.

CAPITALIZATION ON DEBT AND EQUITY CAPITAL. If the utility capitalizes interest on its construction work and the funds are provided both by debt and equity capital, both entries are required. However, the entry recording the interest capitalization not only will include the actual interest paid on debt capital but also will include an imputed interest on equity capital and any other internal funds utilized. The interest capitalized and charged to "Interest during construction—cr." is greater than the actual interest paid because of the imputed interest factor.

TREATMENT ON THE INCOME STATEMENT. The regulated industry accountant should be apprized of the treatment of the interest during construction account under the several uniform classifications. The uniform systems of accounts issued by the NARUC for Class A and B electric, gas, and water utilities classifies "Interest charged to construction—cr.," account 432, under the general title of "Interest charges."[22] Since "Interest expense" and "Interest during construction—cr." will appear in the income statement, the effect reduces total interest charges.

The Federal Power Commission in its Docket No. R-416 dated 9 August 1971 amended the FPC uniform system for large Class A and B electric and gas utilities.[23] The account now is titled account

---

[22]NARUC, *Uniform System of Accounts for Class A and B Electric Utilities* (Washington, D.C.: NARUC, 1958 [hereafter cited as *Class A and B Electric Utilities*]), p. 113.

[23]Federal Power Commission, Docket No. R-416, Order No. 436, 9 August 1971.

419.1, "Allowance for funds used during construction," and is relocated under "Other income and deductions," similar to its placement under the FCC telephone accounting system.

Accounting for interest during construction for telephone utilities gives one an impression and interpretation of the account different from the methods advocated by the NARUC systems, but similar to that of the FPC. The instructions for telephone plant accounts say:

> (i) Reasonable amounts for interest during the construction period (before the property is received or is completely ready for telephone service) on general funds expended for the acquisition or construction of telephone plant shall be charged to the telephone plant accounts and credited to account 313, "Interest" income, except, however, that such interest shall be only on amounts in Account 100.2, "Telephone plant under construction."
>
> (ii) When funds, derived from the sale of bonds, notes, and other interest-bearing debt, are specifically acquired and separately held for use in the construction of telephone plant, the total interest, discount, or premium, and expense of such debt, less interest earned on such funds, applicable to the accounting period shall be included in the cost of telephone plant and credited to Account 313, "Interest income," provided, however, that no interest charge for a longer period than 6 months prior to the commencement of construction work shall be made unless specifically authorized by this Commission.[24]

By including interest during construction in account 313, "Interest income," this capitalized cost is embedded in the income statement under "Other income." Such treatment enhances the amount of the income received by the utility. Yet, under no circumstances should this income be interpreted as revenue.[25] Note that the Interstate Commerce Commission will allow interest during construction capitalization only to the extent that funds are pro-

---

[24]FCC, *Rules and Regulations—Part 31,* para. 31.2–22, p. 27.

[25]See, for example: *Re New England Telephone and Telegraph Company* (1950) 83 PUR (NS) 414 (Vermont); and *Re Diamond State Teleph. Company* (1959) 51 Del 525, 28 PUR 3d 113, 149 A2d 324 (Delaware Supreme Court).

vided through long-term debt. The ICC does not allow imputed interest on equity capital.[26]

Figure 4 simulates an income statement showing, first, conditions when there are no construction projects in progress; second, construction work is in progress, with interest being paid on outstanding debt but interest during construction not capitalized; and, finally, two situations where construction work is in progress, interest is being paid on outstanding debt, and interest during construction is being capitalized.

Treatment on the Balance Sheet. Capitalization of construction interest also has balance sheet effects. When capitalization of interest does take place, the fixed assets increase not only by the amount of work in progress but by the additional interest factor. A more controversial issue is raised when consideration is given to the offsetting credit.

If capitalized interest is allowed to flow through the income statement thereby offsetting that part of interest expense capitalized, any amount transferred to retained earnings is increased. If these earnings are not distributed as dividends, equity ownership is increased. The serious theoretical question is this: Retained earnings represent undivided income available to equity security holders. Undivided income results from operations, and it is only by this avenue that a company will add to its retained earnings account. If an imputed interest factor calculated on equity funds is included as part of the addition to retained earnings, such addition results from the utility neither operating nor producing a utility service. In fact, the very opposite is the case and, as stated above, was the justification for calculating interest during construction. That is, the utility was utilizing investors' capital in long-term construction over which time revenue was not being earned. The actual effect, as is true when accounting for a number of items under the uniform systems, is that interest expenses are being delayed until sometime in the future. This is based on the regulatory theory of charging customers who will be receiving the benefits.

Financial Effects. There also are financial implications which

[26]Interstate Commerce Commission, *Uniform System of Accounts for Railroad Companies* (Washington, D.C.: ICC, 1 January 1962), Account no. 76, pp. 45–46.

Income statement	*No interest*	*Interest paid but not capitalized*	*NARUC electric, gas, and water utilities interest paid and capitalized*	*FPC electric and gas utilities and FCC telephone utilities interest paid and capitalized*
Operating revenue	$100,000	$100,000	$100,000	$100,000
Operating expenses	80,000	80,000	80,000	80,000
Net operating income	$ 20,000	$ 20,000	$ 20,000	$ 20,000
Interest charged to construction (cr.)	—0—	—0—	—0—	4,000
Gross income	$ 20,000	$ 20,000	$ 20,000	$ 24,000
Interest expense		5,000	5,000	5,000
Interest charged to construction	—0—	—0—	(4,000)	—0—
Net income	$ 20,000	$ 16,000	$ 19,000	$ 19,000
Times bond interest earned	—0—	4 times	20 times	4.8 times
Earnings/share (10,000 shares)	$ 2.00	$ 1.60	$ 1.90	$ 1.90

FIGURE 4. *Interest Charged to Construction*

require discussion. If interest during construction is capitalized, regardless of an actual interest or an imputed charge, there will be an effect on earnings per share of common equity. Earnings per share will increase, but there were no earnings as such.

Further financial analysis concerns interest coverage. Using the accounting techniques advocated by the Federal Communications Commission and the Federal Power Commission, times interest earned is calculated to be much lower than that calculated under the NARUC accounting systems. Using the NARUC uniform accounting system for electric, gas, and water utilities, where interest during construction is an "Other income" deduction following the deduction for bond interest, interest coverage is inflated. It is imperative that the accountant be aware of these conditions; they cannot be taken lightly in view of the fact that during a recent three-year period, 1960–1962, interest during construction averaged about $91 million annually.[27]

TAX EFFECTS. One final element which bears consideration is the income tax effect. The majority of utilities currently deduct this interest for income tax purposes. If the expense is reflected in the financial records of the company the effect is a reduction in income tax expense. Future implications also probably would lead to lower tax payments caused by a larger rate base, greater depreciation charges (a tax deductible item), and, consequently, lower tax liabilities. The opposite effects, *ceteris paribus*, would result if the company chose not to reflect the expense, or if regulation precluded the capitalization of interest during construction. Timing of expenditures in relation to benefits must be considered.

The above comments are particularly critical in the regulated industry sector since the effect ultimately influences rates paid by consumers of utility service. In the nonregulated sector of the economy these factors may be thought provoking, but any direct effect on product price may be remote indeed. In the regulated sector, where price depends upon identified expenses of operation as well as magnitude of rate base, the impact must be recognized. Although interest during construction is not revenue, at some later date when work under construction is added to the rate base such work may be revenue producing.

---

[27]Ferd Rydell, "Interest During Construction," *Public Utilities Fortnightly* 79 (11 May 1967):40.

Customer Contributions

In order to offer utility services to certain customers or groups of customers, utilities may request or regulation may demand that the potential consumers provide funds for construction of facilities which enable the utility to deliver its services. The rationale behind requesting such contributions has a quasi-legal-economic origin. Although public utilities are forbidden to discriminate unduly against specific customers, they have been mandated to supply reasonable and adequate service to all those who want such service and are willing to pay for it. In effect, the utility has been offered the legal opportunity to charge nondiscriminatory rates such that in the aggregate it will earn a reasonable and adequate return on its investment.

The utility would not be confronted with the issue of customer contributions if all consumers or potential consumers were near existing facilities and if the service demanded not only was of reasonable quantity but also required no unusual facilities. Since such utopian conditions are rare, alternative provisions must be arranged. Utilities thus have been provided with the opportunity to request advances from consumers who demand the unusual or extraordinary and/or who are located in sparsely populated areas far from existing utility equipment. Both regulatory commissions and the courts have upheld this requirement.[28]

Customer Advances for Construction

Account 252 in the *Uniform System of Accounts Prescribed for Public Utilities and Licensees* is entitled "Customer advances for construction." The account is part of the utility's liability ledger,

---

[28]"The test of where the customer contribution toward the cost of constructing lateral gasline facilities to serve new communities is to be required is whether customer contribution is necessary to the economic feasibility of the project." *Re Kansas-Nebraska Natural Gas Company* (1963) 29 FPC 1058, 48 PUR 3d 308 (Federal Power Commission).

"An electric company properly required a customer to pay for the installation of electric service where the company had no power line in the immediate vicinity of the customer's premises, where the company had to acquire rights-of-way across other properties, and where there was no contention that the charge demanded was unreasonable." *Douthit* v. *Arkansas Power & Light Company* (1966) 240 Ark 153, 398 SW2d 521 (Arkansas Supreme Court).

classified under "Deferred credits," and is set up to accept all advances made by customers or potential customers for construction work. Subsequently, such advances may be refunded, or they may be retained permanently by the constructing utility.[29] The amount may be determined by several methods. In certain jurisdictions commissions restrict a utility from constructing facilities and expending amounts greater than a specified number of dollars per customer. Other financing plans provide for capital expenditures based on anticipated revenues. When these estimates fall short due to the type or number of customers, the potential consumer is required to advance money if he desires service.

Once the utility receives an advance it is recorded as follows:

Dr. Cash or alternative asset accounts	xxx	
Cr. Customer Advances for Construction		xxx

If at some future date a customer is refunded part or all of the advance, according to the agreement or rule under which the advance was made (sufficient revenue generation or a minimum number of on-line customers), the utility then would make the following entry:

Dr. Customer Advances for Construction	xxx	
Cr. Accounts Payable or similar liability or Cash		xxx

If the agreement called for only partial refund, or if the utility cannot refund the advance, for example, because it cannot locate the contributor, and it has waited a specified length of time, all remaining balances in account 252 should be transferred to account 271, "Contributions in aid of construction."

Dr. Customer Advances for Construction	xxx	
Cr. Contributions in Aid of Construction		xxx

[29]"A Commission rule, providing that if further extension of waterline is required within corporate limits of any city or town, a customer may be required to deposit excess costs of such extension, and the deposit shall thereafter be rebated as other customers are added to the line, is not applicable to an area which is sparsely settled and rural in character." *Hixon* v. *Snug Harbor Water and Gas Company* (1963) ______ Okla ______, 381 P2d 308 (Oklahoma Supreme Court).

Contributions in Aid of Construction

"Contributions in aid of construction" is an account peculiar to regulated industries. In addition to the transfers from account 252, the accounting utility also is required to record in account 271 any donations or contributions in cash, services, or property from states, municipalities, or other governmental agencies and individuals for construction purposes. The difference between these particular contributions and those initially recorded in "Customer advances for construction" is that the latter are made with the full knowledge and intention of being outright contributions to the utility. No future refund is anticipated. Thus the New Jersey Public Service Commission said: "The cost of transmission and distribution mains to supply water service to a land development area, to be paid for by a parent land development company and donated to its subsidiary water company, should be recorded on the books of the water company in the account contributions in aid of construction pursuant to the applicable uniform system of accounts."[30] Furthermore, in most jurisdictions the account does not regress. It may remain stable or, as additional contributions are received, increase. Even if service is abandoned, the utility appears to be under no obligation to refund customer contributions.[31]

No distinction is made between utility property which is purchased from contributed funds and that which is purchased from funds provided through normal security and financial channels. Contributed property is entered into the "Electric plant in service" account on a par with all security financed items. Depreciation is recorded on contributed property, and when its service life is ended the property is retired in the normal fashion. The contributions account is not disturbed. Customers' advances, contributions, and donated property generally are treated the same for rate-making

---

[30]*Re Central Jersey Water Company* (1966) 66 PUR 3d 377 (New Jersey).

[31]"Where a company was authorized to abandon steam-heating service to some 260 customers in a city, no basis appeared for imposing the customer's conversion costs upon a company or for requiring a company to refund customer contributions in aid of construction." *Re Southern Indiana Gas and Electric Company* (1965) 61 PUR 3d 232 (Indiana).

purposes, that is, regulatory commissions eliminate such property when calculating a rate base.[32]

Before any amounts may be transferred from "Contributions in aid of construction" commission permission is required (see Table 18). Without prior approval it is impossible for a utility to transfer such contributions to retained earnings (earned surplus); such contributions are, in fact, financial matters and are not directly related to earnings from service supplied. They are neither revenue nor income, and income taxes are not assessed. "Contributions by customers for the construction of plant, which are no longer refundable under a company's contracts, should not be credited to 'Other Income' but should be accounted for as 'Contributions in Aid of Construction'; and a contention that no adjustment should be made because income tax has been paid on this account is not logical for the reason that it is not income."[33] Likewise, no depreciation may be deducted on this property for tax purposes.

Although contributions usually are interpreted as not requiring refunding, under certain conditions the commission may make such a demand. For example, if property is sold which originally was purchased through contributions, a refund might be justified. At least this is the interpretation given by the Oklahoma Supreme Court in a 1963 case: "Where a water company's customers have deposited with the company substantial sums in the nature of contributions in aid of construction or connection charges for the purpose of obtaining lower rates and subsequently the company seeks authority to sell its system, including the portion paid for by the customer deposits under circumstances precluding the customers from the ability to retain the benefits to which they are entitled by virtue of such contributions, the same may be approved subject to a condition that the seller refund to such customers all of such deposits."[34]

Similarly, if service is abandoned by the utility, this may be grounds for the commission to request refunding. "Although no

---

[32]See, for example, *Re Commonwealth Edison Company* (1970) 85 PUR 3d 199 (Illinois); *Re Alton Water Company* (1970) 82 PUR 3d 178 (Illinois); and *Re Detroit Edison Company* (1970) 83 PUR 3d 463 (Michigan).

[33]*Re Kansas City Suburban Water Company* (1953) Docket No. 44519-U, 18 November 1953 (Kansas).

[34]*Hixon* v. *Snug Harbor Water and Gas Company* (1963) ——— Okla ———, 381 P2d 313 (Oklahoma Supreme Court).

legal basis exists for requiring an electric company which had been authorized to abandon its hot water space-heating utility operations to make payments to customers in connection with the costs of converting their premises to other sources of heat, the commission held that if such payments were offered they should be made to all customers on the same terms and conditions, without discrimination."[35] If at some future time inequities arise between customers which lead to discriminatory rate structures, the commission also may order refunding of initial contributions. "An electric utility was ordered to refund contributions in aid of construction to remove a possibility of inequitable treatment of customers which might arise from different rules for customer financed and utility financed service extensions."[36]

The mere accounting for contributions is sometimes questioned. Transactions which have been consummated and which have appeared to be something other than contributions have been ruled as contributions by regulatory commissions: "Where a land development company spent a large sum for the account of a utility company and proposed to turn over such costs for a few shares of $10 par value stock, the utility would be required to credit the excess over par value to Contributions in Aid of Construction rather than to Premium on Capital Stock."[37] In another case, "a water and sewer company was ordered to change its accounting procedures to properly recognized revenue collected through tap fees as contributions in aid of construction rather than income."[38] Finally, the New York Public Service Commission ruled that rather than transfer a balance from "Contributions in aid of construction" to "Earned surplus" which the company had requested, it should be transferred to the "Reserve for depreciation" which was designed to remove a partial deficiency in the reserve that persisted with the company.[39] The rationale is not altogether clear.

---

[35]*Re Northern States Power Company* (1967) 2-U-6410, 17 August 1967 (Wisconsin).

[36]*Re Northwestern Wisconsin Electric Company* (1965) 2-U-6328, 4 November 1965 (Wisconsin).

[37]*Re Berkeley Shore Estates Sewerage Company* (1962) Docket Nos. 626-422 and 627-448, 23 August 1962 (New Jersey).

[38]*Re Utilities Operating Company* (1968) 72 PUR 3d 267 (Florida).

[39]*Re Consolidated Edison Company of New York* (1962) Cases 12718, 12515, 9027, 11 December 1962 (New York).

There has been an interesting development in the uniform system of accounts for Class A and B electric corporations used in the state of New York. As of 1 January 1969 electric utilities were directed to eliminate the "Contributions in aid of construction account."[40] Any contributions for construction made in cash or property by any governmental agency, individual, or others is to be credited directly to the plant account chargeable with the cost of construction. The accounting system does retain an account number 252, "Customer advances for construction," which is similar to the account in the NARUC and FPC classifications. However, it provides for nonrefundable balances to be charged to the electric plant accounts to which the cost of the property was charged. In eliminating the contributions account, the uniform system of the state of New York states:

> (e) As of the effective date of this Uniform System of Accounts, the account "Contributions in Aid of Construction" is discontinued. Amounts for contributions in aid of construction still remaining in such account at the effective date of the Uniform System of Accounts prescribed herein shall be transferred temporarily to an appropriate subdivision of Account 253, "Other Deferred Credits." The amount which can be identified with property and electric plant accounts and with property which has been retired shall be charged to Account 253 and concurrently credited to the electric plant accounts or to the accumulated provision for depreciation as appropriate. With respect to the remaining amounts of contributions, which cannot be identified or associated with specific electric plant, the utility shall submit a proposal for an accounting disposition of such remaining balance to the commission for its consideration and determination. Except as provided herein, such amounts representing contributions in aid of construction shall not be transferred to any other account without approval of the commission.[41]

This new thinking may be an indication of the demise of a rather incongruous accounting procedure. In the past it was dictated that property purchased with customer contributions should be segregated so that customers would not pay a return on investment in property which they had provided. In rate-making proceedings

---

[40]16 NYCRR, *Uniform System of Accounts for Electric Corporations, Classes A and B* (New York: New York Public Service Commission, 1 January 1969), section 168.2(e), p. 20.

[41]Ibid.

contributions in aid of construction normally have been deducted from the rate base. As noted earlier, however, all utilities have operated on the theory that, regardless of the source of investment, all plant has a limited service life. Therefore, utilities always have been allowed to include depreciation on contributed property as a legitimate operating expense. Theory assumed that the only way a utility could keep its property investment intact was through depreciation expense. Now, under the New York classification, either the contributions account is obsolete and is no longer needed due to the lack of new contributions, and/or net utility plant used in rate making will be figured from the accounting data based upon *all* utility plant in operation. It is interesting to note, however, that the New York classification still requires contributed property to be itemized so that such property not only may be identified but also may be identified by contributor.

Accounting for Nuclear Fuel: A Digression

The FPC *Uniform System of Accounts Prescribed for Public Utilities and Licensees* provides for accounting for energy production through the use of nuclear fuels. The production plant section of the electric plant accounts is subdivided to cover nuclear production and includes accounts 320–325. Furthermore, accounts 157, 158, and 159 provide for current asset classifications of nuclear fuel, its components, and by-products. Finally, the section of operation and maintenance expense accounts is subdivided for nuclear power generation. This subsection includes accounts 517–532. Operation account 518, specifically entitled "Nuclear fuel expense," was devised during a period when enriched uranium was leased by the Atomic Energy Commission.

The AEC subsequently modified its arrangements with regard to fuel leasing to utilities. After 1 January 1971 utilities no longer are allowed to enter into new leases with the AEC, and after 30 June 1973 utilities now holding leases will be unable to retain them. This change prompted commission action in devising new accounting and reporting instructions for nuclear fuel ownership.

Balance Sheet Classification

Proper classification of nuclear fuel presents a unique accounting problem. In effect, it is a hybrid fixed asset–current asset. Since uranium has a life of from three to six years it meets the qualifications of being a fixed item to be so classified and subject to depreciation or amortization. At the same time, it possesses well-defined characteristics as a fuel, which normally is classified as a current asset, and its cycle is definite. After uranium has been enriched, refined, converted, and fabricated into nuclear fuel elements, it either is inserted into a reactor or held as stock on hand awaiting insertion. While in the reactor, the elements gradually lose enrichment until it becomes necessary to remove them. The spent fuel contains not only quantities of uranium that may be reenriched and reprocessed to a usable form, but also plutonium, thorium, and other recoverable nuclear by-products.

Fuel Ownership

The new AEC ownership arrangement prompted certain changes in both asset and expense accounting for electric utilities involved in nuclear power generation. Certain additions to and deletions from the system of accounts became necessary. The additions are designed to account for each process of the fuel cycle and for the salvage value of the by-product materials, which either may be sold when reprocessed or retained by the utility for future sale at perhaps a higher price. Those accounts added include: 120.1, "Nuclear fuel in process of refinement, conversion, enrichment and fabrication"; 120.2, "Nuclear fuel materials and assemblies—stock account"; 120.3, "Nuclear fuel assemblies in reactor"; 120.4, "Spent nuclear fuel"; 120.5, "Accumulated amortization of nuclear fuel assemblies"; 157, "Nuclear byproduct materials"; and 158, "Nuclear fuel." Those accounts deleted include: 157, "Nuclear fuel assemblies and components—in reactor"; 158, "Nuclear fuel assemblies and components—stock account"; 159, "Nuclear byproduct materials"; and 518, "Fuel." These changes alter the classification of nuclear fuel from merely leased or rental expense items to asset accounts. Accounts 120.0–120.5 are fixed asset accounts, while accounts 157 and 158 are classified as current and accrued assets of materials and supplies. This new classification was necessary in order to carry out the Federal Power Commission's order.[42]

[42]Federal Power Commission, Docket No. R-363, Order Nos. 393 and 393A, 18 December 1969 and 2 April 1970.

9

Utility Accounting for Business Combinations

Accounting for business combinations raises many issues of a legal and economic nature for both regulated and nonregulated firms. Those combinations involving regulated public utilities add a number of social considerations as well.

Early History of Consolidations

Perhaps the first business combinations in the regulated sector of the economy were made in the railroad industry. While some combining took place in the early days of railroading, the merger movement did not become popular until the last half of the nineteenth and first decade of the twentieth century. The general public looked upon this movement with fear, and as a result certain legislation was enacted; however, little control was exercised over these mergers until the Transportation Act of 1920 granted specific authority to the Interstate Commerce Commission. Mergers and combinations in the utility field sometimes are remembered for the infamous holding company scandals of the 1920s, but proper government control has provided a new and acceptable holding company arrangement today.

Among the more evident examples of combinations within the utility industries are the Bell system and several holding company arrangements of large electric systems. When properly controlled, these combinations must be viewed differently from those holding companies of the 1920s and 1930s, which were designed for individual financial gain. Although combination eliminates competition, well-administered rules can provide for better service to the public while eliminating costly duplicate facilities.

Combinations within the utility industries come about in a number of ways. (1) One utility company may purchase another. (2) A utility may purchase the securities of another. (3) By utilizing a holding company arrangement, a parent organization, either operating or nonoperating, merely may hold securities in a number of operating firms. (4) Several utility companies may combine with the resulting organization emerging as a new entity. (5) Combination may result from a utility's leasing another utility's property. As evidenced by the conglomerate movement of the last decade, these possible combinations could involve both utility and nonutility functions.

Accounting Methods

Formerly, stress was placed upon legal definition of the terms *merger* and *consolidation*. Today, for accounting purposes, the legal formalities may be incidental; the substance of the problem currently revolves around proper treatment for the assets, liabilities, and equities involved in the combination. The major issue may well be the prospects of continuity of the former organization under the new financial arrangements.

Two generally accepted methods of accounting for business combinations are now available to the public utility: pooling of interests and purchases. Since the method used may have a significant effect upon the company's financial position and net income for the current as well as future accounting periods, an elaboration of each approach is necessary.

Opinion No. 16, issued in August 1970 by the Accounting Principles Board, concluded that both the pooling-of-interests and the purchase methods were acceptable.[1] The board stipulated, however, that unlike alternatives existing prior to *Opinion No. 16*, whereby

[1]Accounting Principles Board, *Opinion No. 16—Business Combinations* (New York: AICPA, August 1970).

a company could choose the method of accounting for a business combination—either a pooling of interests or a purchase—which would be to his advantage, the new opinion specifying guidelines makes it impossible to consider the two procedures as alternatives. In other words, given the specified criteria, the combination is either a pooling of interests or a purchase.

Pooling of Interests

Under the pooling-of-interests method, union is achieved by combining two or more companies through the exchange of equity securities. The parties to the combination, utility or otherwise, in effect continue with their given economic activity, and no acquisition as such is recognized. Accounting methods used by each of the combined companies prior to the pooling are retained. The recorded amounts of both assets and liabilities of the members of the combination are carried forward, income for the members is recorded as a combined income for the entire fiscal year in which the pooling occurs, and income of the members for prior years is combined and restated as if the combination existed prior to the pooling arrangement.

When a business combination meets certain specified conditions, accounting requires the use of the pooling-of-interests method.[2] The Accounting Principles Board stated that transactions involving the payment of cash or other assets or the incurring of liabilities usually are considered purchases. However, when the situation involves primarily a stock-for-stock exchange, the question arises as to whether a pooling of interests or a purchase is involved. In such a situation, if additional conditions are met, the business combination must be accounted for as a pooling of interests; there is no alternative. A summary of the additional conditions follows.

1. Attributes of the combining companies:
   a. Each of the combining companies must be autonomous and must not have been a subsidiary or division of another corporation within two years prior to initiation of the plan to combine.
   b. Each of the combining companies must be independent of the

[2]Ibid.

other combining companies. If the combining companies hold as intercorporate investments more than ten percent voting common stock of any of the other combining companies, the test of independence is not met.

2. The manner of combining interests:
   a. The combination must be affected in a single transaction or completed within one year after a plan is initiated. This means that no subsequent shares are to be issued.
   b. A corporation issues only voting common stock with rights identical to those of the majority of its voting common stock for ninety percent or more of the outstanding voting common stock of the acquired corporation at the date the plan is consummated.
      i. Excluded are shares acquired before and held by the issuing corporation at the date the plan is consummated.
      ii. A transfer of net assets of a combining company to effect a business combination is allowable provided all net assets of the company at the date the plan is consummated are transferred in exchange for stock of the issuing corporation.
   c. The combining company cannot change the equity interest of the voting common stock in contemplation of effecting the combination within two years before the plan of combination is initiated and until the plan is consummated. This includes additional distributions to stockholders, exchanges, and retirements.
   d. The combining company may reacquire shares of voting common stock only for purposes other than business combinations. This is to prevent the combining company from decreasing its outstanding shares at the date the plan is consummated.
   e. The ratio of the interest of an individual common stockholder to other common stockholders must remain the same after the exchange of stock to effect the combination. This means that each shareholder must keep his proportionate percentage of interest in the combined corporation.
   f. The stockholders must keep their voting rights; stock cannot be transferred to a voting trust to effect the combination.
   g. The combination is resolved at the date the plan is consummated and no provisions of the plan relating to the issue of

securities or other consideration may be left pending. This prevents the issuance of additional consideration at a later date.

3. The absence of planned transactions:
   a. There can be no agreement to acquire directly or indirectly any of the common stock issued to effect the combination.
   b. The resultant corporation cannot enter into other financial arrangements for the benefit of former stockholders. This prevents agreements to guarantee loans by accepting the stock originally issued as security.
   c. The resultant corporation cannot intend or plan to dispose of a significant part of the assets of the combining companies within two years after the combination except in the normal course of business.[3]

If all of these conditions are met, the combination must be accounted for by the pooling-of-interests method. In so doing, the results of operations for the period in which the combination occurs are to be reported "as though the companies had been combined as of the beginning of the period."[4] Costs incurred in effecting the combination are to be considered as expenses in the period incurred.

Purchase

When the business combination is classified as a purchase, any amount paid for identifiable assets, whether they be tangible or intangible, should be recorded at the cost of such assets. Normally, the cost of such assets will be equal to their fair market values at the date of acquisition. "The excess of the cost of the acquired company over the sum of the amounts assigned to identifiable assets acquired less liabilities assumed should be recorded as goodwill."[5]

The earnings in future years will be affected by the write-off, if any, of the goodwill. This situation does not arise when the pooling-of-interests method is applied since the assets are recorded at their book values. The accounting profession in the past has not had any

[3]Ibid., pp. 295–305.

[4]Ibid., p. 306.

[5]Ibid., p. 318.

specific statement regarding goodwill created as a result of a business combination. However, when *Opinion No. 16* was issued, the Accounting Principles Board also issued *Opinion No. 17*, "Intangible Assets."[6] It states that goodwill acquired when a business combination is effected should be amortized and that the straight-line method of amortization should be applied unless the company demonstrates that another method is more appropriate. The goodwill should be amortized over its estimated useful life and should not be written off in the period of acquisition. In addition, the period of amortization should not exceed forty years.[7]

Advantages and Disadvantages

Pooling of Interests

Those favoring the pooling-of-interests method argue that business combination is only the exchange of common shares of equity capital. The net assets of the combination remain as they were prior to the combination, stockholders remain intact, and income does not change since all of these merely are combined. The historical costs and earnings of the separate corporations are properly accounted for simply by summation. While each stockholder involved in the combination necessarily gives up certain interest in assets which he formerly held, he nevertheless acquires a new interest in assets formerly held by other members of the combination.

Pooling-of-interests arrangements also are in conformity with the precedent-setting historical cost concept. The accounting combination of recording assets and liabilities at their respective partners' costs is in keeping with this standard. Any difference between these historical costs would be reflected in the bargaining which took place in the exchange of stock, that is, the ratio of exchange which was agreed upon. The results of the combination from an economic point of view probably are best measured by using historical costs and best reflected in any economic advantages of the combination. Since most combinations, in fact, involve the

---

[6]Accounting Principles Board, *Opinion No. 17—Intangible Assets* (New York: AICPA, August 1970).

[7]Ibid., pp. 339–40.

exchange of stock rather than a disbursing of cash or other form of indebtedness, the pooling-of-interests method appears to be the favored one.

Those who oppose this approach would argue that it is not based upon an accepted accounting concept. Disregard for the fair values of assets and goodwill which underlie the combined transaction fail to recognize one of the important elements of the combination. Thus, the economic substance of the resulting combination is indeed ignored, that is, the arm's-length bargaining which took place in the determination of the fair value of the acquired companies.

Purchase

Those in favor of the purchase method of accounting for combinations argue that, regardless of the intent, almost every business combination results in one of the companies emerging as the dominant member, that is, all other partners exist in a subservient capacity and no longer control their assets and operations. While the dominant member may be somewhat difficult to identify when companies of equal stature combine, the purchase method forces identification of the dominant partner, who, in effect, becomes the purchaser. Since the combination usually involves arm's-length bargaining between the proposed marriage partners, accounting for the ultimate combination essentially recognizes the bargained value or cost incurred by the companies. The historical costs of the separate partners may be unknown or at least are recognized only incidentally in the final accounting work. Any expenses and income which occur from the combination are recognized as such, and no costs of prior owners nor retained earnings of prior owners are evident. It is the results of the combined operation that are reflected in the books of account under a purchase agreement.

Those opposed to the method argue that establishing fair value may be very difficult, particularly if there are no benchmarks to aid in the determination of present market value of assets over original purchase price, which is necessary to provide assurance that the intangible goodwill is, in fact, reasonable. If stock is exchanged in the purchase agreement, the shares represent the cost of the acquired company measured in terms of market price. Market price of equities for both the acquiring as well as the acquired company is obviously a factor ultimately represented in the market price of goodwill. Thus, if the cost of the acquired company exceeds fair market value of its assets, a question arises concerning the double counting of goodwill. A somewhat related argument criticizes the purchase method because goodwill and fair values are recognized only for the purchased company. Those using this particular attack believe that both the sale and the purchase should be recorded at fair values.

Accounting for Combinations

Original Cost

While the Accounting Principles Board has agreed to recognize both methods to record business combination which meet specified conditions, it is highly unlikely that both approaches are available when accounting for combinations of regulated industry. The uniform systems of account require that any acquisition of other utility property be recorded at the *original cost* to the first utility placing the asset in public service. If this original cost is represented in the book value of the purchased property, the market value or the price actually paid for the facilities cannot be recognized as an intrinsic value upon which the acquiring company may earn a return in the future. In other words, the rate base of a utility determined after the combination can include only those original costs of the combined used and useful property and plant. The exception might be in states where fair value or reproduction cost standards are used for rate base determination. In these jurisdictions the valued rate base may recognize part of the true market value of the investment, even though original cost is reflected in the financial books of account.

Acquisition Adjustments

The difference between book cost (original cost) and market value (purchase price) must be reflected by the utility in acquisition adjustment accounts. Normally such acquisition adjustments are required to be written off below the line, but under certain circumstances they may be interpreted as above-the-line expenses.[8] Following is an example of one utility acquiring another.

Question:

Utility Y purchases the utility plant of utility Z for $200,000 in cash. The plant constructed and property depreciated by utility Z are carried on their accounts as follows:

Dr. *Electric Plant in Service*	$300,000	
Cr. *Accumulated Provision for Depreciation of Utility Plant in Service*		$100,000
Contributions in Aid of Construction		25,000
Net amount		$175,000

What is the proper accounting for utility Y in recording the purchase?

Answer:

Dr. *Electric Plant in Service*	$300,000	
Electric Plant Acquisition Adjustment	25,000	
Cr. *Accumulated Provision for Depreciation of Utility Plant in Service*		$100,000
Contributions in Aid of Construction		25,000
Cash		200,000
	$325,000	$325,000

Under the uniform accounting systems used by the majority of utilities, it appears that the purchase method of business combination involving only utility functions is not an acceptable approach. However, the pooling-of-interests accounting technique is acceptable. Yet, the pooling-of-interests method may be discouraging because the rigid accounting requirements might prove impractical.

---

[8]See, for example: *Board of Supervisors* v. *Virginia Electric & Power Company* (1955) 196 Va 1102, 87 SE 2d 139, 8 PUR 3d 120 (Virginia Supreme Court of Appeals); *Re Southern California Edison Company* (1954) 6 PUR 3d 161 (California); and *Re LaCrosse Telephone Corporation* (1950) 85 P.U.R.(N.S.) 401 (Wisconsin).

TABLE 19. ***Authority of Commissions Over Sale, Purchase, Merger, and Consolidation of Facilities***

State	*Prior approval required*[1]	*State*	*Prior approval required*[1]
FPC	X[6]	Missouri	X
FCC	—[3]	Montana	
		Nebraska[2, 3]	X
Alabama	X	Nevada	X
Alaska	X	New Hampshire	X
Arizona	X[8]		
Arkansas	X	New Jersey	X[8]
California	X[9]	New Mexico	X[15]
		New York	X[8]
Colorado	X	North Carolina	X
Connecticut	X	North Dakota	X
Delaware	X[8]		
District of Columbia	X	Ohio	X
Florida		Oklahoma	X[14]
		Oregon	X[9]
Georgia	X	Pennsylvania	X
Hawaii	X	Puerto Rico	X
Idaho	X		
Illinois	X[10]	Rhode Island	X
Indiana	X	South Carolina	X
		South Dakota[2]	—[16]
Iowa	—[11]	Tennessee	X
Kansas	X	Texas[4]	X
Kentucky	X		
Louisiana	X	Utah	X
Maine	X	Vermont	X
		Virginia	X
Maryland	—[12]	Virgin Islands[5]	X
Massachusetts	X	Washington	X
Michigan	—[13]	West Virginia	X
Minnesota[2]	X[14]	Wisconsin	X
Mississippi	X[14]	Wyoming	X

SOURCE: Federal Power Commission, *Federal and State Commission Jurisdiction and Regulation of Electric, Gas, and Telephone Utilities* (Washington, D.C.: U.S. Government Printing Office, 1967), pp. 22–23.

NOTE: X = "Yes."

[1]Unless otherwise noted, submission of proposed accounting also required.
[2]No commission regulation of electric or gas utilities.
[3]Jurisdiction limited to common carriers which are not regulated by a federal regulatory agency.
[4]No commission regulation of electric or telephone utilities.
[5]Electric facilities are government owned and operated and are not regulated by the commission. No natural gas service in the Virgin Islands other than bottled gas, which is not regulated by the commission.
[6]"Yes" for gas utilities. In the case of electric utilities, "yes" for the sale of

jurisdictional facilities and purchase, merger, or consolidation of any facilities of a value of $50,000 or more.

[7]"No," except for the sale of facilities. Securing commission approval of purchase is optional. Obtaining such approval makes antitrust laws inapplicable.

[8]"No" for purchase of facilities.

[9]For purchases, approval required only if from another utility.

[10]Sales of privately owned public utility property to a municipal authority are exempt from jurisdiction.

[11]Commission approval not required, but proposed accounting is required prior to sale, purchase, merger, or consolidation of facilities.

[12]"No" for the purchase or sale of facilities. "Yes" for merger or consolidation.

[13]"Yes" for telephone, "no" for electric and gas.

[14]Submission of proposed accounting not required.

[15]"No" for telephone utilities.

[16]Mergers and consolidations only (and then only if companies are competitive). Submission of proposed accounting not required.

Commission Approval Before Combining

In addition to following prescribed accounting systems, utilities usually are required to obtain commission approval prior to any sale, purchase, merger, or combination of facilities. Table 19 details these requirements by state and federal regulatory agencies.

Initial Recording

Completed units of property acquired through purchase, combination, liquidation, or some other means must be recorded initially in utility plant account 102, "Utility plant purchased or sold."[9] This account is temporary, and within six months after the date of property acquisition or sale the accounting utility must file with the appropriate regulatory commission its proposed accounting entries transferring the amounts from account 102 to other utility or nonutility plant accounts.

Final Recording

The accounting utility must follow detailed instructions in its suggested accounting treatment for final disposition of account 102.

---

[9]When a utility sells property or when property is transferred to another, the disposing utility initially must credit the transfer to this account.

For example, all transfers from that account for Class A and B electric utilities must be made according to the following instructions:

> (1) The original cost of plant, estimated if not known, shall be credited to account 102, Electric Plant Purchased or Sold, and concurrently charged to the appropriate electric plant in service accounts and to account 104, Electric Plant Leased to Others; account 105, Electric Plant Held for Future Use; and account 107, Construction Work in Progress—Electric, as appropriate.
>
> (2) The depreciation and amortization applicable to the original cost of the properties purchased shall be charged to account 102, Electric Plant Purchased or Sold, and concurrently credited to the appropriate account for accumulated provision for depreciation or amortization.
>
> (3) The cost to the utility of any property includable in account 121, Nonutility Property, shall be transferred thereto.
>
> (4) The amount of contributions in aid of construction applicable to the property acquired shall be charged to account 102, Electric Plant Purchased or Sold, and concurrently credited to account 271, Contributions in Aid of Construction, unless otherwise authorized by the Commission.
>
> (5) The amount remaining in account 102, Electric Plant Purchased or Sold, shall then be closed to account 114, Electric Plant Acquisition Adjustments.[10]

The system provides the full complement of accounts necessary to handle these adjustments, including the recording of the asset, its amortization as an expense or income deduction, and accumulation of the write-off. These include: account 114, "Electric plant acquisition adjustments" (asset); account 115, "Accumulated provision for amortization of electric plant acquisition adjustments" (contra-asset); account 116, "Other electric plant adjustments" (asset); account 406, "Amortization of electric plant acquisition adjustments" (operating expense); and account 425, "Miscellaneous amortization" (income deduction).

Recording as an Asset

The electric plant adjustment accounts are peculiar to regulated industry accounting techniques. Essentially, they are designed to

[10]FPC, *Uniform System,* p. 101-8.

bridge the gap between allocations, based on *original cost* requirements, and the market price or consideration which actually was relinquished for the property unit. In one sense, they replace the goodwill account. They also represent changes in the value of the dollar.

Amortization as an Expense. Utility plant acquisition adjustments are subject to amortization as the commission may direct. It would be simple if one could assume the reason for acquisition adjustments was merely to comply with the accounting rule regarding original cost which makes it impossible to add the purchase price directly to the plant account involved. However, this is not the case. The point at issue is the utility's justification for paying a price or giving consideration of value greater than the original cost of the property purchased or sold. If the utility has conducted negotiations for the acquisition of the property under arm's-length conditions, one could say that the difference in purchase price and original cost is reasonable under present economic conditions and is a justifiable expenditure. Thus, the amount should be includable in account 114, "Electric plant acquisition adjustments."

If, however, the commission found such payment by the utility to have been made through negotiations other than those considered arm's length, the difference between original cost and the purchaser's sales price would have to be included in account 116, "Other electric plant adjustments." The system of accounts defines this to "include the difference between the original cost, estimated if not known, and the cost of utility plant to the extent that such difference is not properly includable in Account 114."[11] Like account 114, account 116 is disposed of at the discretion of the regulatory commission. The disposition presents the second accounting problem to be solved.

Account 115, "Accumulative provision for amortization of electric plant acquisition adjustments," is the contra-account for 114. The uniform system explains: "This account shall be credited or debited with amounts which are includable in account 406, Amortization of Electric Plant and Acquisition Adjustments or account 425, Miscellaneous Amortization, for the purpose of providing for the extinguishment of amounts in account 114, Electric Plant Acquisition Adjustments, in instances where the amortization of

[11]Ibid., p. 101-23.

account 114 is not being made by direct write-off of the account."[12] There are a number of points to be made regarding this explanation. The account may have either a debit or credit balance arising from paying either more or less than the original cost of property.[13] In addition, one must be aware of the fact that the use of account 115 appears to be at the discretion of the commission. That is, write-offs or amortizations might be made directly to account 114 as opposed to keeping a separate contra-account 115.

Finally, periodic amortization, whether directly to account 114 or the separate contra-account 115, may be interpreted as an above-the-line expense or a below-the-line income deduction. Account 406, "Amortization of electric plant acquisition adjustment," is an above-the-line entry. The amortization to this account implies not only that the excess paid over original cost was arm's length and legitimate, but also that the rate payer is receiving benefits through better service.[14] Amortization of utility plant acquisition adjustments are thus chargeable to the rate payer as a legitimate expense of operation.

Account 425, "Miscellaneous amortization," is a below-the-line write-off reflecting a reduction in earnings available for equity holders.[15] It is classified within the accounting system as a miscellaneous income deduction.

AMORTIZATION AS AN INCOME DEDUCTION. When a utility submits proposed accounting for acquisitions, the commission must decide how the subsequent amortization is to be treated, that is, whether

---

[12]Ibid.

[13]The debit and credit balances also arise from accounting through account 114 for purchases as well as sales of plant.

[14]See the previous discussion regarding Bonbright's analysis, chap. 8, p. 167.

[15]See, for example, a case involving the Pennsylvania Electric Company where the Federal Power Commission said: "An electric utility under the jurisdiction of the Federal Power Commission which pays for local distribution facilities a substantial sum over and above depreciated cost will not be permitted to classify the excess in Account 100.5 [114], Electric Plant Acquisition Adjustments, and amortize it through charges to Account 505 [406], Amortization of Electric Plant Acquisition Adjustments, in the operating expense section of the income statement, above the line of return on investment, but on the contrary, will be required to amortize the excess over depreciation original cost to Account 537 [425], Miscellaneous Amortization, below the line." *Re Pennsylvania Electric Company* (1950) 84 PUR NS 97 (Federal Power Commission).

it is to be extinguished through account 406 or 425, or whether both are to be used in the amortization process. It is possible for the commission to consider part of the arm's-length cost over original cost as being an above-the-line expense and to authorize amortization in this way; at the same time, it may consider part of the purchase price in excess of original cost as a below-the-line income deduction.

Amortization to Retained Earnings. With certain accounting systems, utility plant acquisition adjustments also may be amortized in a lump sum in account 435, "Miscellaneous debits to surplus." As the NARUC uniform system explains, this account shall include "write-off of utility plant acquisition adjustments or of intangibles when not done under an *orderly, systematic program* indicating the propriety of inclusion of the annual charges to Account 425, Miscellaneous Amortization" [emphasis added].[16] In this instance, the utility may be instructed by the regulatory commission to make a lump-sum write-off to account 435 as opposed to amortization over a given period of time to below-the-line income deductions through account 425.[17] Any lump-sum write-off to retained earnings automatically precludes the possibility of inclusion in the rate base for rate-making purposes. Likewise, a write-off to retained earnings, depending on the magnitude of the acquisition adjustment, could have an impact on equity book values and even alter the leverage of the utility.

Disposition of account 116, "Other utility plant adjustments," implies two things. First, the difference between original cost and purchase or selling price for some reason does not represent arm's-length bargaining with subsequent benefit to the consumer. Second, the amortization or write-off must be below the line. This disposition may be either a systemized write-off or a lump-sum write-off to retained earnings.

Another decision which must be made by the regulatory commission concerns the period involved for amortizing acquisition adjustments. A lump-sum write-off to retained earnings through

---

[16]NARUC, *Class A and B Electric Utilities,* p. 114.

[17]A small telephone company was authorized to transfer a telephone plant acquisition adjustment account to the surplus account, thereby eliminating the adjustment account. *Re Swayzee Telephone Company* (1962) Cause No. 29683, 3 October 1962 (Indiana); and *Re Woodburn Home Telephone Company* (1962) Cause No. 29752, 6 December 1962 (Indiana).

the acquisition adjustment accounts or directly to retained earnings presents no problem. However, rather than advocate immediate write-off, the commission may choose to amortize the adjustments over some period of time. This might cover at a maximum the remaining life of the utility plant, or it could be a somewhat shorter time period. The latter seems favored by most commissions. It is likely a commission would advocate amortization over the remaining life only in those circumstances where approval was given to charge the amortization as a legitimate, above-the-line expense. Examples of such write-offs do exist, but they are rare; most amortizations are to either account 425 or 435 over a period of from five to ten years.[18]

Acquisition Adjustments and Rate Making

There remains a final point of discussion, one not directly related to accounting, but which involves accounting data. Commissions also must prescribe treatment of plant acquisition adjustments and subsequent write-offs for rate making. It was indicated earlier that the utility's accounting records serve as a guide, but that in no way are they designed to dictate to the commission or inhibit it from conducting its rate-making function. Thus, the commission may specify a certain method of accounting for acquisition adjustments but may specify different treatment for rate making. With respect to acquisition adjustments, one is inclined, therefore, to question at least the extremes.

For example, if a utility purchased property at a cost greater than the original cost, and the commission subsequently found that the excess was both arm's length and contributed to better or improved customer service, how should account 114, "Electric plant acquisition adjustments," be treated in the rate base? Inclusion in the rate base seems not only proper but also a foregone conclusion. Likewise, if acquisition adjustments are included in account 116 and amortized through account 425, it would be doubt-

[18]For example, "a company being authorized to issue securities to effectuate a merger was authorized to amortize plant acquisition adjustments resulting from the merger over a 10-year period by monthly charges to Miscellaneous Income Charges account." *Re General Telephone Company of Wisconsin* (1954) 2-FB-560, 8 June 1954 (Wisconsin).

ful that such items would be approved for inclusion in the rate base and subsequently charged to operating expenses.

One may visualize many of the themes and variations on these two extremes which might occur. The following is a good example.

> In approving the sale and transfer of water utility properties to a parent corporation for a price substantially in excess of the original cost, the Commission held that annual amortization to account 505 (406), Amortization of Utility Plant Acquisition Adjustments, should not be approved since such authorization might imply that it is proper to amortize the excess cost of properties by annual charges to operating revenue deductions which are considered in determining the reasonableness of rates paid by consumers, but that the annual amortization of such excess cost should be accounted for as an income deduction charge to Account 537 (425), Miscellaneous Amortization, and the company was advised that such authorization was for accounting purposes only and not to be construed as a finding of value in determining just and reasonable rates.[19]

Summary

When a commission decision regarding accounting of acquisition adjustments differs from subsequent decisions concerning rate making, the procedure becomes not only incongruous but also rather meaningless. For example, if a utility was authorized to amortize utility plant acquisition adjustments above the line, and in a subsequent rate hearing was forbidden to include these items as an operating expense, the latter decision negates the former. Likewise, once the commission has established a general rate level for the public utility, authorization to write off acquisition adjustments above the line apparently is meaningless until a further rate hearing is held. Such procedures are outmoded and fail to achieve good regulatory objectives.

[19] *Re California Water and Telephone Company* (1966) Decision No. 70418, Application No. 48170, 8 March 1966 (California).

10

Deferred Accounts and Operating Reserves

Regardless of the completeness and uniformity of any accounting system, there are a number of items which are peculiar to and difficult to categorize within it. Two such—deferred debits and credits and operating revenues—are the topic of this chapter; they are not at home under the more commonly captioned divisions of accounting.

Deferred Debits

Among the deferred debit accounts, "Unamortized debt discount and expenses," "Extraordinary property losses," various clearing accounts, and expenditures for research and development appear to be the most common.

Unamortized Debt Discount and Expense

Long-term debt frequently is sold at a price other than stated or par value. As a result, the utility receives more or less than the dollar amount printed upon the bond certificate. If the securities are sold at a discount, proceeds to the utility are less than the bond's face value. The sale is recorded as:

Dr. Cash	xxx	
Unamortized Bond Discount and Expense	xxx	
Cr. Bonds		xxx

The discounts are recorded in the uniform system of accounts under "Other debits" to be amortized monthly over the life of the bond using a straight-line method.[1]

With the abundance of debt capital outstanding, this form of financing essentially becomes a permanent part of a utility's total capital. Since the bonds have a stated life, the utility may, and often does, practice refunding of new bonds for old. Likewise, during periods of declining interest rates it is to the company's advantage to refinance securities at the lower rate. When refunding takes place prior to a bond's maturity, any discount and expense attached to the bonds at the time that they were sold must be accounted for. At least three alternatives are available. (1) The remaining discount and expense may be written off immediately to income.[2] (2) The remaining discount and expense may be amortized over the remaining life of the original bond issue. (3) The unamortized discount and expense on the original issue may be written off over the life of the new issue.

The first method appears more conservative and seems to be the generally accepted accounting approach since the immediate write-off will reduce charges against income in the future. However, this practice is not one of conservatism when viewed in terms of the income statement. If one considers the fact that refunding was done for financial purposes to readjust the costs of outstanding money, the logic of immediate write-off is unclear. The AICPA supports the second alternative, that is, writing off the unamortized debt discount and expense over the remaining life of the original bond issue to better reflect financial expenses in future income

---

[1]In nonregulated industries firms often will account for debt discount and expense as a valuation item, deducted from "Bonds payable," to reflect a net obligation or liability. To show debt discount as a debit may give the impression of a prepaid future benefit.

[2]The NARUC systems of accounts allow write-offs to retained earnings. For tax purposes, immediate write-off is mandatory.

statements anticipated in the original commitment.[3] The final alternative of writing off the old discount over the life of the new bond issue, while not inconsistent with the cost standard, has the least support. Proponents maintain that the remaining discount from the old issue is the result of the company being able to acquire cheaper money; thus, the unamortized discounts and expenses of the old bond issue are merely financial costs of the new issue—a continuation of the original debt. The opposition states that the new issue is a new contract, unrelated to the old.

The uniform accounting systems do allow the utilities some flexibility in handling discount and expense write-offs. The instruction given for electric and gas utilities states:

> E. When the redemption of one issue or series of bonds or other long-term obligations is financed by another issue or series before the maturity date of the first issue, account 421, Miscellaneous Nonoperating Income, or account 426.5, Other Deductions, shall be credited or debited, as appropriate, with any unamortized discount, expense, or premium on the first issue and any premium paid or discount earned on the redemption. If the utility desires to amortize any of the discount, expense, or premium associated with the issuance or redemption, of the first issue over a period subsequent to the date of redemption, the permission of the commission must be obtained; provided, however, that special permission of the commission shall not be necessary, if the utility proceeds with a plan of disposition of the discount, expense, and redemption premiums associated with the refunded bonds, as follows:
>
> (1) A special charge is recorded in the year of refunding in account 428, Amortization of Debt Discount and Expense, equal to the saving in income taxes arising from the refunding transactions;
>
> (2) There is charged to account 426.5, Other Deductions, in the year of refunding, any amounts of unamortized discount and expenses or redemption premiums relating to bonds or other long-term obligations previously refunded by the refunded bonds under immediate consideration, such amounts sometimes being referred to as "grandfather items"; and
>
> (3) The utility proceeds to amortize by equal monthly charges, from the date of refunding, the remainder of the charges associated with the refunded bonds, over a period not longer than that in which the saving in net annual interest and amortization charges equals the

[3]American Institute of Certified Public Accountants, *Accounting Research and Terminology Bulletins—Final Edition* (New York: AICPA, 1961), chap. 15.

> remainder of charges to be amortized, after taking into consideration the estimated additional taxes on income attributable to the saving in net annual interest and amortization charges.[4]

Extraordinary Property Losses

Periodically a utility will sustain an unusual or nonrecurring property loss which will not be covered by depreciation, insurance, or other provision. Examples of these losses include storm damage and other acts of God, regulatory requirements, and technological changes. With proper application to the regulatory commission, a utility is allowed to amortize the loss over a period of time.[5] This procedure, while somewhat inconsistent with generally accepted accounting principles, allows the extraordinary item to be spread over a longer period of time, thus reducing the possibility of wide fluctuations in periodic income caused by the nonrecurring item. Since the uniform systems do not provide for the creation of reserves to cover these extraordinary expenses—such a reservation of profit might be open to question—recovery of the loss is always after the fact. Consequently, *The Uniform System of Accounts Prescribed for Public Utilities and Licensees* incorporates into the system a deferred debit account 182, "Extraordinary property losses," and a companion write-off account 407.1, "Amortization of property losses," the latter being an above-the-line operating expense.

Accounting for extraordinary losses usually requires that the lost property be removed from the asset accounts; the cost of removal and salvage be recognized; the extraordinary property loss be established; and the first year write-off, including the income tax

---

[4]FPC, *Uniform System,* p. 101-31.

[5]See, for example: "Storm damage expense of a telephone company was amortized over a period of five years for ratemaking purposes with normalization of maintenance expense." *Re Southern Bell Telephone and Telegraph Company* (1966) 66 PUR 3d 1 (Florida); "Amortization of extraordinary expenses incurred by a telephone company to maintain its plant in serviceable condition after a severe storm was allowed over a five-year period. The interest on such expenses was not allowed in operating expenses as well as under interest expense, as had been done by the company." *Re Chrisp's Telephone Company* (1966) 65 PUR 3d 317 (Nebraska); and "the cost of a water company for the testing of a well was considered a nonrecurring charge, and not a normal expense, and was amortized over a period of ten years." *Re Mantua Water Company* (1966) 67 PUR 3d 264 (New Jersey).

effect for that year plus a percentage of the unamortized balance (usually established on a straight-line basis over five to ten years), be recorded.[6] The entries would include:

To remove the original plant from the records,		
Dr. Accumulated Provision for Depreciation of Utility Plant in Service	xxx	
Cr. Utility Plant in Service		xxx
To account for cost of removal,		
Dr. Accumulated Provision for Depreciation of Utility Plant in Service	xxx	
Cr. Cash		xxx
To record salvage from plant,		
Dr. Cash or Materials and Supplies	xxx	
Cr. Accumulated Provision for Depreciation of Utility Plant in Service		xxx
To record extraordinary loss,		
Dr. Extraordinary Property Losses	xxx	
Cr. Accumulated Provision for Depreciation of Utility Plant in Service		xxx
To record tax effect and annual amortization of write-off,		
Dr. Amortization of Property Losses	xxx	
Cr. Extraordinary Property Losses		xxx

Commission rate making requires thorough scrutiny of extraordinary losses. Without careful analysis some of these could be incorporated as legitimate above-the-line expenses for a particular test year and thus reflect an expense to be incurred for an indefinite time into the future. The Ohio Public Service Commission expressed itself clearly on the subject of accounting for abnormal expenses: "Extraordinary expense incurred by a telephone company in moving toll positions and switching equipment to a new location would not be charged to expenses during the test year but would be amortized to expense over a period of five years."[7] In a rather cautious statement in a 1954 decision, the New Hampshire

[6]Accounting for the tax loss generally requires that the total loss be recognized in the year in which it occurred. In addition, most utilities probably will adjust interperiod tax allocations.

[7]*Re Chillicothe Telephone Company* (1965) 60 PUR 3d 270 (Ohio).

commission interpreted *abnormal circumstances* and said that "the Commission will not normalize every abnormal circumstance occurring during an electric company's test year since the effect would be to remove any margin of safety necessary to protect the company against sleet storms, floods, and other contingencies."[8]

Clearing Accounts

Clearing accounts are required by all uniform accounting systems to provide for items that have not been distributed to other accounts as of the balance sheet date. These accounts, however, must be cleared within the following calendar year. Account 184, "Clearing accounts," is the general one listed in the uniform systems for recording such items; however, this account may be subdivided as the utility deems necessary. The New York commission's classification lists the following: "184.1, Building service expenses—clearing; 184.2, Electronic data processing expenses—clearing; 184.3, Laboratory expenses—clearing; 184.4, Shop expenses—clearing; 184.5, Tools and work equipment expenses—clearing; and 184.6, Transportation expenses—clearing." Furthermore, the uniform system states that the "utility shall maintain any other clearing accounts necessary as a medium through which to accumulate initial costs and expenses with respect to particular types of transactions in order to facilitate the distribution and apportionment of charges on equitable bases among the appropriate accounts to which such charges are applicable."[9]

Research and Development Expenditures

The wisdom of public utilities engaging in research and development has not always been clear. On the one hand, there are sound arguments that any progressive going concern, regulated or unregulated, will experiment with new and, hopefully, better ways and methods of providing a good or service. This work ultimately benefits the consumer. On the other hand, convincing arguments

---

[8] *Re Public Service Company of New Hampshire* (1954) 3 PUR 3d 361 (New Hampshire).

[9] 16 NYCRR, *Uniform System of Accounts for Electric Corporations, Classes A and B* (New York: New York State Public Service Commission, 1 January 1969), p. 65.

are made that public utilities exist to provide a necessary service and consumers should be required to pay only for the necessity.

In view of recent recognition by regulatory commissions that a utility must assume responsibility for costs to improve service and meet service requirements of an ecological and environmental nature, compensation by the rate payer appears eminently fair. The Federal Power Commission has issued revised accounting instructions to all electric and gas utilities under their jurisdiction regarding research and development expenditures.[10] Under the new rules, utilities may select between two alternatives for recording these costs. The first alternative, generally considered the preferred method under good accounting principles, recognizes research and development as a deferred debit. Accordingly, account 188, "Research and development expenditures," has been created, which the commission defines in the following way:

> A. This account shall include the cost of all expenditures coming within the meaning of Definition 24.B of the Uniform System of Accounts, except those properly includable in account 107, Construction Work in Progress.
>
> B. Costs that are minor or of a general or recurring nature shall be transferred from this account to the appropriate operating expense function or if such costs are common to the overall operations or cannot be feasibly allocated to the various operating accounts, then such costs shall be recorded in Account 930, Miscellaneous General Expenses.[11]

The other alternative allows research and development expenditures to be accounted for in account 107, "Construction work in progress." The explanation to this account states: "C. Expenditures on research and development projects for construction of utility facilities are to be included in a separate subdivision in this account. Records must be maintained to show separately each project along with complete detail of the nature and purpose of the research and development project together with the related costs."[12]

The commission also has provided for subsequent treatment of these expenditures depending upon their initial recording. If

---

[10]Federal Power Commission, Docket No. R-381, Order No. 408, 26 August 1970.

[11]Ibid.

[12]Ibid.

research and development is recorded as a deferred debit, and this may include expenditures of an operational nature as well as for new construction, such amounts should be written off over a period of five years.[13] The write-off should be done on a functional basis above the line in the appropriate "Operations and maintenance" accounts. Furthermore, any balance remaining in the account at a closing date should be given strong consideration for addition to the rate base. If the utility initially records construction research and development in "Construction work in progress" accounts, any rate base treatment accorded would be similar to that of interest during construction and the interest thus would be added to the rate base.

There is an encouraging point. The commission strongly advocates synonymous treatment for both accounting as well as rate-making purposes. This should remove any doubts on the part of the utility as to probable future rate-making treatment if such expenditures are made and, at the same time, should encourage use of these accounts by utility management.

Deferred Credits

Those deferred credits which require some elaboration are "Unamortized premium on debt," "Customer advances for construction," and "Accumulated deferred investment tax credits."

Unamortized Premium on Debt

Just as certain issues of debt capital are sold at discounts, so certain issues must be sold at a premium. Futhermore, the premiums as established are recorded and amortized over the life of the bonds.

To record the sale of long-term debt at a premium,

Dr. Cash	xxx	
Cr. Bonds		xxx
Unamortized Premium on Debt		xxx

[13]Under commission approved circumstances, the write-off period may be extended to a longer period of time.

To record the annual write-off of debt premium,

Dr. Unamortized Premium on Debt	xxx	
Cr. Amortization of Premium on Debt—Cr.		xxx

The other provisions and comments made regarding debt discount and expense (see pages 206–209) also are applicable to any discussion of bond premiums.

Customer Advances for Construction

Because of the extreme capital intensity of public utilities, the company itself or regulatory requirements ask that customers or potential customers contribute cash before facilities will be erected. Utilities generally have guidelines as to revenue requirements per dollar of investment, or commissions specify maximum utility contribution per unit of investment. If costs exceed these minimum or maximum requirements, and if customers still desire service, the customer is required to make a contribution of cash or labor.

At the time such advances are made, agreement usually is established for whole or partial refund of the deposit. If these are not totally refunded, any balance is transferred to the "Contributions in aid of construction" account. A full discussion of these contributions is contained in chapter 8.

Investment Tax Credits

The Internal Revenue Act of 1962 allowed public utilities to deduct from their income tax liabilities, within certain limits, 3 percent of the cost of qualifying assets purchased during the firm's fiscal year. Subsequently, a number of arguments arose as to the purpose of the credit. What was congressional intent? Was it a reduction in the cost of new plant or was it a tax reduction? Should the credit be accounted for during the year of occurrence or should it be deferred over some longer period? If the latter, is that period less than or equal to the service life of the assets?

Commissions have not fully agreed on the proper accounting treatment. For example, the Connecticut commission said: "Since use of the investment tax credit represents a reduction of income taxes for the current year, it should be accounted for on the initial year flow-through basis which is preferable because it recognizes that the credit is earned by making investment in newly acquired facilities, and such credit is *not* related to the period in which the asset is used" [emphasis added].[14] Others have used a normalizing or deferral approach in accounting for the investment credit. The Kansas Public Service Commission is one of these: "So-called tax reductions resulting from the investment credit allowed under the Revenue Act of 1962 should be spread over the life of the assets to which the credit applies."[15]

In 1964 the Federal Power Commission said: "Public utilities and licensees under the Federal Power Act have the option in accounting for the federal investment tax credit to elect between (1) prorating by deferral account the tax credit benefits over a period of years not exceeding the useful life of the property involved, or (2) reflecting the benefits of the investment tax credit in the income statement of the year in which the credit is used to reduce income taxes."[16] Accordingly, the FPC has provided in its accounting systems the needed accounts to record the investment credit. Account 225, "Accumulated deferred investment tax credit," is used by those utilities who have elected to normalize and amortize the credit over a period of time up to the full service life of the asset. Account 411.3, "Investment tax credit adjustments," an operating expense account, is debited with the deferral. The transaction is as if no tax credit were taken. Account 225 must be maintained so as to reflect utility and nonutility credits. Similarly, account 411.3 is subdivided into accounts 411.4 and 411.5 for utility and nonutility operations respectively.

Operating Reserves

The uniform systems of accounts provide for a number of operating reserves to be maintained at the discretion of the utility. These

---

[14]*Re Southern New England Telephone Company* (1969) 78 PUR 3d 504 (Connecticut). See also: *Re California Water and Telephone Company* (1964) Decision No. 66879, Application No. 44611, 25 February 1964 (California).

[15]*Re Accounting Procedure for Investment Tax Credit* (1962) 47 PUR 3d 4 (Kansas).

[16]*Re Accounting Procedure for Investment Tax Credit* (1964) 32 FPC 1470, 56 PUR 3d 306 (Federal Power Commission).

reserves are established and increased by charges to operating expenses and credits to the appropriate reserve account. Unlike extraordinary losses whose occurrence is unpredictable, operating reserves cover losses whose probability of occurrence is predictable. Thus each accretion should be based on what might be interpreted as a reasonable provision for the expense.[17] When a utility does establish such reserves for what appear to be legitimate purposes, the commissions are prone to allow such as sound business practices and operating expenses.[18] The following two commission decisions are examples. "An adequate annual accrual by an electric company for storm damage was a sound business practice and a proper charge against operating expenses."[19] "An electric company should be allowed to charge to operating expenses each year amounts which will create a reserve to take care of possible future storm damages."[20]

A number of these reserves are listed in the balance sheet accounts of most uniform systems and include accounts 261, "Property insurance reserve"; 262, "Injuries and damages reserve"; 263, "Pensions and benefits reserve"; 264, "Amortization reserve—federal"; and 265, "Miscellaneous operating reserves."[21] Account 261 is designed for the utility which, by choice, requirement, or the inability to procure outside coverage, self-insures against losses through accident, fire, flood, or other hazards which may afflict its own property or property leased from others. The companion operating expense debited with these charges is account 924, "Property insurance."

---

[17]"No allowance will be made for expenses which are purely speculative and based on contingencies, such as loss due to regulatory lag; future increases in labor, materials, or taxes; possible traffic decline; and possible work stoppages due to strikes." *Re San Diego Transit System* (1955) 10 PUR 3d 233 (California). "No allowance for contingent risks should be included in a transit company's operating expense." *Re Metropolitan Coach Lines* (1955) 10 PUR 3d 337 (California).

[18]The apparent conflict which exists between reserves established for storm damage and accounting for extraordinary property loss is based on the predictability of the occurence of the event. Property loss in the former case is evident, while in the latter it is unpredictable. Geographical location often accounts for these differences.

[19]*Re Florida Power and Light Company* (1967) 19 PUR 3d 417 (Florida).

[20]*Re Long Island Light Company* (1955) 7 PUR 3d 140 (New York).

[21]As specified in FPC, *Uniform System,* p. 101-19.

From time to time utilities will encounter liability suits by injured parties. The injury may be to property or person and the utility is found at fault. To protect itself against adverse decisions the utility establishes a reserve. Account 262, "Injuries and damages reserve," is designed to meet such occurrences; the companion account is 925, "Injuries and damages." In an attempt to guide the utility on the magnitude of this reserve, the Kansas Supreme Court said: "In a rate investigation the allowance for anticipated casualty repair expense should be so calculated as to produce a sum sufficient to make the repair at the cost anticipated at the time of the casualty."[22]

There are times when a commission, in its review of utility accounting, may feel that certain reserves have been accumulated to sufficient amounts for predicted requirements and may order a discontinuance of such an expense allocation.[23] Furthermore, a utility is not allowed to divert from these reserve accounts for other uses without specific approval by the commission.[24] Since the reserves are not specifically incurred expenses, they generally are not deducted for income tax purposes.

Accounting for Uncollectible Receivables

Account 144, "Accumulative provision for uncollectible accounts —credit," provides for a valuation procedure; its companion account is 904, "Uncollectible accounts." Like other valuation

---

[22]*Southwestern Bell Telephone Company* v. *Kansas State Corporation Commission* (1963) 192 Kan 39, 51 PUR 3d 113, 386 P2d 515 (Kansas Supreme Court).

[23]See, for example: "Further accumulations to a telephone company's reserve for cyclone losses by way of charges to current expense were held not to be warranted where there existed substantial reserves and insurance coverage in relation to the value of the plant exposed and their probability of loss." *Re Puerto Rico Telephone Company* (1964) 55 PUR 3d 1 (Puerto Rico); and "an electric utility was ordered to discontinue its annual charge for storm damage reserve where the reserve had grown so large that there was no need for this benefit." *Re Florida Power and Light Company* (1965) Docket No. 7759-EU, Order No. 3926, 10 November 1965 (Florida).

[24]"An electric company was authorized to transfer an excess portion of its injuries and damages reserve to earned surplus, since the reserve had been maintained principally by charges to operating expenses." *Re Consolidated Edison Company of New York* (1962) Cases 12718, 12515, and 9027, 11 December 1962 (New York).

accounts, 144 is credited with systematic additions simultaneously debited to customer expense account 904. Any losses which ultimately are incurred by the utility from uncollected items are then charged to account 144 with a debit to that account and credit to "Accounts receivable." This procedure is similar to that found in any nonregulated industry, and the measurement of the periodic addition to the uncollectible reserve can be based on a percentage of anticipated revenues or on an average of past experience for bad debts.[25]

With proper evidence, commissions are sympathetic toward bad debt allowances, but if the claim is unreasonable or unsubstantiated, the commission may be rather critical. The Florida commission expressed itself thus: "A telephone company's claim for bad debts of 1.3% of gross operating revenues was considered indefensible since the normal range for uncollectibles is approximately .4–.8% and the Commission disapproved a deduction from operating revenues to allow for an increase in the reserve for uncollectibles which was intended primarily to rectify deficiencies for prior years."[26]

The importance in discussing bad debts or uncollectible accounts as far as utilities are concerned revolves around the legitimacy of including an amount for uncollectibles as an above-the-line expense. This is particularly true when customers are required to make security deposits in advance of the utility supplying service. Allowing the utility to collect security deposits and at the same time collect, through the rate-making structure, added amounts for uncollectible accounts may be interpreted as double charge to the consumer. There are a number of regulatory commissions which

---

[25]"An allowance for a gas company's uncollectible account should reflect or be related to those to be expected from each current year's sales rather than those incurred for prior years' sales." *Re Michigan Consolidated Gas Company* (1960) 36 PUR 3d 289 (Michigan).

[26]See, for example: "A gas company's claim for uncollectible accounts, based on application of the per cent of bad debt net losses to revenues for the last five years, was allowed in operating expenses." *Pennsylvania Public Utility Commission* v. *Equitable Gas Company* (1965) 61 PUR 3d 1 (Pennsylvania); and "a telephone company's claim for uncollectibles was limited, for rate-making purposes, to the average rate of uncollectibles actually written off for the preceeding five years." *Re General Telephone Company of Upstate New York* (1961) 41 PUR 3d 1 (New York).

allow utilities to collect security deposits, and, when such deposits are held by the utility, law requires the payment of interest.[27]

Several approaches or combinations of approaches may be authorized by a commission and used by a utility in allowing for nonpayment of bills for services rendered. In those instances where security deposits are maintained and where the utility has the prerogative of denying service for nonpayment,[28] it is questionable whether or not uncollectible account expense is indeed necessary. This is not to say that the utility might not continue to maintain such an expense and reserve account, but including the item as a legitimate expense of operation might be disallowed by the commission. Under such conditions, the amounts included by the utility in its uncollectible expense account in effect become an allocation of equity capital's earnings.

---

[27]*Re General Telephone Company of Florida* (1967) Docket No. 7766-TP, Order No. 4137, 15 February 1967 (Florida).

[28]See, for example: *Re Kalida Telephone Company* (1964) 55 PUR 3d 525 (Ohio); and *Re Ayersville Telephone Company* (1966) 56 PUR 3d 475 (Ohio).

[29]"The general rule is that a utility company supplying services to the public—such as water, gas, and electricity—may adopt and enforce reasonable regulations in conducting its business, including one providing that services supplied to a customer may be discontinued if he faults in his payments." *Siedel* v. *Minneapolis Gas Company* (1965) 271 Minn 127, 59 PUR 3d 267, 135 NW2d 60 (Minnesota Supreme Court).

"A gas and electric company may not discontinue service to a person at his place of residence because of his failure to pay bills for service at his place of business where there is nothing either by private agreement or statutory regulation which warrants the use of this course of force." *Dworman* v. *Consolidated Edison Company of New York* (1965) 49 Misc 2d 204, 63 PUR 3d 288, 267 NYS2d 291 (New York Supreme Court).

11

Analysis of Financial Statements

Among all economic enterprises, the public utility provides a unique collection of financial and accounting data for detailed analysis. The uniform regulatory requirements of accounting insist upon such information and require that it be reported to the regulatory bodies in specified form. Any industry whose prices (rates) depend upon knowledge of all expenses of operation make detailed data not only essential but also mandatory. Furthermore, these data, while of utmost importance to the utility manager and the regulator, also provide a wealth of knowledge to any interested outsider. All such data are in the public domain. For this reason, the utility industries' financial aspects are more thoroughly dissected than those of any other sector of the economy. It therefore behooves the regulator to provide the utilities with proper financial statement requirements which, when met by the utility, will generate data beneficial to all interested parties. Accounting is that tool which prepares useful, informative, timely, and valid statements of financial and operating results so essential to further analysis.

Required Financial Statements

The balance sheet and income statement are examples of periodic classifications for information basic to any further study. The balance sheet, defined as a representative indication of a firm's financial position at some point in time, indicates costs of various assets purchased with resources indicated as liabilities and capitalization.

The income statement is the periodic estimation of income based on revenues earned, whether received or not, and expenses incurred, whether as cash outlays or as allocations of converted or expired costs. The statement of retained earnings reconciles operating changes reflected in the income statement between balance sheet dates; it connects the income statement and balance sheet.

While these three statements may be of primary importance in measuring management and regulatory efficiency, utility management and regulators may or should require schedules which show greater detail of such items as sales and operating expenses, statements of sources and applications of funds, analysis of working capital, and variance reports concerning budgeted and actual performance. Much of this data, while not required regularly, generally is presented to the commission to support rate requests.

Once the accounting function is performed and the statements are synthesized, they are ready for further analysis and scrutiny. Those concerned with studying a utility's operations (see chapter 2) now may dissect, compare, and contrast data in order to provide interesting and meaningful information to management, regulatory agencies, stockholders, auditors, or other interested groups. This analysis can be of a vertical nature—relationships within one accounting period—or horizontal—a comparison over a number of periods.

Analysis by Management

Management obviously is interested in further analysis. A good executive always seeks to minimize expenses and place the resources at his disposal to the best use in accordance with the utility's objectives. In this context, management might compare present with past performance and indicate desired future performance. It may question performance critically when the results adversely affect the company and praise itself mightily when the analyses indicate superior performance.

One approach to this type of evaluation is to subject the income statement to ratio analysis, that is, compare total expenses of operations to total revenues, profit margins to total revenues, and individual expense items to total expenses. Table 20 provides key income statement relationships utilizing the composite statistics for privately owned Class A and B electric utilities as reported by the Federal Power Commission.[1] Ratio analysis comparison generally is more meaningful than comparison in absolute terms. For example, a year-by-year comparison of absolute dollars may show increases or declines; yet, on a percentage basis, the figures may be quite stable. In the former case, management would be inclined to accept the analysis without further explanation. Absolute expense such as depreciation and property taxes may present little cause for alarm if plant has increased proportionately over the period analyzed. If fixed expenses increase as a percentage of total expenses or total revenues, the data will require further analysis. However, the situation might be acceptable if fixed expenses decline relative to variable expenses as revenues increase.

An analysis of variable expenses on an absolute basis indicating a downward trend is probably more demanding of an explanation than an upward trend, particularly if revenues are increasing. On a relative basis, variable expenses might be expected to increase proportionately to revenue increases. An analysis over a number of years may be of particular interest and value to the company. While change may be expected, utility management should be prepared to explain why such differences occur. Inflation may account for certain increases in expenses, or changing to more efficient plant facilities might cause both fixed and variable expenses to be altered, neither of which may be cause for celebration or alarm.

Since a regulated industry's financial success or failure is dependent upon rates it can charge the consumer, more detailed analysis of operating revenues and expenses is critical. Tables 21 and 22 present such an analysis for Class A and B electric utilities based on Federal Power Commission composite data. Revenues are analyzed by type of customer, as a percentage of total customers, total revenues, units of sales (kwh), average kwh of sales per customer, average annual customer bills, and average revenue in

[1]Tables 20–24 are based on annual aggregate data of privately owned Class A and B electric utilities. The discussion concentrates upon this type of analysis for inhouse use by individual utilities.

TABLE 20. *Income Account Relationships*

Relationship	*Year ended 31 December*					
	1968	*1966*	*1964*	*1962*	*1960*	*1958*
Electric operating revenues as a percentage of total operating revenues	85.2	84.7	84.5	84.6	84.9	85.4
Percentage of electric operating revenues:						
Electric operation and maintenance	45.1	44.6	44.0	43.9	44.8	46.1
Electric depreciation and amortization	11.2	11.2	11.3	11.0	10.7	10.4
Federal income taxes—electric	9.2	9.9	10.7	10.9	10.9	10.0
Other taxes—electric	10.9	10.5	10.4	10.3	10.1	9.8
Provision for deferred taxes on income—electric	.7	.6	.8	1.5	2.0	2.5
Income taxes deferred in prior years—credit	.3	.3	.3	.3	.2	.1
Investment tax credit adjustments—(net)	.5	.4	.4	.4		
Total electric operating expenses	77.3	76.9	77.3	77.3	78.3	78.7
Electric operating income	22.7	23.1	22.7	22.7	21.7	21.3
Electric depreciation and amortization as a percentage of electric utility plant	2.4	2.5	2.5	2.5	2.4	2.4
Interest on long-term debt:						
Percentage of operating revenues	7.0	6.1	6.0	6.1	6.1	6.0
Average interest rate	4.3	3.9	3.7	3.7	3.6	3.4
Times earned	3.1	3.6	3.6	3.5	3.4	3.4
Net income as a percentage of operating revenues	15.4	16.2	16.0	15.2	15.0	14.9
Dividend appropriations, preferred stock:						
Percentage of operating revenues	1.4	1.3	1.4	1.5	1.6	1.7
Average dividend rate	4.9	4.6	4.6	4.6	4.6	4.6
Times earned	10.7	12.5	11.5	10.0	9.3	8.5
Dividend appropriations, common stock:						
Percentage of operating revenues	9.9	10.1	9.8	9.3	9.3	9.4
Percentage of earnings available for common stock	70.7	67.9	67.4	68.0	69.6	71.3
Percentage of average common equity:						
Earnings available for common stock	12.3	12.8	12.3	11.7	11.3	11.0
Dividend appropriations, common stock	8.7	8.7	8.3	7.9	7.9	7.9

SOURCE: Federal Power Commission, *Statistics of Privately Owned Electric Utilities in the United States, 1968, Class A and B* (Washington, D.C.: U.S. Government Printing Office, 1969), p. XXVII.

cents per kwh sold. Thus the utility can detect shifts in customer types, changes in usage by customer types, and variations among customers as contributors to total operating revenue.

Table 22 illustrates a number of statistics provided by the FPC relative to electric utility operation and maintenance expense. The analysis performed on the major expense categories—maintenance, production, transmission, distribution, customer accounting, sales, and administrative and general expenses—relates each expense item to revenues and units of output (kwh). A similar ratio analysis performed on the composite balance sheet for Class A and B electric utilities is illustrated in Tables 23 and 24.

Ratio analysis is a useful analytical device. Under certain circumstances it gives more meaningful information than does an analysis of absolute numbers, but more detailed statistical analysis can provide further useful information. Two techniques are regression and correlation analysis, which, together with tests for statistical significance, are designed to show relationships between dependent and independent variables and relationships to some hypothetical trend. Any variance from this trend may be tested for statistical significance of variation. One might analyze a particular expense against revenues over time, or one expense against all other expenses. With this type of analysis management could concentrate its efforts in the "exceptional" areas, that is, investigate those items which vary in a statistically significant amount from expectations based on a hypothetical trend.

Analysis by Regulatory Commissions

Analysis of individual company data is useful not only to utility management, but also to utility regulators. As was shown in Tables 20–24, analysis of similar data on an aggregate basis will give the regulators clues about management efficiency in controlling expenses or about areas which require further investigation.

Public Utility Commissions

It often is alleged that one of the tasks of the regulator is to make comparisons among utilities, and the dangers in such comparative analysis have been noted. Nevertheless, there are certain norms, which may be one device, for commissions to use in their

TABLE 21. *Electric Operating Revenue Relationships*

Relationship	*Year ended 31 December* 1968	1966	1964	1962	1960	1958
Residential sales:						
Percentage of total customers	87.8	87.5	87.4	87.4	83.4	82.9
Percentage of total revenues	37.1	36.8	37.2	37.1	35.1	35.2
Percentage of total kwh sales	24.6	24.0	24.3	24.1	22.7	22.8
Average annual number of kwh sold per customer	5,706	4,931	4,377	3,878	3,454	3,101
Average annual bill per customer, dollars	128.43	115.37	107.25	99.36	90.51	82.52
Average revenue per kwh sold, cents	2.25	2.34	2.45	2.56	2.62	2.66
Commercial sales:						
Percentage of total customers	11.4	11.7	11.8	11.8	—	—
Percentage of total revenues	27.2	27.4	26.8	26.7	—	—
Percentage of total kwh sales	19.7	19.6	19.0	18.7	—	—
Average annual number of kwh sold per customer	35,009	30,239	25,448	22,378	—	—
Average annual bill per customer, dollars	725.30	643.81	574.60	531.67	—	—
Average revenue per kwh sold, cents	2.07	2.13	2.26	2.38	—	—
Industrial sales:						
Percentage of total customers	0.5	0.5	0.5	0.5	11.7	11.9
Percentage of total revenues	23.9	24.3	24.9	24.9	50.3	50.1
Percentage of total kwh sales	36.7	37.9	39.1	39.3	57.2	57.0
Average annual number of kwh sold per customer	1,581,801	1,443,952	1,219,650	1,123,281	61,944	54,091
Average annual bill per customer, dollars	15,399.55	14,126.36	12,425.65	11,794.94	922.71	815.69
Average revenue per kwh sold, cents	0.97	0.98	1.02	1.05	1.49	1.51

SOURCE: Federal Power Commission, *Statistics of Privately Owned Electric Utilities in the United States, 1968, Class A and B* (Washington, D.C.: U.S. Government Printing Office, 1969), p. XXXIII.

TABLE 22. *Electric Operation and Maintenance Expense Relationships*

Relationship	*Year ended 31 December*					
	1968	*1966*	*1964*	*1962*	*1960*	*1958*
Operation and maintenance expense as a percentage of operating revenues	45.1	44.7	44.0	43.9	44.8	46.1
Maintenance charges:						
Percentage of total operation and maintenance expenses	14.3	14.5	14.8	14.7	13.3	13.3
Percentage of operating revenues	6.4	6.5	6.5	6.5	6.0	6.2
Maintenance and depreciation charges as a percentage of operating revenues	17.7	17.7	17.8	17.4	16.6	16.5
Production expenses:						
Percentage of operating revenues	27.3	26.3	25.0	24.8	24.8	25.5
Per kwh sold, mills	4.09	4.01	4.00	4.12	4.20	4.38
Transmission expenses:						
Percentage of operating revenues	1.4	1.4	1.4	1.4	1.5	1.5
Per kwh sold, mills	0.21	0.21	0.22	0.24	0.25	0.26
Distribution expenses:						
Percentage of operating revenues	6.3	6.5	6.8	6.8	7.5	7.9
Per customer, dollars	19.31	17.84	17.18	16.00	16.19	15.27
Customer accounts expenses:						
Percentage of operating revenues	2.5	2.6	2.8	2.8	3.0	3.1
Per customer, dollars	7.68	7.18	6.99	6.54	6.38	6.04
Sales expenses as a percentage of operating revenues	1.7	1.8	1.8	1.7	1.7	1.6
Administrative and general expenses as a percentage of operating revenues	5.7	6.0	6.3	6.4	6.3	6.5

SOURCE: Federal Power Commission, *Statistics of Privately Owned Electric Utilities in the United States, 1968, Class A and B* (Washington, D.C.: U.S. Government Printing Office, 1969), p. XXXIX.

TABLE 23. *Balance Sheet Relationships*

Relationship	*Year ended 31 December*					
	1968	*1966*	*1964*	*1962*	*1960*	*1958*
Electric utility plant per dollar of revenue	4.60	4.46	4.44	4.45	4.49	4.51
Other utility plant per dollar of revenue	2.76	2.73	2.67	2.63	2.69	2.84
Total utility plant per dollar of revenue	4.33	4.19	4.17	4.17	4.22	4.27
Current assets times current liabilities	.79	.89	.97	1.01	.99	1.00
Percentage of capitalization and surplus:						
Long-term debt	53.8	52.3	51.8	52.4	52.8	52.8
Preferred stock	9.6	9.5	9.6	10.3	10.7	11.4
Common stock and other paid-in capital	24.1	26.1	27.8	27.1	27.1	27.1
Earned surplus (retained income)	12.5	12.1	10.8	10.2	9.4	8.7
Long-term debt:						
Percentage of gross utility plant	39.9	39.0	39.3	40.8	41.8	42.7
Percentage of net utility plant	51.6	50.6	50.5	51.5	52.0	52.6
Accumulated provision for depreciation as a percentage of total utility plant	22.7	23.0	22.2	20.8	19.6	18.8

SOURCE: Federal Power Commission, *Statistics of Privately Owned Electric Utilities in the United States, 1968, Class A and B* (Washington, D.C.: U.S. Government Printing Office, 1969), p. XX.

TABLE 24. *Percentage Relationships of Electric Plant in Service*

Relationship	*Year ended 31 December*											
	1968		*1966*		*1964*		*1962*		*1958*		*1960*	
Production plant	40.0		40.0		41.7		42.6		42.6		41.6	
Intangible		—		—		—		—		—		—
Steam		83.4		84.3		84.5		84.8		85.0		83.4
Nuclear		1.7		1.3		1.3		1.2		Part of steam		
Hydraulic		12.7		13.4		13.6		13.4		14.4		15.9
Other		2.2		1.0		.6		.6		.6		.7
Transmission plant	18.1		17.0		16.2		15.9		15.7		16.0	
Distribution plant	39.0		39.6		39.2		38.6		38.7		39.4	
General plant	2.9		2.9		2.9		2.9		3.0		3.0	
Electric plant purchased and sold (net)	—		.1		—		—		—		—	
Total plant in service	100.0		100.0		100.0		100.0		100.0		100.0	

SOURCE: Federal Power Commission, *Statistics of Privately Owned Electric Utilities in the United States, 1968, Class A and B* (Washington, D.C.: U.S. Government Printing Office, 1969). Author's calculations based on Table 20, pp. XXXIX and XL.

regulatory work. The analysis of composite income statements and balance sheets has been used for all privately owned Class A and B electric utilities in the United States, and it also might be a useful guide for analysis of like utilities in a given geographical area. Furthermore, like utilities in one state are comparable in several ways, and a particular utility within a state can be analyzed in relation to general trends or norms in the state which certainly will be apparent. Such analysis may give clues to the liberalism or conservativism of the regulatory authority and, at the same time, may provide a measure of constant surveillance in regulation.

The Missouri Public Service Commission has embarked on a program for analyzing thirty-five major financial and operating characteristics. Data are supplied to the commission for its "Monthly Utility Analysis Report" by individual utilities. Information comes from thirty-nine balance sheet and income statement accounts. The balance sheet information is month-end data, while income statement data cover the preceding twelve months just ended. The output is grouped into seven functional categories (pages) of a financial and operating nature. Each page displays data for fifty-four consecutive months showing actual and least-squares trend values. On a utility-by-utility basis, the commission is able to readily recognize seasonal, cyclical, and, perhaps most important, unusual performance, a type of continuous surveillance expected of regulatory bodies.

A word of caution is necessary: Few utilities operate under so-called ideal conditions with a good consumer mix, including different types of customers—residential, commercial, and industrial—and within each class a good mix of subclasses. In addition, the company may be operating in a rather compacted area, which requires a minimal distribution system. Distribution costs often represent a substantial amount of a utility's investment, and their minimization significantly could reduce expenses. Under these conditions consumer rates could be quite acceptable, perhaps even lower than those of surrounding utilities, while the utility would earn greater than normal net income.

Cost also may be analyzed on the basis of identified units of installed capacity or output, which was illustrated in Table 21. With proper facilities it might be well for a utility and regulators to make such analyses on the basis of certain segments of the utility's operating system, such as substations or exchanges. Obviously, there are certain segments in any utility which are more profitable, and data should be analyzed to see why this is so. Furthermore, such investigation might enable a marketing or sales organization to increase or reduce the amount of advertising directed toward a specific segment of the consuming public.

Securities and Exchange Commission

The Securities and Exchange Commission, as a regulatory agency, also is interested in a company's past financial history, particularly when it is called upon to authorize—or at least to approve—a utility's issue of additional securities. The SEC is obligated by law to ensure potential investors adequate information for analysis and decision making.

In like manner, creditors and investors will make a critical analysis of a utility's financial statements. The former are interested in analyzing capital ratios and times bond interest earned, while the latter will utilize both company financial data and investment market information to aid in their evaluation of a utility's performance. Important financial data include: price earnings, or reciprocal earnings-price ratios; dividends-market price ratios; capital turnover ratios; profit margin (net income related to gross revenue); growth in dividends over a period of time; growth in earnings over a similar period; and changes in the market price of securities. If it is assumed that investors purchase securities on a comparability of risk basis, then the investor also is interested in data of other utilities in addition to the one being analyzed. He might compare utilities of similar size based on investment in assets or, more likely, on gross operating revenues.

Bureau of Internal Revenue

Of course, one cannot ignore the Internal Revenue Service and its need for financial data. Tax accounting often is at variance with financial accounting. This is particularly true with respect to the types of expenses which are tax deductible, the limits as to the amount of the deduction, and the timing of the deduction. Referring to the latter, tax accounting frequently recognizes lump-sum deductions to be taken the year in which the expense occurs, whereas utility financial accounting treatment often requires deferral or at least a spreading of the expense over a number of years. The utility must be able to provide supporting data to the IRS in order to reconcile these differences.

Summary

To satisfy all parties, it is obvious that certain common elements must exist. Within a company, consistency is extremely important. If one wants to compare distribution expenses over a period of years, accounting techniques must be similar, or data would have to be adjusted for inconsistencies. Consistency, however, must be employed with discretion, or it is meaningless. If economic conditions change, or better ways of data presentation are found, consistence with past performance decreases the validity of the results. Proper disclosure of changes adds to clarity, consistency, and comparability of these data.

To be effective, financial data must be available promptly. Firms in many sectors of the economy produce daily income statements so that management tends to operate almost on a real time basis. Results of prior day's operations are available for the following morning's review; if changes are needed, they can be made before a problem becomes acute. Adequate data processing equipment can produce timely financial information.

Obviously, a number of individuals or groups have a strong interest in financial data provided by accounting departments. It is even more obvious that each individual or group desires data somewhat different from the others. To be effective, data must be adequate, and the uniform systems of accounts attempt to ensure this. However, it may be well to look more deeply for a common denominator of information which would allow those interested in aggregating data to meet their needs more easily. These needs are particularly acute within the firm: the cost accounting department requires a much different breakdown of data than does the engineering department, the finance department, or the sales department. Again, the electronic data processing equipment available to utilities certainly could be one solution to meeting such varied requirements.

Selected References

Foulke, Roy A. *Practical Financial Statement Analysis.* New York: McGraw-Hill Book Company, Inc., 1957.

Iulo, William. *Electric Utilities—Costs and Performances.* Pullman: Washington State University Press, 1961.

Kennedy, Ralph Dale, and McMullen, S. Y. *Financial Statements—Form Analysis and Interpretation.* Homewood, Ill.: Richard D. Irwin, Inc., 1952.

12

Cost Accounting: Analysis and Apportionment

Cost accounting and analysis is important to any business which produces a product for sale. In a nonregulated firm, whose prime market structure is dictated by competitive forces, cost accounting is somewhat less important in determining financial success. Such analysis is not irrelevant for fixing prices, but its import is probably more indirect than in noncompetitive enterprises.

The public utility requires cost information and analysis to distribute operating expenses and fixed asset costs into proper service or customer groups to determine prices or rates charged to the consumer. Cost analysis and apportionment are important to the nonregulated firm in determining the cost of its products, or current assets, but in the regulated sector of the economy they are critical in determining the associated costs of long-lived, fixed assets and in pricing the services produced by these assets.

Construction Costs

Direct Costs of Construction

The cost of service producing assets, whether constructed by utility personnel or provided by contract with outside construction companies, requires evaluation through the utility's work order system for assignment to proper continuing property records (CPRs) and asset ledger accounts.

Property and plant constructed by a utility's own personnel will utilize both materials and labor. Direct costs of these expenditures are capitalized and assigned to the proper project work order based upon material requisition and labor time cards. Information must be provided in sufficient detail to permit subsequent assignment to CPRs and asset ledger accounts. If construction work is contracted with outside sources, sufficient detail must be obtained to permit evaluation of the completed assets into retirement and CPR units.

In addition to these identifiable direct costs, a number of indirect costs, which are properly capitalized, must be assigned by arbitrary formula.

Indirect Costs of Construction

Those indirect costs assignable to construction work include: indirect salaries and wages of engineering, supervisory, and administrative personnel; costs of special shop machinery and services; transportation costs; and costs of taxes and interest during construction. The difficulty surrounding the assignment of these lies in the fact that they are partially operating expenses and costs of construction. While division of these costs is arbitrary, construction projects should be awarded a fair and equitable share. The problem involves finding a formula which will produce valid and acceptable results.

Although other methods are available, two are suggested for allocating indirect costs: an incremental cost approach and a benefit-realized method. If a utility uses the former, an analysis is made of the cost of indirect items to determine those expenditures which would have been incurred without the construction project. The difference, or incremental amount, between the costs actually incurred and those which would have been incurred is then assigned to the project. Under the latter method, all indirect labor costs are assigned to construction projects based on the ratio of time spent by personnel on construction work versus daily operations. Those indirect costs other than personnel labor charges must be capitalized and assigned by some reasonable method based on the benefits received in the construction project.

Using the benefit-realized method has the effect of reducing expenses and thus increasing net income during periods of heavy construction activity. At the same time, capitalization of these expenditures increases the rate base. The incremental cost approach tends to avoid the effects of showing greater net income when construction activity is increased.

LABOR. Cost of time spent by engineering, supervisory, and administrative personnel which are associated with construction work should be so assigned. If time reports are maintained, assignment is not difficult. When such information is unavailable, assignment is usually made in relationship to direct labor costs or hours devoted to the project.

SPECIAL SHOP MACHINERY AND SERVICES. Any materials, labor, and appropriate overhead costs incurred in a utility machine shop must be capitalized against the project work order directing the expenditure. Materials used can be identified, while labor, together with budgeted overhead, generally will be based on time spent in such work.

TRANSPORTATION. Transportation costs provided by outside or utility-owned vehicles and not directly assignable to construction work must be capitalized at reasonable rates. Outside costs often are based on the value of items carried or space required. Most in-house facilities have been assigned a predetermined rate designed to cover the cost of fuel, oil, maintenance, and depreciation.

TAXES DURING CONSTRUCTION. Any taxes incurred and attributable to construction projects should be assigned thereto. These include all payroll taxes on both direct and indirect labor, property taxes, and any sales taxes paid on materials used in the construction work.

INTEREST DURING CONSTRUCTION. Interest during construction includes all reasonable costs of money, whether paid out or not, utilized in the project during its construction stages. Interest on debt capital, whether paid or accrued, is properly capitalized; furthermore, an imputed interest on equity capital also is properly charged to the project. While the rates on long-term debt are readily available, no rate is available on equity money since the assets are not yet producing a service. The capitalization for all construction funds might be imputed at the utility's legally authorized rate of return. Some commissions specify a definite rate to be used on all funds regardless of source, while others are not as specific.[1]

Many of the indirect construction costs require arbitrary allocation, but the cost accountant should strive for a formula(s) which will allocate these costs in an equitable manner and at the same time be clerically feasible. If properly performed, the costs of utility plant will be functionally allocated to utility plant in service, which includes facilities for production, transmission, distribution, or general purposes. This functional allocation, however, does not provide the necessary cost analysis for rate-making purposes. A reclassification of plant costs (return on investment) and expenses of operation and maintenance must be made in order to associate costs with those customers who utilize the service.

Cost Analysis for Rate Making

One of the principal functions of a regulatory commission is to determine a utility's general rate level or revenue requirement so that rates in the aggregate will cover all legitimate expenses of operation and earn a just and reasonable return on investment. An economist would describe the situation as producing an output where total cost equals total revenue ($TC = TR$). Furthermore, regulation has influenced individual rates to produce an output such that, in the aggregate, average unit cost is equal to average unit revenue ($AC = AR$). In an accounting sense this function might better be described as the determination of gross operating revenue. While the determination of overall revenues, including expenses and earnings, is of primary regulatory importance, the determination of individual rates usually is viewed as a managerial function. The latter represents a working compromise between theory and practice. Cost analysis aids in bridging this gap and is one of the numerous tools and considerations available to management in producing reasonable rate structures. Since rate structure design goes beyond accounting and involves the expertise of engineers, economists, and statisticians, no attempt will be made to

---

[1]See, for example: *Re Muncie Water Works Company* (1963) No. 29674, 26 July 1963 (Indiana); and *Re Southwest Gas Corporation* (1967) 69 PUR 3d 348 (Nevada).

produce actual rate schedules; the emphasis will be on cost accounting principles only.

The basic data used in cost analysis are functionally classified by the uniform accounting system. Plant and expense accounts are grouped on a functional basis with respect to production, transmission, distribution, customer accounts, sales, and administrative and general items. Unfortunately, such a grouping does not lend itself particularly well to rate making, although a functional analysis can be made. A better classification would be based on customer, energy, and capacity expense categories. The cost analysis problem is one of taking information found in utilities' accounting records and regrouping and allocating these data to serve the rate analysis study.

Justification for the new functional allocation is an economic one since it is an attempt to separate fixed and variable cost components. Because public utilities have relatively large amounts of fixed investments, most of their costs are fixed. A large portion of these costs is related to the number of customers and their demand for service from the utility system. The relatively smaller amount of variable costs is dependent upon the actual amount of service supplied.

Customer Costs

Customer costs are those which vary with the number of customers served and which can be directly attributable to a particular individual. Included in this category are investment charges and expenses related to a portion of the general distribution system; the service drop, or connection from the distribution line to the point of consumption (residence, store, factory, and so forth); metering equipment; and meter reading, billing, and accounting. Most of these items are of a fixed nature, and costs per customer tend to be fairly constant. Total absolute dollars will vary with the number of customers served.

Energy Costs

The electric utility, in supplying kilowatt hours of electric energy to fulfill customer requirements, incurs costs which vary with the number of kwhs demanded. Fuel costs, together with attendant labor costs, are the major components of this functional category.

Capacity Costs

Load, capacity, or customer demand costs often are described as common or joint costs; consequently, it is impossible to assign them to a particular customer. Each customer using the plant facilities both shares and utilizes them to varying degrees. Different customers may utilize the same facilities at different times. The costs vary with the customer's load or demand on the utility system and, in a functional sense, include capital costs as well as expenses connected with the generating plant, transmission lines, substations, and a more general portion of the distribution system which bears a common element among a number of customers.[2] Demand or load costs bear little relationship to the amount of energy used, but they are related to the amount of plant capacity required to fulfill a demand at a particular time.

An example may be helpful. Two customers utilize a particular utility system. Both use an equal amount of energy during one month, but each places a different demand upon the system. Customer A has a demand or load of ten kilowatts which he operates 100 hours per month; his monthly consumption is 1,000 kwh (10 kw × 100 hours). Customer B has a demand of 20 kilowatts which he operates 50 hours per month. The monthly consumption is the same as customer A's—1,000 kwh. Needless to say, the cost of serving the second customer is more than the cost of serving the first—the investment in equipment needed to supply this larger load is greater.

Table 25 lists the major plant and expense accounts by uniform system account numbers and demonstrates the functional transformation from accounting classifications to the customer-energy-demand classification. Transformation is essentially a four-step procedure. (1) All directly assignable costs should be segregated in order to eliminate them from further concern and allocation problems. These assignable costs are attributable only to specific uses such as street lighting or urban transit systems. (2) The

[2]The latter is distinguished from the distribution system expense which was directly allocable under customer cost.

functional allocation of items relating to customer, capacity, and energy components must be made. (3) The allocation of the demand component of joint and common costs not attributable to any particular customer or customer class must be arbitrarily allocated on the basis of formula. (4) Customer, demand, and energy costs must be subdivided into fairly homogeneous groups by types of customers.

The most general classification of homogeneous groups to use might be those basic revenue accounts listed in the uniform system. These include "Residential sales," "Commercial and industrial sales," "Public street and highway lighting," "Other sales to public authorities," "Sales to railroads and railways," "Sales for resale," and "Interdepartmental sales."[3] This does not preclude many individual rate structures being devised within each of these revenue classifications.

Cost determination would be relatively simple if there was only one class of service, but with so many classes being supplied from common facilities, cost allocation becomes extremely complex. In most unregulated businesses, product costs tend to be variable, and the allocation process is much simpler. In a utility, a large segment of the costs are fixed and are of the common or joint variety. The complexity, however, does not relieve the utility from separating fixed and variable items.

Functional Allocation

There still remains the need for a general discussion of functional allocation.[4] Basic functional allocations are derived from careful inspection of the nature of the cost. The dominating influences of customer, energy, and demand components will aid in separating the items. Although hard-and-fast rules for this allocation are rare, a systematic approach with a generous sprinkling of logic seems required. The subsequent discussion leans heavily on this philosophy.

---

[3]FPC, *Uniform System,* p. 101-69.

[4]The following discussion relies on much of the material presented in Russell E. Caywood, *Electric Utility Rate Economics* (New York: McGraw-Hill, 1956), chap. 11.

TABLE 25. *Reallocation of Costs for Rate-making Purposes*

Name of item	*Plant account numbers*	*Operation and maintenance account numbers*	*Customer costs*	*Demand or capacity costs*	*Energy costs*
Intangible plant	301–303		X	X	
Production plant	301–316, 320–325, 330–336, 340–346	500–557		X	X
Transmission plant:					
Lines	350, 351, 354–359	560, 563–568, 571–573		X	
Substations	352, 353	561, 562, 569, 570		X	
Distribution plant:					
Lines and services	360, 364–367, 369, 371 372	580, 581, 583, 584, 588, 589, 590, 593, 594, 598	X	X	
Substations	361–363	582, 591, 592		X	
Line transformers	368	595	X	X	
Meters	370	568, 587, 597		X	
Street lighting	373	585, 596	X	X	
General plant	389–399	932	X	X	
Customer accounting and collection expenses		901–905	X		
Sales promotion expenses		911–916	X		
Administrative and general expenses		920–931	X	X	

SOURCE: Adapted from Russell E. Caywood, *Electric Utility Rate Economies* (New York: McGraw-Hill, 1956), p. 148.
NOTE: X denotes the new categories to which the functional accounts have been reclassified.

Allocation of Basic Plant

The basic plant, which is represented by the primary plant accounts illustrated in Table 25, generally has no energy elements. Thus, allocation is a matter of separating the customer and capacity or demand functions. Usage dictates that all generation and transmission facilities, including substations, are demand related, while services and meters are allocated to the customer function. However, there are certain demand elements in services and meters, and these might be handled by segregating the items based on customer sizes. Similarly, distribution transformers and primary and secondary distribution lines, including conductors and devices (account 365, "Distribution plant") and poles and towers (account 364, "Distribution"), all contain capacity and customer costs. Perhaps one of the best rules to follow is this: The closer one approaches the ultimate consumer, the more easily one can identify plant used; therefore, such costs will be allocated directly to customers or customer classes on a use basis. As one nears the substation or the transmission and generating facilities, the costs become more common or joint. The items more distant from the customer should be included within the basic demand or capacity category.

Provision for accumulated depreciation is a negative consideration; as such, it must be allocated to the various primary plant accounts as applicable.

General and Intangible Plant. Allocation of general and intangible plant is usually on some ratio basis. It can be allocated to the functional classes based on the amount of investment in that function as related to total investment. Each function's share is then allocated to customer classes on the basis of either the demand or customer component.

Working Capital. Working capital includes cash requirements as well as materials and supplies, prepaid expenses, and a percentage of operating expenses. If cash working capital is to be allocated, it usually is done as a percentage of either gross revenue or operating expenses.[5]

Materials and supplies as an element of working capital should

[5]If large tax accruals exist, cash working capital is eliminated from rate-making requirements. This accrual may be much less relevant today due to the timing of tax payments.

be allocated between those used for operation and maintenance and those directly related to construction materials. The latter can be apportioned on the basis of the plant accounts to which the materials and supplies are related. In the case of operation and maintenance materials, these usually are associated with operation and maintenance expenses; with the exception of the power source, for example, coal, which has a direct allocation to energy, they generally are allocated to the materials component of operation and maintenance expenses.

These allocations functionally have subdivided that portion of the revenue requirements related to investment, or what is commonly interpreted as $(V - d)$.[6] In order to determine the dollar amount which must be used in cost analysis, the allowed and approved rate of return is then applied. The result represents the cost of money as part of the total cost of service. Other expense items now must be allocated, which may be done by various methods. The following discussion relates to a number of the more prominent components.

Operating Expense Allocations

Depreciation. Depreciation expense generally is allocated on the same basis as was the negative figure, accumulated depreciation, discussed above.

Taxes. Taxes include income, property, employer related, and miscellaneous taxes. The first type is allocated on the basis of income generated by each customer group. The second type can be apportioned on the basis of property allocation. Employer related taxes are best distributed on the basis of labor charges.

Plant Operation and Maintenance. There are several different approaches available, but one method suggests that all fuel and maintenance be classed as energy costs and the remainder as demand costs. Admittedly, there is a basic fuel requirement which might be apportioned as demand, and there are certain minimal maintenance requirements which might be interpreted similarly.

---

[6]The rule of rate making used by regulators and utilities is expressed as follows: Gross operating revenue = Operating expenses + Annual depreciation + All taxes + $(V - d)r$, where $(V - d)$ is property value less accumulated depreciation, and r represents a reasonable rate of return.

The demand component in fuel more or less offsets the energy component in maintenance.

CUSTOMER ACCOUNTING AND COLLECTION. Customer accounting and collection costs usually are allocated on the basis of customer classes; these further can be reduced to a unit cost per customer based upon the number of customers served.

SALES PROMOTION EXPENSES. Sales promotion expenses generally are spread on the basis of revenue by customer class, number of customers served, or some combination of the two. If the apportionment is on the basis of revenue, customers contributing a large amount of revenue may be assessed an unduly high proportion of sales promotion expenditures. Thus, general customer classification allocations may be the best alternative.

ADMINISTRATIVE AND GENERAL EXPENSES. Administrative and general expenses can be related to plant investment or to revenues generated by customer class. A relatively simple yet reasonable method is to allocate on the basis of payroll.

Summary

Up to this point the various cost components reflected in the financial accounting system have been reallocated into customer, energy, and demand or capacity elements. These three functional divisions must be allocated to the several customer groupings that were mentioned previously. Customer and energy cost allocations present little difficulty; the basis for their allocation is evident. The problem arises in just and reasonable distribution of the capacity or demand costs among customer groups. To date, some thirty-five or forty methods have been described and utilized. Inasmuch as expertise in areas other than accounting are necessary to make many of these allocations, this particular study made only some very general comments, and the reader is referred to other discussions of demand cost allocations.

Theory would state that proper allocation of the inallocable, that is, the common or joint costs of capacity, should result in the distribution of economic resources in the best possible manner and should enable all customers requiring service to purchase same (statute has declared public utility service a necessity). The resulting price should neither discourage needed use nor encourage wasteful use; the plant should be utilized to its desired capacity, thereby reducing unit costs and providing a reasonably sanctioned and allowed profit element; and no customer group should be penalized at the expense of any other group. If capacity is, in fact, reached and costs increase, rates likewise must increase.

The FPC's Cost Analysis Program

Traditional cost analysis for rate making is based upon total revenue requirements or cost of service as designated by a regulatory commission. Unfortunately, this accepted rate-of-return/rate base approach provides little in the way of useful cost data for analyzing *specific* rate structures. Using aggregate data, the above discussion developed the generally accepted approach to the formation of individual utility rates. This method of revenue determination and eventual rate structures has been criticized since it gives management little, if any, incentive to seek new and more efficient ways of providing service. In short, the utility is not encouraged to improve either its performance or its productivity.

With the increase in competition faced by many sectors of utility services, utilities are forced to act more like unregulated business in setting prices. Public utility earnings should be similar to those of general business activity. As most businesses attempt to set prices by applying a mark-up to total cost, utilities could do the same. Such an approach has been developed by the Federal Power Commission in their Cost Analysis Program (CAP) with respect to utility cost allocation. The program directs attention to the cost of operation and investment as the cornerstone of rate-making analysis. Basic to the analysis is the assumption of viewing the utility as any other competitive business with cost based on volume of output. The intent is not to dispose of the traditional rate-making process as described above, but to supplement it and to furnish current data to regulator and manager alike. In essence, CAP determines how many units of output have been produced (kwh, Mcf, and so forth) and the cost per unit. The merit is that volume of output becomes a major factor in the rate-making equation—a type of incremental or marginal cost approach long advocated by public utility economists. Thus, it is designed to overcome one of the major weaknesses of the current methods, namely, application of the costs developed for a given output to every future unit of output regardless of the magnitude of total production, which fails to recognize the importance of declining unit costs as output rises or increasing unit costs as output declines.

The result of CAP is the establishment of a profit margin per unit rather than a rate of return for total investment. In addition, CAP should allow the commission a continuous overview of the utility's operations—a type of continuous surveillance—in place of the infrequent and laborious formal rate hearing. Furthermore, the approach also should serve management with data on costs of seeking added business which might require new investment. "The big plus resulting from the use of CAP in the electric utility field is its service as one of the key financial management tools. In the hands of executives, CAP clearly reveals the effect of volume of sales in determining profits, losses, or break-even points, and/or the cost of efficient or inefficient use of the total investment dollars, over extended periods of time."[7]

The topic cannot be dismissed without a cautious note. Standardized unit costs during periods of rapid price changes for even a single utility may have little value. Under the same conditions, when standard costs are suggested for a number of utilities, the problem becomes more acute, especially when one considers such differences as market, geographical, and operating cost variations.

Marginal or Incremental Cost Rate Making

Cost accounting and the rate-making process are not synonymous. Rates or prices for any good or service must be determined under supply and demand conditions. Therefore, cost data are only one factor to be considered in setting rates for public utilities. The general analysis described on pages 236–44 assumes the characteristics of an average cost (fully allocated cost divided by total output) approach. All costs for the utility's operations are allocated to various customer classifications, or groups. Directly assignable costs are apportioned on a responsibility basis, and joint or common costs by formula. Each customer then identified within a group has a rate(s) set on the basis of average costs for the customers within the group. No overt attempt is made to identify specific

---

[7]Gordon F. Heim, "Cost-Analysis Program—An Indicator of Volume Effect," in *Public Utility Accounting: Models, Mergers, and Information Systems,* ed. Roland F. Salmonson (East Lansing: M.S.U. Public Utilities Papers, 1971), p. 87.

costs with specific customers to determine the incremental or marginal costs either incurred by attaching a customer to the system, or avoided when a customer selects an alternative source.

In any competitive industry this approach is theoretically and practically correct. In the competitive analysis, under equilibrium conditions, average costs for the last unit of output as well as marginal costs are identical (see Figure 1). Subsequently, prices for the individual firm facing a completely inelastic demand function are equated with the two cost functions, and the firm is economically sound. Firms with market structures which differ from the competitive model, such as the public utility, find that their cost functions do not neatly align in an equilibrium position. Rather, the negatively sloping demand curve bisects the average cost curve at a point to the left of the marginal cost-demand intersection (see Figure 2). In the first instance, an example of average cost pricing (D or $AR = AC$), a substantial number of customers remain unsatisfied because they have a demand, D, with an attendant price, (AR), greater than additional cost, (MC). However, producing output at a point where $D = MC$ places the utility or any firm with similar market structure in an untenable position because total revenues will not cover all costs, including a reasonable profit. Thus the firm must be subsidized or the owners must support the deficit.

The proposition that marginal cost is important in evaluating pricing of utility service cannot be denied. In fact, this information is essential to pricing decisions. With the increased competition faced by utilities, both direct and indirect, marginal cost information becomes even more desirable.

Marginal Cost Defined

Defining *marginal cost* in theoretical terms is not difficult. The mathematician describes it by use of the calculus as the first derivative of total cost. For example, it is the ratio of the change of total cost to a very small corresponding change in output if the increment of output is infinitesimally small.[8] The economist describes it as the extra cost incurred to produce one extra unit of

[8]Clark Lee Allen, *Elementary Mathematics of Price Theory* (Belmont, Calif.: Wadsworth Publishing Company, Inc., 1962), p. 33.

output in the cheapest way possible.[9] The accountant has used direct cost analysis as a surrogate for marginal cost. At times, the concept is defined as variable, out-of-pocket, or incremental cost. Regardless of the precise definition chosen, all have a common thread: added cost, that is, additional costs to be incurred if there is added output or monetary outlay for an alternative good or service.

SHORT- VERSUS LONG-RUN COSTS. If marginal cost data is utilized by the utility, it must be decided whether or not these costs will be of a short- or a long-run nature. In the economic short run, plant capacity is assumed to be fixed, that is, added capital is not expended to increase the size of the plant. Existing facilities merely are utilized to greater advantage by consuming variable inputs such as fuel or labor. The amount of available capacity may show that marginal costs can be less than, equal to, or greater than average costs. Furthermore, they are more volatile than those of a longer run variety.

Long-run marginal costs, by definition, assume that plant size or capacity also may vary. According to economic interpretation, added output will be performed at the lowest possible cost, which allows the firm to take advantage of scale economies. Public utilities always have tried to maintain stability of rates or prices, and the long-run marginal cost concept allows for such stability.

PAST VERSUS FUTURE COSTS. Because marginal cost is identified with future costs, the information available from normal functional accounting records fails to provide such data. In fact, many have claimed quite rationally that determination of marginal cost is impossible, since future costs are unknown. However inexact these projections may be, one still might argue that they are of greater assistance than inappropriate average cost data.

PLANT CAPACITY. Availability of plant capacity and time of use are probably two important problems to be resolved when utilizing marginal cost data. In a practical sense, increased demand or output cannot be identified as an infinitesimal amount or even as one additional unit of output. Furthermore, plant capacity, in the long run, cannot be precisely adjusted to provide service only for the last or marginal unit. Rather, most changes in plant capacity

---

[9]Paul A. Samuelson, *Economics An Introductory Analysis,* 5th ed. (New York: McGraw-Hill Book Company, Inc., 1961), p. 464.

are gross alterations. The addition of a generator will increase capacity and potential output by several million kilowatts, not just one kilowatt or a fraction thereof; the installation of a telephone cable may provide thousands of new circuits, not just a single pair for a specific customer. Furthermore, only part of the firm's capacity may need to be supplemented. Removal of bottleneck constraints on capacity may enable a utility to realize the full potential use of total plant. The installation of a larger diameter gas distribution main, for example, may be all that is required to provide service to many more customers or to existing customers in greater amounts.

Timing the use of facilities—existing or new—will help to determine the proper interpretation of marginal cost. If excess capacity exists at off-peak periods only, short-run cost is appropriate. If pricing is contemplated for a service at peak-use periods requiring capacity alterations, long-run costs must be used.

DEMAND ELASTICITY. The final setting of a utility rate will depend upon the potential customers' elasticity of demand. Certain customers will present definite inelasticities, while others will possess definite elasticities. This latter group increases as substitute or alternative services or suppliers emerge—as competition grows. Since some subscribers to a utility's output will be required to pay rates greater than marginal cost—all costs must be covered if no subsidy is allowed—who will pay the higher rate will depend upon which customers have the least elastic demand.

Uses of Marginal Costs

Marginal cost may be used in the rate-making process to set exact rates, as one input in the total rate-making process, or at least as a floor in identifying minimum rates. The concept emerges that no customer should be served unless he pays for the added cost of serving him. Again, whether or not the cost analysis is long or short run depends on the considerations and problems outlined above.

Applications of Marginal Cost Pricing

The use of incremental or marginal cost data in pricing of regulated industry services is not new. The Interstate Commerce

Commission has utilized long-run, out-of-pocket costs for many years, and rates for off-season or off-peak services are closely allied to incremental costs. The familiar expression of out-of-pocket cost, plus a contribution to fixed costs, however slight, is a worthwhile rate for providing service during times of unused or excess capacities. Stand-by or student air fares are good examples of this philosophy. Others include off-peak uses of electric energy or gas for water heating or interruptable industrial use; rates for "dump" power from hydrofacilities; and lower priced telephone services during off-peak evening and late night hours. Two more prominent examples of marginal cost pricing, one in electric energy, and one in communications, should illustrate the phenomenon.

The Green Tariff

Most applications of incremental cost pricing are based on offering a new service under specific operating conditions. These were mentioned above. The Green Tariff of Électricité de France, however, was designed and implemented for existing classes of service, including wholesale and high-voltage industrial customers. The rates were not specifically designed to ward off competition or attract new customers.

A number of theoretical studies preceded the actual setting of rate schedules. The results were to improve the load factor and operating characteristics for the entire system.[10] The goal was a system load factor as close as possible to 100 percent, which would allow for more complete use of plant and optimum use of national economic resources. Rates were based on the time of use as related to the system load. Lower rates were established for off-peak usage, average rates for usage during normal hours, and high rates for users demanding service at peak periods.

The structures developed are demand-energy rates which are differentiated by time of use, voltage of service supplied, and geographical location of the user by identified rate zones. The latter was to give recognition to the different methods of energy production—steam or hydrogeneration. Time differentials were represented by dividing the year into five periods and the days within

---

[10]*Load factor* is defined as the average demand on the utility system expressed as a ratio to the peak or maximum demand on the system.

each into from one to three time periods. Average incremental costs were calculated for the marginal generating plant with the highest fuel cost—in this case a thermal coal-fired unit. Depending on the other factors discussed above, average marginal costs, either short or long run, were added to determine rates.

The results of the Green Tariff are encouraging. The basic objectives apparently have been realized. By shaving anticipated peaks which would have occurred under the old rate structure, savings have been effected in reduced requirements for new investment and lower operating costs for existing facilities through better plant utilization.

The Bell System's LRIC

In recent years the communications industry has found certain segments of once monopolistic markets being seriously challenged, with regulatory commission approval. The Bell system's management determined that long-run incremental costs (LRIC) are relevant to determining rates of principal categories of system interstate services.[11] Full additional cost or LRIC is advocated for minimum rate determination in these service categories. The LRIC studies provide data for decisions in selecting or establishing rate alternatives. These alternatives indicate differences in *future* costs and *future* revenues and are concerned with rate structures for new service. Costs used were based on the latest information that Bell had available. The LRIC thus derived were interpreted as forward-looking cost studies. That is, marginal analysis, by definition, ignores past costs and relies on those costs that will be incurred for producing added units of output.

Like other utilities, the telephone industry employs vast amounts of common plant in furnishing a number of different services. This phenomenon makes it impossible to precisely earmark specific expenses of operation and plant costs for particular services. In prior discussions in this chapter mention was made of allocating such costs by formula, although many would argue such costs are inherently unallocable.

As the cost analysis was developed, the long-run incremental cost

---

[11]Testimony presented in FCC Dockets 16258 Phase 1-B, 18128 and 18684.

study sought to identify or estimate the additional costs which would be incurred in the long run if added services were furnished. These costs would be over and above those normally incurred without the added service being offered. Based on current and projected market estimates, total incremental or added costs were derived. Among these were: costs associated with increases in plant capacity, including return on the investment and related income taxes; costs of plant provided for use in common with other services when it was estimated such plant would be added because of the increased service; and an amount of common overhead expenses attributable to the new service. Thus, all expense items—maintenance, depreciation, accounting, commercial, and administrative—were included to represent full additional costs or LRIC. Although this approach received criticism, most of it was from a theoretical viewpoint. However imperfect, one might conclude that this was a valiant initial attempt at a practical application of economic theory.

The Role of the Accountant

The general consensus is that incremental or marginal costs are not the final word in a particular pricing situation. Rather, the identification of such costs, imprecise as they may be, is only the point of departure. Incremental cost of the short- or long-run variety is the floor below which rates should not fall. The introduction of demand elasticity or inelasticity aids in allocating the fixed joint or common costs as an added factor over the marginal cost attributable to a particular customer or service. Whatever the extent to which such costs are utilized in the rate-making process—and they will be used as competitive elements increase—the accountant will be called upon to provide usable data.

The functional approach to recording cost information today ignores any necessary breakdowns between fixed and variable costs. Even more important, recorded costs are not identified with particular customers, classes of customers, or types of service for which facilities are being used. With a substantial amount of utility costs being either common or joint, certain classifications seem impossible. Nevertheless, it is becoming increasingly more difficult to rely on this excuse. The accountant must begin devising ways by which costs may be separated into workable groupings for identifying short- and long-run incremental or marginal costs, although some imprecision may result.

Selected References

Cost Accounting

Hornegren, Charles T. *Cost Accounting: A Managerial Emphasis.* 2d ed. Englewood Cliffs, N.J.: Prentice-Hall, Inc., 1967.

Neuner, J. J. W., and Frumer, Samuel. *Cost Accounting: Principles and Practice.* 7th ed. Homewood, Ill.: Richard D. Irwin, Inc., 1967.

Cost Allocations

Bonbright, James C. *Public Utility Rates.* New York: Columbia University Press, 1961.

Bushnell, Curtis M. "Regulatory Responsibilities in Telephone Cost Allocations," *Public Utilities Fortnightly* 72 (7 and 21 November 1963): 52; 32.

Caywood, Russell E. *Electric Utility Rate Economics.* New York: McGraw-Hill Book Company, 1956.

Nelson, J. R., ed. *Marginal Cost Pricing in Practice.* Englewood Cliffs, N.J.: Prentice-Hall, Inc., 1964.

Salmonson, Roland F., ed. *Public Utility Accounting: Models, Mergers, and Information Systems.* East Lansing: M.S.U. Public Utilities Papers, 1971, especially pp. 81–135.

Trebing, Harry M., ed. *Essays on Public Utility Pricing and Regulation.* East Lansing: M.S.U. Public Utilities Studies, 1971, especially pp. 69–212.

13

Electronic Data Processing and Management Information Systems

The introduction of computers and electronic data processing equipment over the last quarter century is, without a doubt, one of the most dramatic events of our generation. Not only does the computer relieve operating personnel from the often repetitive and menial tasks involved in data gathering, recording, summarizing, analysis, and reporting, but, more to the point, the computer is capable of challenging management's imagination by providing facilities for extended analysis to aid in improved planning and control within the firm. The use of such equipment by public utilities has made substantial inroads into the firm's overall operations. Although many small utilities rely on computer equipment for customer billing, fewer have developed a fully integrated data processing system. Those which have frequently rely on computer service bureaus or time-sharing facilities, mainly because of the costs involved. The larger utilities—particularly those in the Class A and B categories—have found it to their advantage either to rent or to purchase some or all of the components of the data processing system. They can justify computer installation for routine customer billing and accounting as a first step toward a complete management information system.

The purpose of this chapter is to acquaint the public utility accountant with a number of data processing and management information system (MIS) terms, to outline the role of the accountant in the system, to develop a workable guide for investigating the feasibility of a management information system, and to indicate the functions within the utility which are most adaptable to the electronic data processing technique.

Electronic Data Processing

Electronic data processing, as opposed to manual or mechanical recording and analysis of accounting data, accomplishes the same tasks through the electronic data computer and its attendant facilities. The principal advantage of such a system is its ability to handle tremendous amounts of information within a very short period of time; speed of operation is the hallmark of the system. Accountants find that the electronic data processing approach is ideal for many routinized procedures requiring the recording and analysis of large amounts of data; payroll computations and billing procedures associated with customer sales are typical examples.

Management Information Systems

Management information systems, or the total systems concept, have received considerable attention over the past decade. The growth and complexity of business organizations require that management teams no longer concentrate on small segments of the enterprise and ignore the total economic function. Brush fighting and troubleshooting, although techniques that cannot be ignored, are not adequate for managment of an ongoing organized institution. Management now has recognized the importance of the total systems concept and the fact that there are a number of subsystems within the firm which interact in creating the whole. Computers are capable of producing more accurate and much more timely information than was available in the past; they are able to take massive amounts of data and, with unusually high speed, translate these data into usable form for alternative courses of action.

The management information system has been defined as "an approach to information systems design that conceives of a business as an integrated entity composed of interrelated systems and subsystems, and which, with the use of appropriate automatic systems tools, attempts to provide a timely and accurate management information system for optimum managerial decision-making."[1]

The Role of Accounting

An organization often is defined to include the functions of operating personnel as well as those appointed to the highest managerial posts. This managerial hierarchy frequently is illustrated with the diagram in Figure 5. The broad base of the

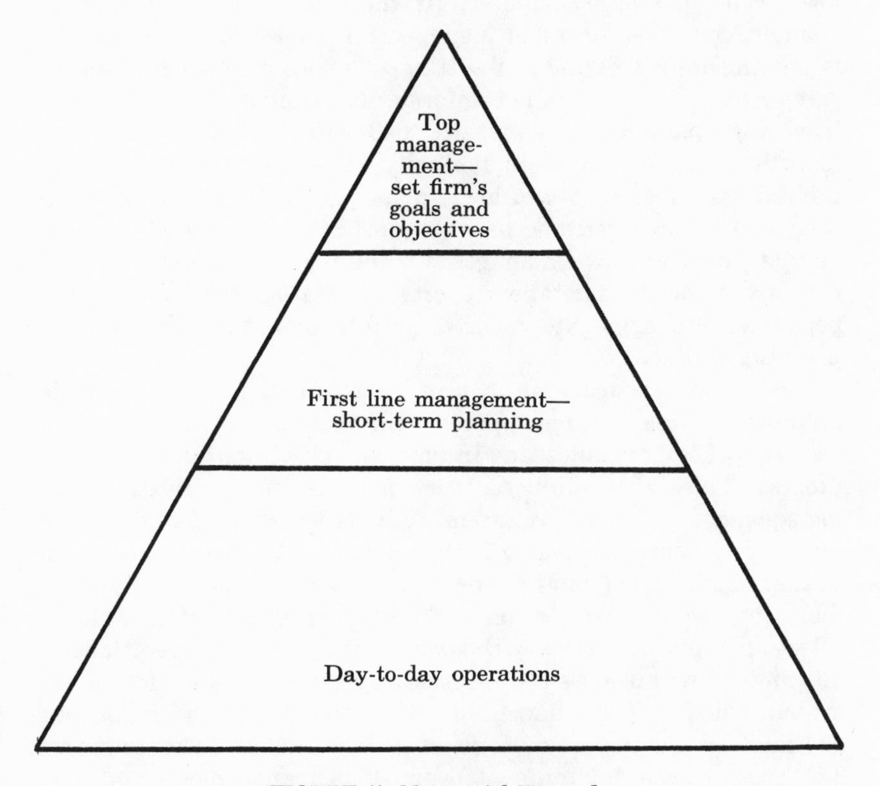

FIGURE 5. *Managerial Hierarchy*

[1]*Business Systems* (Cleveland: Association for Systems Management, 1970), p. 7.

illustration depicts the firm's work or operational force. Lower level supervisors and managers produce huge quantities of data and, in turn, require detailed reports and analyses concerning operational activities. Proceeding upward to middle and top management, one notices needs for further information, but these requirements generally are filled on a more aggregate basis. That is, middle management, in achieving its goals and objectives, requires information not only for operational purposes, but also for limited or short-range planning. Since the planning function of middle management is somewhat removed from day-to-day operations, aggregation of data and reporting is acceptable, and daily operational reports of the lower echelon are consolidated. At the top of the organizational triangle, composed of upper management, whose primary function is defining objectives and goal setting, one finds long-range planning perspective. While detailed information cannot be overlooked, long-range planning is best performed with still more aggregate reporting. Top management normally will insist on summaries of the reports directed toward lower management levels. Information produced by an electronic data processing system should be configured similarly to the managerial hierarchy. The system must be designed to produce detailed reports and statistics for supervisory personnel and aggregate reports for top management's strategic planning and goal setting.

The role of the accountant in providing input for the electronic data processing system is apparent. Historical data with respect to costs, expenses, revenues, and income emanate from the accounting process. This information becomes the basis for analysis in the management information system. As noted earlier, the advantage of electronic data processing is that it provides timely information so that management can take prompt and effective action. Furthermore, by using a simulation technique, management is able to select among alternatives without disrupting present operations or altering actual business processes. Every management information system worthy of the name should be able to do the following: (1) measure the impact of decisions before or after they are made; (2) measure the environment over which management has little control, but which definitely will affect the decision-making process; and (3) provide reports within a current time framework which allow management to see necessary changes and to take meaningful action. Any simulated system analysis permits management to ask many "what if" questions, receive detailed responses, and then choose among alternatives which best fulfill management's goals and objectives.

Data Banks

The chief source of historical information is the electronic data processing system's data bank. In computer language, this is the warehouse or storage place for the collection of accounting and statistical information; it is deposited in the bank and, when needed for analysis, is withdrawn by various users. Debate continues as to whether or not a management information system should contain a single or several data banks. Advantages can be cited for either technique. A single storage facility usually assembles a tremendous amount of data in a single file and necessitates that all subinformation system functions be able to access that material, but redundancy of data generally is eliminated. For a number of data banks, smaller storage facilities are required and interconnection of facilities is less important, but redundant information often is accumulated.

To overcome either the monumental size of a single data bank or the redundancy within a number of banks, a network type of file organization is suggested. This combination attempts to utilize the best features of both approaches. Each element within the system maintains its own file of data, but each file is accessible to all other users of the computer. The results of a single storage facility are reduction in storage facility needs and elimination of information redundancy.

Modular or Total Information Systems

Debate continues over the merits of introducing electronic data processing and management information systems either through smaller, modular subsystems, or through the total information system. In the former, data processing techniques may be introduced center by center. The latter approach advocates a switchover from manual or mechanical methods, or an upgrading of the existing tabulation facilities, to installation of a total and complete management information system in one fell swoop.

The following are advantages and disadvantages of the modular approach. (1) Smaller subsystems generally are straightforward and easier to understand. Examples include the subsystems of customer billing, payroll, and inventory control. (2) Proceeding slowly and cautiously allows elimination of system errors from smaller units. (3) Slow introduction allows operators, supervisory personnel, and management to follow the installation, become acquainted with it, and fully understand its capabilities. Management's cooperation usually is better if they are able to understand what is happening. (4) It recently has been argued that total management information systems, while they have been attempted, never have been fully developed. In fact, such total systems may be at least five to fifteen years in the future. (5) The modular system often is referred to as a bottom-to-top approach. By adapting the simpler accounting and record keeping functions to the computer, some companies find that they never leave this stage of development. (6) Finally, modular facilities often are not compatible with one another. While the bottom-to-top or modular approach often is less painful, the final result may be one in which the pain is everlasting.

The total system approach may be adopted if management suddenly realizes that continued success requires costcutting and more timely information. Evaluation of a complete switchover at one time, often referred to as the *top-down* or *crash* approach, should include several considerations. (1) With the total system program, all management and supervisory personnel must cooperate; everyone is involved together. While this may be more painful, the pain probably is shorter lived. (2) Compatible equipment is available at one time, and incompatibility or redundancies are far more likely to be eliminated. (3) It probably is easier for management to visualize the potential of the information system if all subfunctions are put into operation simultaneously. (4) Among the disadvantages, the cost of such a total system may be prohibitive. (5) Management might rebel because they do not understand all the system's complexities and capabilities. They may feel they are being sold a bill of goods.

Whichever approach is chosen, it should be remembered that the system must provide cost-saving techniques and, at times, a reasonable return on an extremely expensive investment. The total system approach moves from fragmentation to integration with the computer as the focal point, but a caution is in order. The information system is not a panacea for problem solving. If evaluation shows that the electronic data processing system is too costly and time consuming, then problems are better solved by other techniques, and management must consider alternatives.

Time Sharing

For those utilities which find a total system impractical or too costly, computer service bureaus with time-sharing systems may be the solution. Such systems allow a number of clients access to a single, high-speed computer, and service bureaus often will provide programmers to aid in adapting the user's data for input, analysis, reporting, and storage. There are safeguards against unauthorized use of a particular firm's files. These shared facilities allow even the smallest utility to reduce costs on the more repetitive functions, such as customer billing.

Cost of Computer Installation

Instituting the management information system may entail either the introduction of an entirely new operational tool or an upgrading of already existing facilities. Just as demands on electronic data processing equipment are broad and depend upon the utility's desires and objectives, the costs of equipment installation and operation are varied, depending on computer size and capabilities. Since the average life of a system generally is less than five years, cost analysis to the small as well as larger utilities is crucial. Installations generally are categorized and identified as small scale if monthly rental charges are less than $6,000. Medium-size systems average from $6,000 to $25,000 per month, while larger systems have monthly rentals between $25,000 and $150,000.

The simplest small-scale system usually involves an input unit, a central processing unit, and an output unit. The more complex systems include not only these three basic facilities but also larger processing and storage units and many other types of peripheral pieces. Each module or system will have peculiar costs of equipment installation and operation. General industry practice is to quote selling prices for equipment at approximately 50 times their annual rental. On that basis, one must contemplate expenditures of about $300,000 for the purchase of a relatively small system in both size and capabilities. Larger systems, whose monthly rentals approach $150,000, will have a purchase price in the neighborhood of $6 million to $7 million. Purchases of this size probably involve greater expenditures than many of the production facilities of the utility. For this reason, systems analysts maintain that the system not only should be a cost-saving one but also, in many respects, should be considered a profit center.

In addition to purchase or rental of the equipment, the utility must house the installation. Estimates indicate that housing costs average from 3 to 6 percent of the total purchase price. Facilities must include false floors to house wiring and cables, the cable and wire itself, air-conditioning equipment, and electrical equipment, including switches and transformers; engineering supervision also is needed.

Conversion costs must not be overlooked. These and installation costs often are underestimated, and it must be realized that these expenditures include both the design and detail of the system to be used as well as the development of computer programs to perform the operations. Conversion costs, which include translating all historical data into usable form for storage, have been estimated to approximate 40–80 percent of the purchase price of data processing facilities. Again, there will be some variation depending upon the size and degree of equipment sophistication. Also, consideration must be given to batch processing or on-line usage.

Operating costs of the installed facilities include salaries of personnel (operating, programming, maintenance, and supervisory), software or supplies, utility services such as power and communications, and space. The most significant of these are salaries. For small-scale systems, wages are about 2.5 times the monthly rental fee; for medium-sized systems, about 2.2 times; and for larger systems, about 1.7 times. Supplies expenses average about 20 percent of personnel costs, and space occupancy between 25 and 30 percent of personnel costs.

If the utility is contemplating upgrading an existing system, expenses often are greater than for the initial system. This is particularly true when expansion requires additional, incompatible modules. The upgraded system may require completely new programs and other peripheral facilities, and few, if any, items can be salvaged from the old system. If old elements can be utilized, as much as 50–70 percent of the costs of programs and systems may be recovered.

Systems Analysis Needs

All of the preceding factors are relevant considerations for any management information system, simple or complex. The needs of an individual utility can be satisfied only through careful review of the objectives, functions, and requirements of that firm. It is not the purpose of this discussion to provide a utility with full instructions on developing and installing a management information or electronic data processing system. The intention is, first, to offer a guide to aid in determining whether or not a system would be economically beneficial and, second, to provide some basic suggestions for developing a fully integrated management information system. Figure 6 expresses one approach to the necessary steps involved in justifying the installation of this costly equipment.

Numerous outlines have been devised to aid the potential computer user; many differ in form, but the substance is universal. The following steps are advocated: (1) develop workable goals and objectives of the firm; (2) perform a justification study; (3) perform a feasibility study, including an analysis of current data processing and procedures, management needs, and facilities necessary to meet needs in line with management's goals and objectives; (4) identify alternative approaches; and (5) select equipment, install, test, and operate.

During the economic life of any utility or firm, some event is required to trigger the realization that change is necessary. These events may include loss of cost control, rising costs of operation, inadequate reporting facilities, change in management, new technological developments, or merely a desire to keep up with the Joneses. (This latter is highly improbable, but it cannot be ignored.) Step 1 requires a thorough investigation and analysis of the utility's primary objectives which, hopefully, can be translated into quantifiable terms. These undoubtedly will vary from utility to utility, and, in fact, it is not unusual to find firms which have no specifically identifiable long-term plans. Possibilities include such goals as profit maximization, revenue maximization, cost minimization, or exceptional service. Unless these aims are specifically

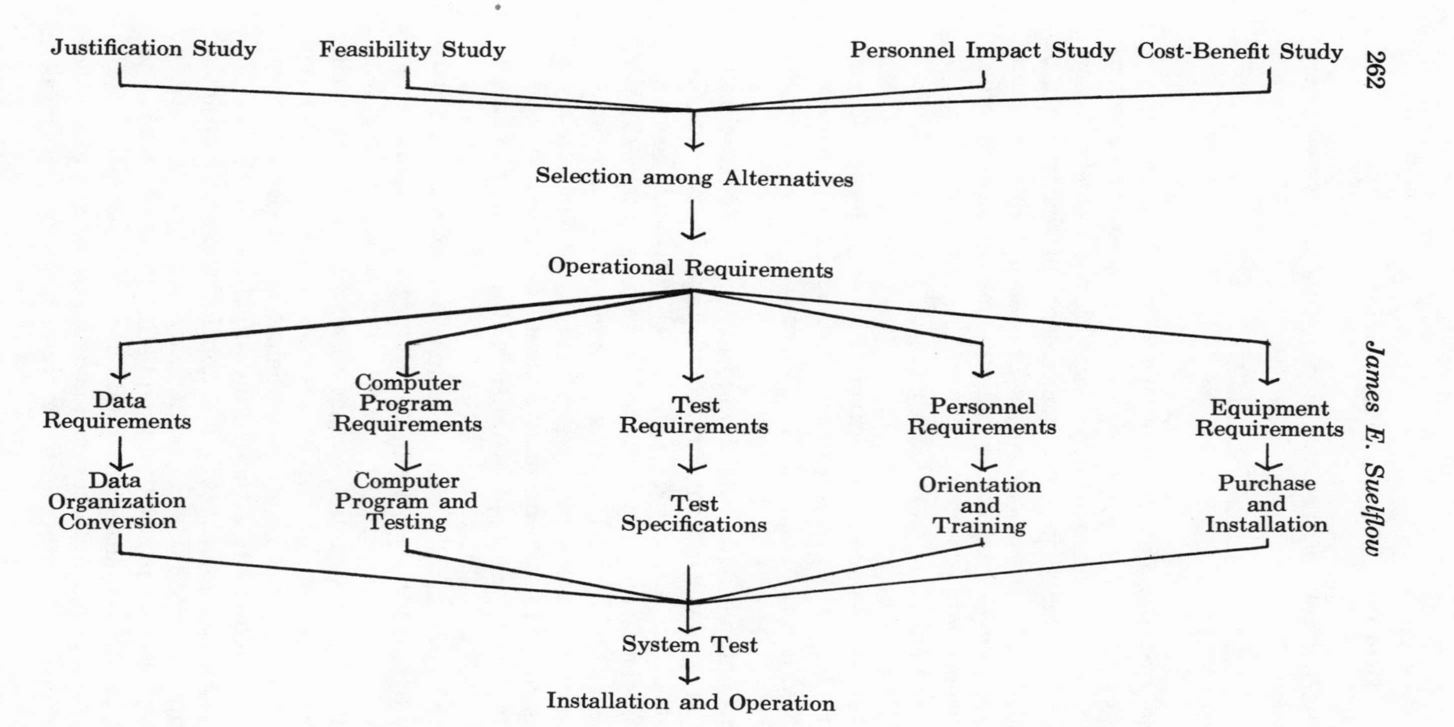

FIGURE 6. *Steps in Adapting to a Management Information System*

SOURCE: American Institute of Certified Public Accountants, *Computer Research Study No. 5* (New York: the Institute, 1966), p. 4.

identified, it is impossible to know whether or not management information systems and procedures currently in use are satisfactory.

The following questions must be answered in any justification study.

1) Is information requested by management for its evaluation, control, and planning functions generally slow in arriving so that decisions are made on partial rather than complete facts? If the present system is causing bottlenecks in certain accounting procedures or other managerial functions, a change may be warranted.
2) Do those requesting information often find data to be incomplete, too general, too specific, or inaccurate?
3) Is it possible to obtain desired information easily?
4) Is it possible for the utility to obtain better economies of operation than are currently being realized through the uses of existing reports and data?
5) Does management find itself desiring more information for evaluation, planning, and control than is readily available under current procedures?
6) Does the utility feel a need to improve service to the public, including billing and ready access to customer information for answering inquiries and improving public relations?
7) Are costs per unit of output increasing? The answer to this question should probe particularly into administrative overhead costs which may be increasing without a corresponding increase in productivity.

If a justification study indicates room for improvement, Step 3, a feasibility study, is called for.

Feasibility Study

The feasibility study has been interpreted in a number of ways, from a general overview of system needs through a detailed study of particular requirements with respect to the installation of a specific system. This discussion will incorporate elements of both viewpoints. A feasibility study involves investigation into the practicability of introducing a management information or electronic data processing system into the utility's management, operating, planning, and control processes. If the utility currently has no electronic data processing equipment, the study must investigate the need for replacing manual and mechanical methods with electronic facilities. If some equipment is already in use, the study will concentrate on replacement and/or additions to the existing system.

In either situation, the results should provide sufficient information to enable management to decide on the use of such equipment, the extent to which facilities should be used, and types of equipment to be employed. There are several steps or formal phases into which a feasibility study may be divided. Each phase has a specific purpose, but it is not always possible to determine the point at which one phase stops and the next begins. Indeed, there is considerable overlap. There are several areas requiring detailed attention. (1) Obtain cooperation from all levels of management, from first-line supervisory personnel to the highest ranking officer. (2) Complete and full knowledge is needed on the data processing system now being used, including all current procedures and methods for gathering and evaluating data as well as the cost of current operations. Copies of all report forms should be obtained. (3) Obtain information as to the desired requirements of any replacement system for operations, planning, and control purposes. This information allows a comparison of current facilities with contemplated needs for new procedures, methods, and equipment to handle these requirements. (4) Investigate purchase and installation costs of the new system.

Internal and External Personnel. Successful completion of the feasibility study depends upon the employment of competent personnel. The first question is whether or not the study will be performed internally or by outside consultants. Experts differ about the proper approach, but the best solution seems to be some combination of in-house and outside talent. The talent mix will depend on the expertise of individuals employed by the utility. Obviously, the more qualified in-house staff available, the less assistance will be required from external sources. If the utility is contemplating installation for the first time, it is likely that little or no internal talent exists; if a system is merely being upgraded and expanded, inside competence may be readily available.

If the utility relies on outside assistance, the hired consultants must become the focal point for all system analysis and design. If work is done by in-house personnel, a focal group or committee must be designated. Only in this manner can full cooperation be expected. Regardless of the approach, management cooperation is imperative for numerous reasons. Less resentment and resistance is likely to occur if all levels of management are made aware of the need for change and become part of the process. Furthermore, individuals involved with a particular subsystem will have more complete information and familiarity with that subfunction. For example, personnel in the customer billing and accounting departments would be able to identify peculiar requirements and analytical and reporting needs for the proper function of those departments; personnel entrusted with materials and supply inventory control will have specific suggestions. Cooperation at all managerial levels, therefore, cannot be overemphasized.

PROMOTING CONFIDENCE IN THE SYSTEM. Engaging the confidence and cooperation of necessary personnel allows the feasibility study committee to begin phase two of its analysis, which involves development of a detailed understanding of the data processing system currently in use. The obvious first step is to gather as much information about the system as possible. Interviews should be conducted with members of the various departments whose functions will be incorporated into the system as well as those groups which will be withdrawing information from the system. Not only in-house personnel but also other similar companies should be interviewed. Data about the type of information they gather and disseminate will be extremely beneficial. In the case of public utilities it also is critical to satisfy the requirements of regulatory agencies, and it might be advisable to discuss the proposed system with members of those bodies.

The emphasis on detail cannot be overstressed. Flow charts are an aid in gathering the necessary information and in tracing its path through the present system. This procedure often will identify the relations between functional areas and point up duplication of information accumulation or demands among various functions. The charts also aid in identifying responsibility centers and the information supplied by and needed by these various groups. The study team should gather cost information on operating the present data system; quantitative measurements are imperative in justifying a changeover to electronic data processing.

In summary, the assessment of current operating techniques is a multistage procedure. (1) Interview employees in line with information flows. (2) Obtain a copy of each form or report originated by the employee and trace it from its origin to final disposition. (3) Study runbooks, machine procedures, and other operating documentation. (4) Account for all functions and estimate the volume of work. (5) List all items of equipment and their cost. (6) Obtain some measure of efficiency of personnel and equipment. (7) Determine work order distribution and its peaks. (8) Determine the cost of each operation. (9) Verify the accuracy of all information with the immediate supervisor.

NEEDS OF THE SYSTEM. Armed with this information, the feasibility committee is prepared to obtain data on information requirements, reports, analysis, and information flow. It is important to stress that desired requirements must be reasonable. Proof should be demanded for the worthiness of each requirement in order to eliminate capricious and worthless requests. It is human nature to ask for more than actually is needed. Constraints imposed by economic considerations and technological feasibility will aid in deciding the extent of a system. The committee must not discourage requests or contributions; to do so could defeat the entire purpose of the study. The goal of any management information system should be to provide every manager or supervisor with information he needs, but not to provide him with unnecessary or excessive information.

A complete management information system should establish a bilateral flow of data inward to the system and outward to management. Decisions by the various departments within a utility, including engineering, research, finance, plant, and personnel, must be quantified and fed into the system. These decisions trigger actions in the operating and functional areas of the organization and return reports to management indicating the results. Forecasts and output data prompt these decisions. Reports must cover the areas of purchasing, production, inventory control, and sales and distribution.

During this phase of the study many utilities will find it useful to call upon outside services for advice. Equipment manufacturers and suppliers will be able to give help with respect to the feasibilities and capabilities of their products. Outside auditors or public accounting firms also should be consulted. These experts will be able to supply information regarding report design and analysis and supplement in-house decisions regarding proper information flow.

COST-BENEFIT ANALYSIS. A cost-benefit study is the next order of business. All costs must be considered, and these can be used as guidelines for a first approximation (see pp. 259–61). Specific installations will require more detailed and exacting cost analysis. Benefits should not be overlooked. Time saving on routine operations, while important, may not constitute the most significant system output. Most utilities, even those of smaller size, also might justify the cost of a system merely because it reduces billing and payroll expenses, but systems capable of providing additional management reports and analysis should be investigated. These latter functions, which often are overlooked, may be slow and laborious; a system that can expedite them may be worth the added expense.

The costs which require specific attention are purchase prices or leasing and rental charges; operating costs, including supplies, salaries, and overhead; conversion costs, including the retraining of personnel, and elimination or addition of employees; and the conversion and storage of historical data in the new record keeping system. Once an assessment of these factors has been made, it is possible to enter the last phases of a feasibility study.

The new system's design must be determined, and alternatives must be enumerated. The utility may decide on a total system, that is, one providing information to all areas of management, including accounting, finance, budgeting, production, personnel, marketing, and engineering. If so, the system design will be more complicated than if the utility had decided merely to install facilities in modular fashion to handle specific bottleneck functions and current operations. Outside consultants should aid in choosing between these two alternatives. On the basis of full cost information, a utility also might investigate alternatives for handling their information system problems. These could vary from retaining the current procedures, to using time-sharing services, to adopting new data processing techniques. Concerning the latter, alternative types and designs of equipment as well as alternative manufacturers of these facilities should be investigated.

RECOMMENDATIONS TO MANAGEMENT. The final segment of the feasibility study should be a report to management. Sufficient information should be available either to recommend installation of a particular system, or to suggest making no change at all. A recommendation to wait for further developments in hardware should be avoided; if immediate benefits are apparent, waiting could be very costly. Because of the large sums of money involved, all final presentations to management should have a financial orientation and should include schedules identifying costs of the present system, costs of the proposed system, savings before conversion costs, and net savings to the company.

In addition, the report should contain a description of the new system's scope and objectives; a detailed presentation of the present system and its deficiencies; those aspects of the proposed system which would eliminate those deficiencies; any organizational changes which may be needed; reasons for selecting the proposed system over alternatives; a summary of required personnel and funds together with proposed training and reassignment of present personnel who no longer would be required; and a schedule of proposed conversion and installation time. With this knowledge, management will be able to reach a decision.

Applications to Particular Areas of Utility Operations

There are a number of accounting and data processing functions performed by utilities which are well suited to electronic data processing operations or management information systems. While these functions are important in an overall management information system, they lend themselves particularly well to a modular approach. They provide a gradual shift from current manual or mechanical methods to the electronic data processing approach. Those functions which are individually adaptable to a total information system, but which are not unique in that they are independent of other functions, include: (1) customer billing and related customer data; (2) payroll processing and selected employee information; (3) materials and supplies accounting and inventory control; and (4) continuing property records, plant data, and depreciation calculations. Interactions still must be recognized, and an initial total system evaluation will provide this information. As modules are added to the system, compatibility is maintained.

Customer Billing and Related Data. Customer billing, a monumental task, is probably the single most important data processing function requiring automation. Because of its routinized nature, computer equipment lends itself extremely well to this function. Even in most small utilities, customer billing alone generally is economic justification for installing a partial or complete computer system. Billing is one of the first items to be recognized when considering computer applications. In addition to the primary function of providing an expedient method to notify customers of their monthly bills, customer information built into this module, including name, address, type of service being supplied, credit information, rate schedule applying to the customer, and evaluations for high-low readings serve important secondary purposes.

Data processing equipment virtually can calculate and prepare monthly bills, but the supplemental data generated is extremely valuable for several reasons. Since it represents sales and demand for service, information can be obtained about customer classes and particular geographical areas having higher or lower demands on the system. In addition, it is invaluable to utility plant engineers in calculating needs for future construction of distribution plant; to the finance department in arranging for this further construction and in providing cash flow projections; to the marketing or sales department by providing leads in advertising and promotion; and, finally, to operating personnel by providing continuing information about need-capacity relations and system overload.

New equipment which now is technologically feasible and, in some limited instances, available for actual use, includes automatic meter reading. Computers, through electrical impulses, are able to read consumers' meters and transmit the data over rented telephone lines during their off-peak periods. It is not difficult to visualize the possibility of individual consumers' meters being read, rates being applied, and bills being mailed virtually untouched by human hands.

PAYROLL. Payroll accounting has been performed by various types of data processing equipment for many years and requires only simple machinery. The payroll function itself usually is not difficult to adapt to the machine, and its repetitive nature makes it an ideal early module addition to any electronic data processing system. In addition to merely writing checks and calculating wages and salaries, a considerable amount of information can be provided by the payroll module, such as locations of employees by residence and personnel information useful for insurance coverage. When linked with other modules, labor costs for work and repair orders could be computed. Further sophistication of the cost accounting procedures could result from modular interaction. The combining of plant, depreciation, maintenance and supplies, and labor statistics, for example, could provide cost distribution and work order data.

UTILITY PLANT IN SERVICE. Computerizing information relative to plant in service includes a recording of all continuing property records with information on particular items of plant, cost, location, depreciation rates, date of installation, and descriptive material about assets such as size, voltage, manufacturer, and so forth. Updating of CPRs is simplified. In an accounting sense, information can be called from the computer to provide a summary ledger of total plant service as well as summaries of any other plant accounts, including leased items, property held for future use, and even nonutility property. Likewise, the data enable calculation of depreciation and amortization charges for each accounting period. Problems concerning composite depreciation rates and past group depreciation techniques, used because of the utility's technological inability to depreciate on an item-by-item basis, certainly can be overcome by electronic processing equipment.

The information made available through this module, however, has more far-reaching implications. Plant accounting data could initiate a repair order to dispatch a service man to repair equipment at a specific location. If the repair involved knowing customer location, customer and plant data could be supplied by linking two modules. Data describing the equipment could provide the repairman with the proper materials before being dispatched. If complete retirement units are replaced, plant accounts can be updated to reflect this new information, and summaries can be made of expenses incurred in the particular project. If a utility practices a set maintenance program, computer data can provide an itinerary in performing this routine function.

MATERIALS AND SUPPLIES AND INVENTORY CONTROL. Adding materials and supplies information as a third module can further enhance the usefulness of plant accounting data. The materials and supplies module not only will serve as an independent summary account of items on hand but also can provide automatic costing of repair and work orders based on information received about items used for maintenance or construction work. This module can alert the purchasing department when additional inventory is needed and can provide information about inventories on hand and orders in process. It also can provide a history of usage or can project usage based on past experience or anticipated demands if certain data are contained in the plant account module. The interconnection of these two modules has several advantages. In addition to simple routine processing, utility functions and operations can be monitored. Thus controls are provided, and management can be alerted to unusual variances which, in a manual system, might go unnoticed for a considerable amount of time.

MIS and the Regulator

It has been suggested that regulatory commissions might be given limited direct access to a utility's computer facilities. A commission could keep abreast of utility functions, interrogate the computer for data and financial information, and, hopefully, provide a real time regulatory atmosphere that looks to the future. This suggestion must be investigated thoroughly; many regulatory advantages are evident, but management's legal property rights must not be overlooked.

Summary

At this point one might be ready to exclaim: "Let the machine do the work!" A word of caution is in order. The electronic data processing system only can be as effective as the information with which it is provided. A computer is not a panacea; substantial effort must be expended in exploring possible use for the data and the information desired therefrom. Many public utility functions do allow for piecemeal system construction, and each module can be investigated and analyzed thoroughly before it is placed into service. This is not to say that at some future date, after subsequent modules have been activated, changes to prior modules might not be necessary. Some utilities have reworked programs several times over the years, but a sound feasibility study could obviate this necessity.

The point should be clear. A utility has an unusually large number of customers; they vary in size, demands, and rates charged, but accounting for their demands is a routine function. A utility also has an inordinate amount of property spread over a wide geographic area. It consists of numerous, small, repetitive or identical units, and an electronic data processing system is ideally suited for handling such information, which, in turn, lends itself to the system. Indeed, cost and price data (the economic supply-demand functions) provide the utility with a wealth of information extending into all aspects of its operation, planning, and control. These include financial, marketing, sales, purchasing, engineering, and even legal aspects. Mention often is made of a last great frontier. In the case of public utilities, while it may not be the last, electronic data processing systems certainly open a new frontier for providing management and regulators with more complete, detailed, and usable information.

This chapter is designed to highlight the importance of electronic data processing and management information systems' advantages and pitfalls. The reader is urged to review the following references and to contact outside consultants when installation of either system is contemplated.

Selected References

Articles and Proceedings

National Conference of Electric and Gas Utility Accountants. *Proceedings,* 5, 6, 7 May 1969. New York: American Gas Association and Edison Electric Institute, 1969, pp. F1–F22.

Piatt, Richard B. "Computer Applications for a Utility." *Municipal Finance* 29, no. 2 (November 1966): 67–73.

Books

The following bibliography was selected to illustrate the type of material available to the public utility accountant who might be considering the use of electronic data processing equipment.

Adamson, Lee J.; Hoglund, Byron E.; and Metcalf, Richard D. *Accountants' Data Processing Service.* New York: The Ronald Press Co., 1964.

American Institute of Certified Public Accountants. *Accounting and the Computer.* A selection of articles from the *Journal of Accountancy and Management Services.* New York: the Institute, 1966.

Association for Systems Management. *Business Systems.* Cleveland, Ohio: the Association, 1970.

Bocchino, William A. *A Simplified Guide to Automatic Data Processing.* Englewood Cliffs, N.J.: Prentice-Hall, Inc., 1966.

Bower, James B., and Welke, William R., eds. *Financial Information Systems—Selected Readings*. Boston: Houghton Mifflin Co., 1968.
Hare, Van Court, Jr., et al. *Management Information Systems for the 1970's*. Kent, Ohio: Center for Business and Economic Research, College of Business Administration, Kent State University, 1970.
Heany, Donald F. *Development of Information Systems*. New York: The Ronald Press Co., 1968.
Li, David H. *Accounting, Computers, Management Information Systems*. New York: McGraw-Hill Book Company, 1968.
Management Conference, Chicago, 1968. *Information Processing for Management*. Elmhurst, Ill.: Business Press, 1969.
Martino, R. L. *MIS—Management Information Systems*. Wayne, Pa.: MTI Publications Management Development Institute, Division of Information Industries, Inc., 1969.
McDonough, Adrian M. *Centralized Systems, Planning and Control*. Wayne, Pa.: Thompson Book Company, Division of Information Industries, Inc., 1969.
Prince, Thomas R. *Information Systems for Management Planning and Control*. Rev. ed. Homewood, Ill.: Richard D. Irwin, Inc., 1970.

In addition to the above, computer manufacturers such as International Business Machines, General Electric, and Honeywell offer information on system designs. The U.S. Government Printing Office, Washington, D.C., also has a number of publications available.

14

Budgeting: Forecasting and Control

The budget is an extremely effective managerial tool. It facilitates performance of the management process of profit planning and control. Unlike accounting, which produces information for a number of individuals other than management, the budget is specifically designed for managerial purposes. That is not to say accounting is unimportant to the planning and control function; the budgeting process must rely heavily on accounting data. By segregating a budget into areas of responsibility, and by means of electronic data processing, management can more effectively measure performance and thus control costs.

The following definitions will be useful in the subsequent discussion of these matters.

> *Budget:* A coordinated financial program or plan of operations, segregated into responsibility areas, indicating amounts expected to be required for specific purposes or received from specific sources, and approved by responsible management. The consolidation of all pertinent budgetary allowances. The term is applied to the combined plans of an entire enterprise, to any of its subdivisions, and to the specific detailed financial plan of a single area, function, project, or account.

> *Forecast:* An estimate of performance for a future period (e.g., sales estimate, profit estimate).

Budgetary Control: The exercise by line management of control over costs through continuous appraisal of actual expenditures, using as a guide the planned costs as expressed in the budget. This principle is also applied to the various types of income and to items that affect the balance sheet, such as receivables, inventories, cash, fixed assets, etc.[1]

Responsibility Accounting

Planning and control are directly related to assigned tasks and responsibilities. The budgeting process aids in assessing the results of those responsible for particular planning and control functions. Since accounting data produce the necessary measurement of actual results against plans and objectives—the control function—the accounting system must be constructed around the organizational responsibilities set forth by the firm. Public utilities, restricted to some extent by the uniform systems of accounts, might organize their responsibility centers around the functional classifications within the system. Revenue generation functions might be organized by district, subdivided into the system's customer classifications. Expenses are best categorized by functional titles —production, transmission, distribution, and general plant. Within this framework, the historical data produced become extremely important for the planning and control process.

The uniform accounting system, and particularly that segment which provides a functional classification for cost accounting purposes, is designed to meet a number of objectives. It allows the utility to identify costs used in establishing effective rate structures; it provides pertinent data for proper cost control; it supplies regulatory authorities with detailed data enabling them to perform their control tasks. Responsibility accounting procedures transcend the traditional cost accounting focus on costs of production and, instead, emphasize cost and revenue control. This approach in no way hinders or eliminates the possibility of proper cost identification for pricing purposes. In fact, the uniform systems are organized in such a way that cost-rate relationships require a recasting of functionally recorded data in order to complete the pricing or rate-making process. In summary, effective budget planning and control require that the accounting system be primarily directed

---

[1]Walter R. Bunge, *Managerial Budgeting for Profit Improvement* (New York: McGraw-Hill Book Company, Inc., 1968), pp. 217–18.

toward the short- and long-range planning and control needs of management. Therefore, the budgeting process under responsibility accounting must be organized to confrom with the functional accounting system. Without such budget structure, comparisons between budgeted plans and actual results are impossible.

Budgeting and the Regulator

Budgets also can be an immeasurable aid in effective regulatory planning and control. While it is reasonable to assume that utilities, particularly those in the Class A and B categories, produce budgets for operations as well as capital expenditures, there appear to be few, if any, regulatory requirements upon the utility to submit these budgets to commission scrutiny. The only possible exception may be those commissions which can require advanced submission of budgets on *capital* expenditures. They have been tabulated by the FPC, and Table 26 indicates those with this authority.[2]

The interesting feature of the table is that neither the FPC nor the FCC requires such advanced submission, and only thirty-seven state commissions have the *authority* to make such demands on the utilities which they regulate. The number which actually require submission is unknown, however. The following probably is typical of the statutory authority given to commissions regarding budgets; it is found in the Wisconsin Statutes, paragraph 196.49 (3): "The commission may provide by general or special order that any public utility shall submit, periodically or at such times as the commission shall specify and in such detail as the commission shall require, plans, specifications and estimated costs of such proposed construction of any new plant, equipment, property or facility, or such extension, improvement or addition to its existing plant, equipment, property apparatus or facilities as the commission finds

---

[2]A 1967 congressional survey conducted by the Committee on Government Operations asked commissions if they required advanced submission of budgets. Twenty commissions answered "yes"; thirty-two "no"; one "don't know"; and five "no response." Unfortunately, the question failed to distinguish or elaborate on the type of budget; therefore, it is difficult to interpret the importance of the response. Subcommittee on Inter-Government Relations, Senate Committee on Government Operations, *State Utility Commissions* (Washington, D.C.: U.S. Government Printing Office, 1967), Docket No. 56, p. 32, and Table V, facing p. 34.

will materially affect the public interest."[3] Professor Eli Clemens considers commission requirements that utilities submit operating budgets for advanced approval "a unique and effective type of accounting regulation." He cites the states of New Jersey, Oregon, and Washington as examples.[4]

In chapter 3 the merits of uniform accounting were extolled, and no one would deny that such uniformity is critical for proper regulation. In fact, evidence indicates that reasonable rate making would be virtually impossible without uniform accounting.[5] However, commissions have regarded accounting as merely a tool for use in their prescribed regulatory work, and one to which they may take exception when performing the rate-making function.[6] Such independent judgment is healthy, but other commissions have disagreed slightly. They deem it expedient and well worth the time and effort to see that, whenever possible, accounting treatment of questionable items follows the procedures which will be utilized in allocating such items in rate proceedings.[7]

In amending its rules and regulations, the Federal Communications Commission said: "Operating expense accounts should reflect only clear-cut current costs, and accounting rules should facilitate expeditious rate proceedings insofar as possible and should not impose upon the Commission, to the possible deteriment of rate

---

[3] *1961 Wisconsin Statutes Administered by or Related to the Public Service Commission of Wisconsin* (Madison: compiled by the Public Service Commission of Wisconsin, July 1962), chap. 196, Paragraph 49(3), p. 2706.

[4] Eli W. Clemens, *Economics and Public Utilities* (New York: Appleton-Century-Crofts, Inc., 1950), p. 459.

[5] "Commission control of accounting and supervision of financial structure are vital to the accomplishment of an agency's primary objective of insuring adequate service to the public at reasonable rates." *Sayre Land Co.* v. *Pennsylvania Public Utility Commission* (1959) 27 PUR 3d 502 (Pennsylvania Court of Common Pleas).

[6] With reference to the fact that a commission in its regulatory process cannot be bound by accounting procedures or the art of accounting. *Re Montana Power Company* (1962) 42 PUR 3d 253 (Montana).

[7] "The power of the commission in rate proceedings to recognize or disallow certain expenditures, such as donations, dues, and lobbying costs, either as to kind or magnitude, is not circumscribed by accounting procedure but, for the sake of convenience, uniformity, and avoidance of confusion and possible misunderstanding, it is desirable that the accounting treatment of these items should follow that used in ratemaking." *Re Accounting Treatment for Donations, Dues, and Lobby Expenditures* (1967) 71 PUR 3d 440 (New York).

TABLE 26. *Commission Budgetary Authority*

State	*The commission has authority to*	
	Require advance submission of budgets on capital expenditures	*Require, in addition,*
FPC		
FCC		
Alabama	×	
Alaska	×	
Arizona		
Arkansas		
California	×	
Colorado	×	
Connecticut		
Delaware	×	
District of Columbia	×	
Florida	×	annual construction budgets
Georgia	×	
Hawaii	×	
Idaho	×	
Illinois		
Indiana	×	
Iowa	×	
Kansas	×	
Kentucky	×	
Louisiana		
Maine	×	
Maryland		
Massachusetts	×	
Michigan	—[4]	
Minnesota[1]		
Mississippi		
Missouri	×	
Montana		
Nebraska[1]	×	
Nevada		
New Hampshire	×	
New Jersey	×	
New Mexico	×[5]	
New York	×	
North Carolina	×	
North Dakota	×	

TABLE 26.—*Continued*

State	*The commission has authority to* Require advance submission of budgets on capital expenditures	Require, in addition,
Ohio	×	
Oklahoma		
Oregon	×	annual expenditures budget
Pennsylvania	×	
Puerto Rico	×	
Rhode Island		
South Carolina		
South Dakota[1]		
Tennessee		
Texas[2]		
Utah	×	
Vermont	×	
Virginia	×	
Virgin Islands[3]	×	
Washington	×	annual expenditures budget
West Virginia	×	
Wisconsin	×	
Wyoming	×	

SOURCE: Federal Power Commission, *Federal and State Commission Jurisdiction and Regulation of Electric, Gas, and Telephone Utilities* (Washington, D.C.: U.S. Government Printing Office, 1967), pp. 24, 52.

NOTE: X = "Yes."

[1]No commission regulation of electric or gas utilities.
[2]No commission regulation of electric or telephone utilities.
[3]Electric facilities are government owned and operated and are not regulated by the commission. No natural gas service in the Virgin Islands other than bottled gas, which is not regulated by the commission.
[4]Possibly under general authority.
[5]"No" for telephone utilities.

payers, the burden of ferreting out doubtful or improper items from the accounts."[8] Such thinking is not only logical, but also is a rational and dignified approach. The old adages "Laws are made to be broken" and "There's an exception to every rule" certainly

[8]*Re Amendments of Part 31 of the Commission's Rules and Regulations* (1956) 13 PUR 3d 163 (Federal Communications Commission).

apply to the regulatory process. No one would deny that under unusual circumstances the regulatory body should have the right to take exception to items accounted for in a specific way. Yet, under this type of regulation the use of accounting data as a regulatory tool is certainly ex post facto control.

Students of public utility regulation are eager to point out that early regulation, of the common law variety, was punitive. That is, corrective action could be taken only after the wrong was committed. The parallel with current administrative regulation is surprisingly similar; disallowance of past expenses for future rate making merely corrects past mistakes. Constructive, forward-looking regulation should give general and, perhaps, rather specific guidelines and pronouncements to the utility before it commits itself to certain operating expenditures or capital investment undertakings. In achieving this goal, budgeting can be extremely valuable not only to utility management but also to the regulator.

Proper budgeting for profit planning and control cannot replace good management or good regulation. Nor can it adequately correct the past errors of an unenlightened group. The budget is merely a managerial tool that provides for a more systematic and effective approach.

Planning the Budgeting Process

A successful budgeting program must be based on realistic expectations incorporating managerial goals, plans, and operating policies. The financial scheduling of both long- and short-run objectives represents this realistic approach. While the overall aims of a utility are fairly well identified—reasonably adequate service at reasonable rates—there are many avenues by which utility management and regulators might achieve this goal. Management objectives must be identified before a successful budgeting process can begin, and all management levels must be involved. One key to successful responsibility budgeting and accounting entails the contributions and cooperation of all supervisory individuals throughout the organizational hierarchy. This involvement also provides checks and balances against unrealistic expectations.

Particularly relevant for a public utility are: (1) operating budgets covering a relatively short timespan of one year which forecast anticipated revenues and expenses; (2) budgets forecasting demands for day-to-day cash requirements as well as long-range projections for additional capital investments; (3) materials and supplies budgets forecasting the needs for materials and supplies used in daily repair and maintenance as well as materials and supplies used for plant construction; and (4) long-range capital budgets forecasting plant expansion for periods of more than one year to as many as ten to fifteen years in the future. Figure 7 is a generalized schematic illustration depicting the entire budgeting process.

Annual Operating Budget

The purpose of preparing an operating budget is to translate management's annual objectives into a plan capable of providing reasonable and adequate earnings. In regulated utilities, where reasonable return is determined by commission dicta, which presumes the supplying of reasonable, adequate service to all present and prospective consumers who are willing and able to pay a just and reasonable rate, accurate revenue and expense forecasting is extremely important. The utility must determine whether allowable gross operating revenues, an interpretation of anticipated sales, in relationship to all production, transmission, distribution, and general administrative expenses will provide remaining net operating income sufficient for a just and reasonable return.

Sales and Revenue Forecasting

Sales generally have been interpreted as the quantity of the product or service sold; revenue is the dollar amount received for such sales. Forecasting sales precedes forecasting revenues, since the latter are derived from sales. Revenue budgeting usually covers periods of one year, but the forecast may be made in weekly, monthly, or quarterly segments within the annual budget.

The techniques used in sales and revenue forecasting are varied; regardless of the one chosen, past records are and should be the basis for this element of the utility's budget. In a most general way, the sales forecast attempts to define the average number of

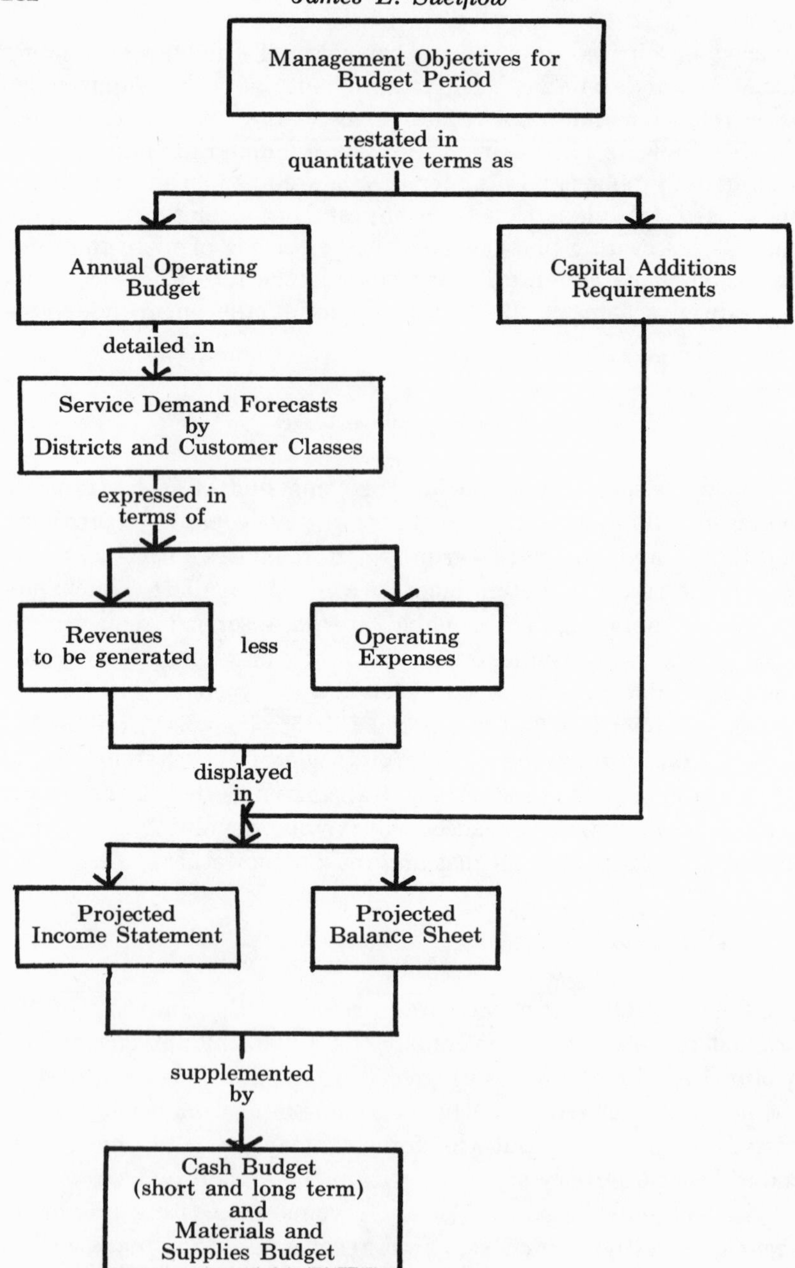

FIGURE 7. *The Budgeting Process*

customers who will be demanding service over the budgeted period and the average amount of consumption per customer. Adjustments for any abnormal conditions and changes in customer demands must be considered.

The utility may choose to segment its sales forecast by customer class, for example, residential, commercial, and industrial. These classifications may be subdivided further by the type of service required. There are residential customers who require only lighting services, others who use electric cooking and water heating facilities, and those with all electric facilities. Further segmentation on the basis of responsibility center, and also encompassing the above, could be by district substation (or other selected geographical area).

There are many factors to be considered in the sales forecast. Weather conditions, new homes being constructed, businesses moving into and out of the community, and population trends all may have an effect. The state of the national economy cannot be overlooked. Indeed, this affects industrial as well as residential and commercial consumption, and it is advisable for the utility to monitor national indicators. Seasonal demand is another factor. Although a breakdown by month or quarter easily can display any seasonal variations, these make it unlikely that an average month for the annual forecast can be determined. Each month may be considered as a separate projection of both customers and consumption, and the annual forecast is merely a summation of the separate monthly projections. Schedule 1 illustrates the concept.

Calculating revenues from the projected sales forecast now can be completed. Detail of the revenue forecast will depend upon the detail of the sales forecast. For example, average kilowatt hours of sales multiplied by the average price per kilowatt hour can produce a total operating revenue figure; or, the total revenue figure might be derived from more detailed breakdowns by customer classes. There may be average kilowatt hour sales by customer group or average rates per customer. Just as the sales forecast was further subdivided into types of customers within each group, so rate schedules may be applied to projected service demands; these then will be summed for total revenue requirements. Schedule 2 summarizes projected income on a district responsibility basis.

Responsibility	*Kwh demand by customer class*											
	Residential				**Commercial**				**Industrial**			
	1968	*Actual* 1969	1970	*Fore-cast* 1971	1968	*Actual* 1969	1970	*Fore-cast* 1971	1968	*Actual* 1969	1970	*Fore-cast* 1971
District A												
District B												
District C												
	—	—	—	—	—	—	—	—	—	—	—	—
Total kwhs												

SCHEDULE 1. *Projected Demand by District, by Customer Classes, on a Monthly Basis*

Responsibility	***Totals***	
	*Kwh**	*Amount*
District A		$
District B		$
District C		$
Total		$

*See Schedule 1 for details.

SCHEDULE 2. ***Operating Revenues by Responsibility-Customer (Districts), Kwh and Dollars, Year Ending 31 December 1971***

Revenue forecasting also may be calculated on a weekly, monthly, or quarterly basis. Again, changes or anticipated changes in rate schedules and shifts in billing periods or dates of meter reading must be considered in projecting revenue schedules. Obviously, the more accurate the input, the more reliable the output.

Good sales and revenue forecasting also provides additional data for various managerial units within the utility. One example is alerting the marketing department to sales advertising needs; projected growth might be an indication of the need for a stepped-up advertising campaign. If the forecasting is done on a district basis, growth projections in an area whose demands already are approaching capacity can assist in planning and developing future capacity requirements. One must not overlook the valuable aid which electronic data processing can provide for this particular budgeting exercise.

Forecasting Operating Expenses

Forecasting operating expenses is a subfunction of the demand forecast. Once sales have been projected in units of output, the utility is made aware of costs per kilowatt hour of energy produced and can project expenses. Since the operating budget usually is portrayed as a pro forma income statement, operating expenses must be subdivided accordingly. They should be categorized as production, transmission, distribution, sales, and general and administrative expenses (including billing and collection costs). The budget officer must be apprized of all changes in expense items. Increases in wages and administrative salaries, rises in fuel prices, general inflationary trends in the cost of maintenance and expense items, and changes in depreciation rates also must be considered. As with revenue forecasting, expense forecasting should place heavy reliance upon past performance. Simple trend-line projections or more sophisticated mathematical techniques may be used for the forecast. It should be remembered that certain expense items are fixed regardless of changes in output, whereas others are variable. A suggested layout is illustrated in Schedule 3.

Providing for commission approval of a utility's projected operating budget could be a worthwhile addition to the regulatory process. Sometimes questionable items such as executives' salaries, advertising expenses, expenses for charitable contributions and donations, and expenditures for research and development either could be approved or disapproved by the commission prior to their being expended. Although the commission could not forbid such expenditures, the utility at least would be aware of its attitude. The utility would know that if the expenditures were made they ultimately would be classified as below-the-line items rather than as legitimate above-the-line operating expenses.

Cash Budget

Cash forecasting has both short- and long-run implications. In fact, it is that element in the total budget which interrelates the operating with the capital expenditures budget. Cash plays a very important role in the day-to-day functions of any business entity. Management is legally and morally obligated to pay its bills when they become due, and meeting these demands requires careful planning and use of available funds. Prudence dictates that there should be ample cash available to meet daily requirements, but too much idle cash would be improvident.

Planning for future growth and development also involves cash forecasting. It is of the long-term variety, and management should devise ways and means of providing funds for capital expansion. With utilities spending billions of dollars each year for capital improvements, and with much of this funding being provided by outside sources, advanced planning is imperative. Cash forecasting for these demands often is done three, five, or more years in advance.

Expenditure	*Responsibility*											
	Production				Transmission				Distribution			
	1968	*Actual* 1969	1970	*Fore-cast* 1971	1968	*Actual* 1969	1970	*Fore-cast* 1971	1968	*Actual* 1969	1970	*Fore-cast* 1971
Classified by uniform systems of accounts numbers 401 and 402, sub-classes 500–932, and accounts 403–411.4 for other operating expenses												
Total	—	—	—	—	—	—	—	—	—	—	—	—

NOTE: Based on projected demand in Schedule 1.

SCHEDULE 3. ***Budgeted Operating Expenditures for 1971***

Accurate cash forecasting is a necessary function of every utility's budgeting officer or committee. Only with reliable projections will the utility find it possible to keep its overall cost of money to a minimum, which is of unquestioned importance today when one considers the high cost of borrowing.

Short-term Cash Forecasting

The nature of a utility's business, like that of most other economic enterprises, is such that cash receipts do not correspond with cash disbursements. This is true on a day-to-day, seasonal, or yearly basis. Receipts coincide with many customers' pay cycles, and they tend to be heavier every other week or near the beginning of each month. The utility can aid in the control of these fluctuations through cycle billing, or distributing due dates equally throughout the month. Disbursements, on the other hand, appear with astounding regularity. Payrolls, interest and dividend payments, various types of taxes, and payments for materials and supplies all have regular due dates. The latter often are dictated by tenth-of-the-month or thirty-day terms granted to the utility.

There are many methods of analyzing short-term cash requirements, but two are most commonly used. One is the projection of the balance sheet cash account itemizing all anticipated receipts and expenditures for a specific period of time, and the other is the adjusted net income method. In the former, weekly, monthly, or quarterly cash forecasts can be made, the shorter term one being the more accurate, of course. Most immediate forecasts are assured since customers are billed and the utility has a record of payments as well as an estimation of the delinquent accounts. Likewise, short-term disbursements, except for unexpected or unanticipated expenditures, are predictable. Known payouts involve payment for purchases already made and for which bills already may have been received. If projections of cash receipts and expenditures are made quarterly or over several months, there may be certain periods of time when cash will be short and others when cash on hand will be excessive. This is precisely the kind of information the utility needs to determine.

Following is a checklist of items to be considered in the cash account analysis.

Cash Receipts:

Cash to be received on accounts considering time of year, growth in customers and service, and modifications for delinquent accounts

Receipts for other services performed, sale of appliances, rents, interest on securities outstanding

Total receipts for forecast period

Cash Disbursements:

Operating disbursements—payroll, materials and supplies, fuel, taxes (property, income, employment), other selling and administrative expenses

Other disbursements—interest on short-term debt, interest on long-term debt due, any principal amounts on maturing securities, dividends on all type of stock, capital expenditures

Total disbursements

A cash budget, in effect, takes cash on hand or in the bank, adds to it all anticipated cash receipts, deducts all anticipated cash expenditures, and arrives at a cash balance at the end of the particular period being analyzed.

The forecasting method used will depend upon the needs of management and upon the size and diversity of the utility. Many small utilities may find it quite sufficient to look at past data and, by a simple trend analysis, project cash receipts and expenditures. Other utilities obviously will require more sophisticated statistical techniques with given error probabilities in reaching a satisfactory forecast.

The adjusted net income method is another approach to budgeting for cash. It is based upon a projection of all anticipated receipts and expenditures in a pro forma income statement with adjustments for noncash items such as depreciation expense, accrued taxes, and amortization of extraordinary items so that the statement is presented on a cash basis. The analysis is, in effect, a cash flow approach. Certain adjustments are required which are not included in the income statement. These involve cash expenditures for capital improvements, cash received on account, expenditures made on account, adjustments to inventory, and cash received from bank loans and sale of new securities. Schedule 4 is an illustration.

Beginning cash balance 1 January 1971		$______
Budgeted cash receipts		
Collections on customer bills		
Other income		
Proceeds on bank loans		
Proceeds on long-term securities issued	______	
Total budgeted receipts		
Total projected cash available		______
Budgeted cash disbursements		
Accounts payable—purchase materials and supplies from Schedule 5		
Total operating expenses—based on Schedule 3		
Production		
Transmission		
Distribution		
General		
Capital additions (construction work)		
Notes payable		
Bonds maturing		
Dividends		
Accrued and deferred items	______	
Total budgeted disbursements		______
Ending cash balance, 31 December 1971		$______

SCHEDULE 4. *Cash Flow Budget, Year Ending 31 December 1971*

One of the largest items of short-term cash forecasting is construction expenditures. They provide both the majority of cash forecasting problems and information which is of greatest aid to the cash forecaster. This budget will offer rather detailed and accurate information with regard to construction cash requirements for the immediate future. However, the farther one forecasts into the future, the more difficult it is to make accurate construction cash estimates.

Long-term Cash Forecasting

The objective of long-term cash forecasting is particularly evident in the type of financing a utility chooses or is required to pursue. Proper forecasting for periods beyond a year or two and extending three, five, or more years into the future will aid the company in achieving a proper capital structure divided among long-term debt, preferred stock, and common equity. This type of planning also will provide for obtaining funds at the lowest possible cost. Long-range cash forecasting is an aid not only to the management of the utility, but also to the financial community at large. Informing outside suppliers of funding needs will help ensure the utility that monies will be available when called for.

Because the long-range cash forecast is more general it is less precise than short-term predictions. The utility must be aware of the task in projecting future revenues and expenditures and must be attuned to changes in wage rates, construction and materials and supplies costs, changing tax structures, and overall inflationary trends. Furthermore, construction programs, both the projects themselves and their timing, are subject to change occasionally.

In relation to long-term prediction, the better of the two approaches suggested for short-term forecasting is undoubtedly cash flow analysis. All changes in utility operations are taken into account, including expenses and revenues, additions to property and plant, retirement of property and plant, and all nonmonetary considerations. The justification for such long-term forecasting obviously relies upon benefits exceeding costs and must be based upon a utility's size and ultimate cash needs.

Materials and Supplies Budget

Like the cash forecast, the materials and supplies budget is largely supplementary. That is, it is an important element in the capital and construction budget and is a key disbursement in the operating or revenue and expense budget. While supplementary, it also has the effect of an inventory control device. Protective in nature, it provides a medium for the interchange of information between the operating and the construction departments. It alerts the budgeting officer about future cash requirements for purchases, and it is an important document for the purchasing department with respect to quantities of future requirements.

A materials and supplies budget includes beginning inventories, additions through purchase or salvage, reductions through maintenance, repair, or new construction, and ending inventories. These budgets usually are developed for annual periods and are subdivided into quarters or bimonthly forecasts. Inasmuch as this particular phase of budgeting is dependent upon other activities of the utility, it is a somewhat short-term prediction. Nevertheless, the budgetary time segments must be so spaced as to allow for change to take place. For example, to be of use to the purchasing department, a materials and supplies budget generally would have to be of sufficient duration to allow the purchasing officer to order, receive, and dispense materials. A daily budget might be quite impractical, but other budgetary factors make a materials and supplies budget of longer than a year's duration highly speculative.

The detail of the materials and supplies budget often will depend on the size and dispersion of a utility's operations. Under certain circumstances, this budget may be incorporated into other forecasting elements, including the construction and operating forecasts. When a separate materials and supplies budget is utilized, it must draw upon information which includes past history of various items and projected future use, this latter based on new construction projections and planned maintenance programs in which the utility participates. In addition, historical data might provide information on probabilities of unforeseen requirements. The materials and supplies budget, in effect, is an extremely detailed plan for purchasing materials and supplies consistent with the operating budget, the capital and construction budget, and the cash forecast. A suggested form to use in budgeting for materials and supplies is shown in Schedule 5.

Capital and Construction Budget

Capital budgeting has been of somewhat more interest to regulators for a number of reasons. First, construction or capital outlay indicates plant expansion. Most regulatory commissions require a utility to procure a certificate of convenience and necessity before proceeding with such work. Second, since plant expansion must meet certain safety and operational specifications, the regulatory commission has a vested interest in knowing of such plans. Third, capital expenditures usually require additional outside financing. Inasmuch as the financial requirements of a utility are closely supervised by regulators, requests for new capital outlays must receive commission blessing.

The capital or construction budget generally is considered to be

	Materials and supplies (by uniform system classification)	
	Fuel stock, and so forth	Accounts 151–165
Units required for operations and maintenance and construction purposes Add desired final inventory as of 31 December 1971		
Total units required Less beginning inventory as of 1 January 1971 Units to be purchased		
Price per unit		
Total cost of purchased materials and supplies		

SCHEDULE 5. *Materials and Supplies Budget, 1971*

long range when compared to the annual operating budget. A construction budget is designed to take into account not only anticipated new construction or gross additions to property and plant, but also estimated retirements from existing property and plant. Costs of removal and dismantling, salvage values, and accumulated depreciation are all factors included in the budget's formulation. While capital budgeting has certain weekly, monthly, or quarterly connotations, it usually is interpreted as a planning forecast extending up to ten or more years into the future. Analysis of anticipated future construction is critical if for no other reason than that major utility plant, such as generating and transmission facilities, requires five to eight years to complete and become operational.

Of primary importance to any capital budget is a forecast identifying potential demands for service. The operations budget forecasts anticipated service demands within existing operation constraints and has a short-run emphasis. The capital expenditure or construction budget attempts to extend the operation or sales forecasts much farther into the future to anticipate demands which will be placed on as yet unconstructed facilities.

It behooves the accountant to provide expense and revenue information necessary for good forecasting. Likewise, the forecaster must take advantage of other information such as economic and demographic data. These facts may be obtained internally through marketing or engineering departments. Outside sources include state and national census figures. Growth areas within an urban or rural region must be investigated, and data relative to this potential growth must be gathered. Answers to such questions as the type of dwelling units, that is, single family or multiple family facilities, must be answered. Trends toward the uses of utility services also should be calculated. For example, are home builders or potential homeowners encouraged to utilize electric versus gas heating or electric versus gas air conditioning? Will these residential regions be developed primarily for young families, or will they be suitable for older and soon to be retired individuals? Will the homes be moderate in size or cater to upper income groups? Forecasting the use of utility service will depend on the answers to these types of questions.

To some extent, industrial development within the region will provide answers to the previous questions, but this development in itself raises a number of queries. Will new industry be attracted to the area? Is this new industry of a type foreign to the region, or is it complementary to already existing manufacturing facilities? If it is new, will these firms attract satellite or complementary enterprises? Are these new industries of a type which will place unusual or at least recognizable burdens upon existing utility facilities? For example, does the firm require an inordinate amount of water and sewerage capacity? Will the industry be of a type which needs a special voltage or unusual amounts of electric energy? What will be the primary source of energy? How important are communications, and will the existing network be ample? Answers to these questions will further aid in determining demands upon which to base construction forecasts.

Other requirements, relating to new commercial or shopping areas, additional street lighting as subdivisions develop, and new recreational facilities are important, as is forecasting employment possibilities. Will the community be able to draw upon existing employment pools, or will new families be moving into the area to fulfill labor needs? If new families immigrate, will they be temporary or permanent? Answers to these questions will depend upon industry, which makes analysis of the types of firms so important. Are they short-lived, perhaps defense industries? Are they stable firms requiring similar raw materials and labor, or are they growth firms which anticipate rather substantial expansion in the future? Information of this kind can lead to much more meaningful capital and construction budgeting forecasts.

Capital budgets, with long-term projections, should be reviewed at least annually. The oldest yearly forecasts should be reassessed and updated and a new year's added. While the total capital budget may be in summary form, it also should be identified by individual projects. Each project forecast within the total construction projection should be assigned a number; contain a description of the proposed capital expenditure; explain the purpose of the project; estimate dates for beginning and completion of the work; estimate costs, revenues, and expenses; and project a return on the new investment. Schedule 6 displays a suggested budget for capital additions.

The operating, construction, cash, and materials and supplies budgets are summarized and integrated in a projected income statement and balance sheet. Actual past experience as well as the forecast for the budgeted year should be displayed. Schedules 7 and 8 are examples.

Analysis of Budget Variations

Producing a realistic budget with full participation is merely the first step in the managerial process of profit planning and control. Of equal importance is the follow-up of performance through an analysis of budget variations. Reports should be issued on a monthly basis, or more frequently if desired, and should display variations between budgeted figures and actual performance. Although the knowledge of variation itself is important, determination of underlying causes is imperative. Only the latter will provide management with the needed information for taking corrective action.

Any evaluation and determination of cause must include: (1) an investigation of both favorable and unfavorable variations for significance; (2) a review for accounting clerical errors; (3) an analysis of management decisions or changes in objectives or goals following budget preparation; (4) variations caused by uncontrollable factors; and (5) unexplained variations requiring additional investigation. Significant variance may be corrected or explained

Addition	*Project number*	*Estimated starting date*	*Estimated date of completion*	*Estimated cost*	*Year budgeted for*				
					1971	*1972*	*1973*	*1974*	*1975*
New office building	11	July 1971	December 1972	$ 500,000	$300,000	$ 200,000			
Additional generator at Main Street station	12	January 1973	August 1975	250,000			$150,000	$ 50,000	$ 50,000
Two hundred miles of 500 kva transmission line	13	March 1971	December 1976	3,500,000	500,000	1,000,000	500,000	500,000	1,000,000
Total cash required by year				$4,250,000	$800,000	$1,200,000	$650,000	$550,000	$1,050,000

SCHEDULE 6. ***Budget for Capital Additions, 1971–1975***

by direct observation or by conferring with the individual responsible for the performance. The variance report aids in identifying areas for further investigation, explanation, or correction.

Budgeting and Financial Modeling

Comprehensive budgeting for planning and control must recognize the advantages of mathematical modeling and electronic data processing systems. These tools not only demand a more quantified definition of management objectives and goals but also add dynamic realism to the budgeting process. The dynamic characteristics of many of the budgeting variables requiring extensive information processing can be accomplished only with high-speed data processing equipment. This simulation technique provides a unique substitute for actual experience. "The computerized financial model is a most worthy new tool now available to public utility management. It is one of the most powerful and potentially useful of those developed since the computer has been commercially available to public utility companies."[9] Machines now can replace man for many of the manual procedures and computations so necessary in the budgeting process. In addition, combining budgeting and accounting with proper quantified inputs of management plans and objectives may put the utility on the road to developing a total information system.

Like the usual accounting process, budgeting involves the handling of massive amounts of data together with testing these data under numerous alternatives. With respect to the budgeting process, the testing of alternatives is a natural extension of the electronic data processing system already used for accounting purposes. Since the system has available revenue data and projections of future demand, anticipated revenues for any designated fiscal period can be added. Likewise, plant and operation and maintenance data, if properly analyzed into cost accounting responsibility centers, can provide unit costs of production and, thus, a budget of anticipated operating expenditures for future accounting periods.

---

[9]Richard Walker, "Financial Models: A Tool for Public Utility Management," in *Public Utility Accounting: Models, Mergers, and Information Systems,* ed. Roland F. Salmonson (East Lansing: M.S.U. Public Utilities Papers, 1971), p. 3.

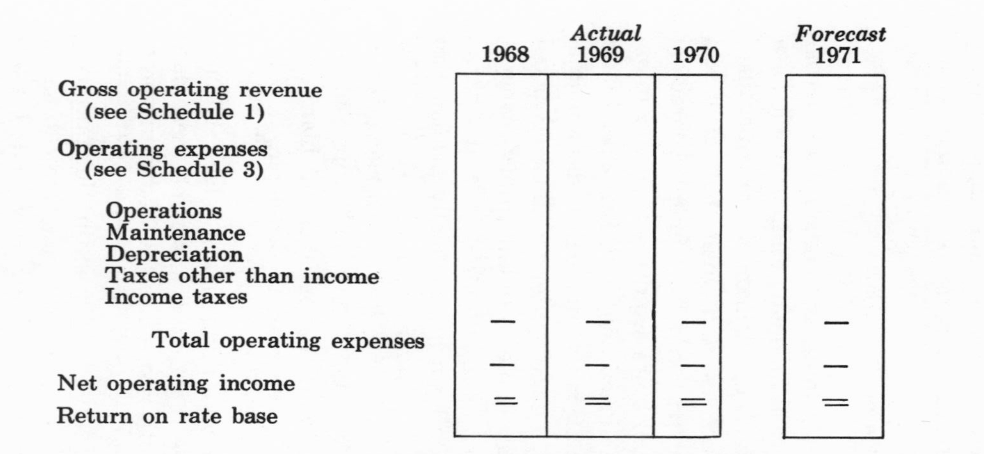

	Actual 1968	Actual 1969	Actual 1970	Forecast 1971
Gross operating revenue (see Schedule 1)				
Operating expenses (see Schedule 3)				
Operations				
Maintenance				
Depreciation				
Taxes other than income				
Income taxes				
Total operating expenses				
Net operating income				
Return on rate base				

SCHEDULE 7. *Projected Annual Income Statement, 1971*

Assets	Actual 1968	Actual 1969	Actual 1970	Forecast 1971
Fixed assets				
Other investments				
Current assets				
Deferred debits				
Total assets				

Liabilities	Actual 1968	Actual 1969	Actual 1970	Forecast 1971
Common equity				
Preferred stock				
Long-term debt				
Current liabilities				
Deferred credits				
Total liabilities				

SCHEDULE 8. *Projected Balance Sheet, Year Ending 31 December 1971*

Providing forecasts of this type to management is essential for planning day-to-day operations and future needs.

The system can be programmed, based on the stored historical data and added calculations for projected budgets, to provide analysis to planning groups on a "what if" basis, which is a type of simulation study. For example, what if revenues did not increase by a projected 10 percent? What if labor costs, as a result of a pending wage contract, increase not by 7 percent, but by 11 percent? What if new business enterprises move into the area, or what if the company vigorously pursues a promotional program for electric heating? The study of such possible changes, which are not reflected in the historical data, allow the utility to visualize a variety of budgets based upon alternative conditions. To provide such information without an electronic data processing system is virtually impossible; with proper programming, several alternative budgets might be available in a matter of seconds or minutes.

Summary

Although budgeting and modeling are not a panacea for management and regulatory ills, they do provide one important input. For all utilities, a company-wide budget is a basic necessity. For smaller firms this general approach may be sufficient, but those utilities which perform several services, cover widely dispersed geographical areas, or which are subdivided by political boundaries usually will require budgetary information identified in smaller, more detailed units. Budget forecasts should be based on responsibility centers, that is, by service performed, districts, substations, city, county, and so forth. The closer budget information approaches operating personnel within the management organizational structure, the more detailed are the requirements.

Submission of the budget to the regulatory commission for its approval can provide useful data for analyzing the potential needs of the utility as well as for producing better regulatory decisions. However, the separation between management and regulatory functions must remain. The regulator should not interfere with management in dictating what expenditures should be made; rather, the commission should give its suggestions about accounting and rate-making treatment under sound regulatory dicta.

Selected References

Burge, Walter R. *Managerial Budgeting for Profit Improvement*. New York: McGraw-Hill Book Co., 1968.

Heiser, Herman C. *Budgeting—Principles and Practice*. New York: The Ronald Press, 1959.

Mattessick, Richard. *Simulation of the Firm Through a Budget Computer Program*. Homewood, Ill.: Richard D. Irwin, Inc., 1964.

Meier, Robert C.; Newell, William T.; and Pazer, Harold L. *Simulation in Business and Economics*. Englewood Cliffs, N.J.: Prentice-Hall, Inc., 1969.

Smidt, Seymour. *The Capital Budgeting Decision*. 2d ed. New York: The MacMillan Company, 1966.

Salmonson, Roland F. *Public Utility Accounting: Models, Mergers, and Information Systems*, Section 1, "Modeling Accounting Data," pp. 3–49. East Lansing: MSU Public Utilities Papers, 1971.

15

Accounting for Nonutility Functions

Public utilities often engage in activities of a nonutility nature for a number of reasons. Electric or gas utilities may find it advantageous to sell and service electric appliances. A company may construct facilities to be used primarily for utility functions, but with excess capacity, which then might be used for nonutility services. Regulated utilities often make outside investments with excess funds either on a short- or long-term basis. Finally, firms, through acquisition or purchase, may acquire businesses which may or may not be related to the supplying of utility service. Thus, a utility might engage in real estate activities, producing parts and equipment to be used eventually in a utility's operations, or other manufacturing or service activities foreign to its regulated functions. Regardless of what is entailed, it is critical that nonutility activity be accounted for separately.

Regulation of Nonutility Functions

Several state commissions have been given specific authority to control a utility's entry into nonutility activities (see Table 27). Whether or not commissions have this authority, they do provide the necessary accounting procedures, through the uniform systems,

TABLE 27. ***Commissions with Authority to Regulate a Utility's Entry into Nonutility Activities Directly or Through Affiliates***

State	*Commission has authority*	*State*	*Commission has authority*
FPC		Missouri	
FCC		Montana	
Alabama		Nebraska	
Alaska		Nevada	
Arizona		New Hampshire	
Arkansas		New Jersey	yes
California		New Mexico	
Colorado	yes	New York	yes
Connecticut		North Carolina	
Delaware		North Dakota	
District of Columbia		Ohio	
Florida		Oklahoma	
Georgia		Oregon	
Hawaii		Pennsylvania	yes
Idaho		Puerto Rico	
Illinois	yes	Rhode Island	
Indiana		South Carolina	
Iowa	not decided	South Dakota	
Kansas		Tennessee	
Kentucky		Texas	
Louisiana		Utah	question has not arisen
Maine		Vermont	
Maryland		Virginia	yes
Massachusetts	yes	Virgin Islands	not decided
Michigan		Washington	yes
Minnesota		West Virginia	
Mississippi		Wisconsin	yes
		Wyoming	

SOURCE: Federal Power Commission, *Federal and State Commission Jurisdiction and Regulation, Electric, Gas and Telephone Utilities, 1967* (Washington, D.C.: U.S. Government Printing Office, 1967), p. 24.

to separate assets, revenues, and expenses of nonutility activities from those of a utility type. This is done specifically to protect the rate payers.[1]

[1]"The Commission may require a public utility to maintain special accounts for its nonutility service, so that the Commission may protect utility rate payers from any burdensome contracts for a nonutility service."

Accounting for Nonutility Functions

Provision for separate accounting of nonutility functions is found in the *Uniform System of Accounts Prescribed for Public Utilities and Licensees.* Balance sheet accounts contained under "Assets and other debits" include Section 2, "Other property and investments." Account 121, "Nonutility property," is described as follows:

> A. This account shall include the book cost of land, structures, equipment or other tangible or intangible property owned by the utility, but not used in utility service and not properly includable in account 105, Electric Plant Held for Future Use.
>
> B. This account shall be subdivided so as to show the amount of property used in operations which are nonutility in character but nevertheless constitute a distinct operating activity of the company (such as operation of an ice department where such activity is not classed as a utility) and the amount of miscellaneous property not used in operations. The records in support of each subaccount shall be maintained so as to show an appropriate classification of the property.[2]

The income accounts provide for income other than that produced from utility functions in account 415, "Revenues from merchandis-

---

[2]Account 121, together with its companion account 122, "Accumulated provision for depreciation and amortization of nonutility property," as well as accounts 123, "Investment in associated companies," 124, "Other investment," and certain other miscellaneous fixed asset accounts allow the utility to record any of its nonutility acquisitions or assets separately from those utilized by the utility. FPC, *Uniform System,* pp. 101-24–101-25.

Uniform accounting systems for gas and water utilities have similar accounts for nonutility functions. Telephone accounting is much less precise and includes nonutility property under investments, account 103, "Miscellaneous physical property." Accumulated depreciation is included along with utility property depreciation under "Liabilities, deferred credits and reserves," account 171, "Depreciation reserve." FCC, *Rules and Regulations—Part 31,* pp. 17, 24.

Re Pacific Telephone and Telegraph Company (1965) 58 PUR 3d 57 (California).

Moreover, the Idaho Public Service Commission, speaking in the *Intermountain Gas* case in 1967, said: "The accounting system for an appliance rental program of a gas company should be separated from the operating statement of the company's business required to fulfill its obligation or provide service as a public utility since the investment in the appliances should not be included in the rate base, and the applicable expenses and revenue should not be included in the utility operations of the company." *Re Intermountain Gas Company* (1967) 67 PUR 3d 511 (Idaho).

ing, jobbing and contract work." A companion account 416, "Cost and expenses of merchandising, jobbing and contract work," covers all expenses incurred in producing such revenue.

Additional accounts required to record income from other nonutility or nonoperating transactions, including interest and dividend income from outside investments, also are available. The New York Public Service Commission spoke for most state and federal commissions in its decision on legitimate operating expenses: "Expenses of a gas company related to merchandising, jobbing, and contract work should be excluded in fixing the company's rates."[3] Moreover, the magnitude of nonutility income is important. The same commission, referring to revenues in the same case, said: "Revenues realized by a gas company from merchandising, jobbing, and contract work should be excluded from consideration in setting the company's rates for gas service but where the credit balance from such activities was very small, its exclusion from total revenues was not deemed necessary."[4] This is not to say that all commissions are in agreement on these items. A decision was carried to the Arkansas Supreme Court, and the court said: "Expenses incidental to merchandising which tend to increase a gas company's sales of gas were properly included in utility expenses for ratemaking purposes."[5]

Often property is jointly used for both regulated and nonregulated functions. Under those conditions, the decision in the *Oklahoma Natural Gas Company* case of 1965 stated: "In determining the rate base of a natural gas company, the Commission properly required the nonutility function to share its portion of the expense of maintaining the central office building and other properties used in connection with its nonutility operations."[6] Costs completely unrelated to the utility's operations, in all probability, should be excluded and recorded as nonutility expense. The following two

---

[3]*Re Columbia Gas of New York* (1965) 61 PUR 3d 491 (New York); and *Re Rocky Mountain Natural Gas Company* (1964) 55 PUR 3d 334 (Colorado).

[4]*Re Columbia Gas of New York* (1965) 61 PUR 3d 491 (New York).

[5]*City of Eldorado et al.* v. *Arkansas Public Service Commission et al.* (1962) 235 Ark 812, 47 PUR 3d 354, 362 SW2d 680 (Arkansas Supreme Court).

[6]*Re Oklahoma Natural Gas Company* (1965) 61 PUR 3d 94, 406 P2d 273 (Oklahoma Supreme Court).

examples illustrate the point. "An amount expended for S&H green stamps to be given to employees as a bonus for leads on appliance sales was deducted from a gas company's test year expenses."[7] "Expenses of a telephone company incurred in furnishing food to employees below cost are not allowable as operating expenses."[8] Yet, this latter example may be one of the least costly but most rewarding fringe benefits accorded employees. In its Order 389, the Federal Power Commission further specified that all taxes, operating and income, must be properly allocated for nonutility functions.[9] Account 408 has been designated for taxes other than income taxes, while account 409 is provided for recording related income taxes.

The point should be clear. Classification of items as operating and nonoperating or utility or nonutility is extremely significant for both proper accounting and regulatory rate-making purposes. One cannot blindly declare certain functions as being either utility or nonutility in nature. The case related to merchandising costs is one such example. While most regulatory bodies would exclude merchandising as an expense for utility operations, there are certain circumstances when the expense is considered above the line. If, for example, such an expense is indeed promotional in nature and expands the demand for the product, it may be deemed socially and economically acceptable and may warrant inclusion as an operating item.

In those instances where regulatory bodies have jurisdiction over a utility's revenues and expenses, and where such income from merchandising, jobbing, and contract work must be reported as an operating item, revenues are recorded in account 914 and expenses in account 915, both of which are subsumed under the title "Sales expense." The revenue derived from and expenses incurred for this activity are operating items. However, if the regulatory commission interprets these items as nonoperating, they must be recorded in accounts 415 and 416.

In those instances where the regulatory body is noncommittal or

---

[7] *Re Iroquois Gas Corporation* (1968) 74 PUR 3d 322 (New York).

[8] *Re New England Telephone & Telegraph Company* (1949) 83 PUR NS 238 (Massachusetts).

[9] Federal Power Commission, Docket No. R-344, Order No. 389, Attachment A, 9 October 1969, p. 26.

at least has not been required to render a decision on such practices, the utility has its choice of using either accounts 415 and 416, which are the nonoperating accounts, or 914 and 915, which are operating accounts. Regardless of the approach taken by the utility, the practice should be consistent,[10] but the final decision rests with the regulatory body or, ultimately, with the courts. To regulate in strict conformance with the accounting used in a particular transaction might not be practical. Thus, while uniformity of accounting persists, regulation reserves the prerogative to alter it.

---

[10]FPC, *Uniform System,* pp. 101-65–101-66.

Index

Part I

Part I lists cases referred to in the text; Part II is a subject index.

Part II

A

B

C

P

U